THE WEAKER SEX IN WAR

A Nation Divided: Studies in the Civil War Era
Orville Vernon Burton and Elizabeth R. Varon, Editors

The Weaker Sex in War

Gender and Nationalism in Civil War Virginia

Kristen Brill

UNIVERSITY OF VIRGINIA PRESS

Charlottesville and London

University of Virginia Press
© 2022 by the Rector and Visitors of the University of Virginia
All rights reserved

First published 2022

1 3 5 7 9 8 6 4 2

Library of Congress Cataloging-in-Publication Data
Names: Brill, Kristen, author.
Title: The weaker sex in war : gender and nationalism in Civil War Virginia / Kristen Brill.
Other titles: Nation divided.
Description: Charlottesville : University of Virginia Press, 2022. | Series: A nation divided: Studies in the Civil War era | Includes bibliographical references and index.
Identifiers: LCCN 2022016245 (print) | LCCN 2022016246 (ebook) | ISBN 9780813947716 (hardcover) | ISBN 9780813947723 (paperback) | ISBN 9780813947730 (ebook)
Subjects: LCSH: Women—Confederate States of America—History. | Women—Virginia—History. | Nationalism—Confederate States of America—History. | United States—History—Civil War, 1861–1865—Women. | Virginia—History—Civil War, 1861–1865.
Classification: LCC E628 .B84 2022 (print) | LCC E628 (ebook) | DDC 973.7/13082—dc23/eng/20220510
LC record available at https://lccn.loc.gov/2022016245
LC ebook record available at https://lccn.loc.gov/2022016246

Cover art: Detail from design drawing for Captain Sally Louisa Tompkins Memorial Window, St. James Episcopal Church, Richmond, Virginia. Designer, Katharine Lamb Tait, J. & R. Lamb Studios. (Library of Congress, Prints and Photographs Division, LC-DIG-ppmsca-10813)

S|H   **The Sustainable History Monograph Pilot**
M|P   Opening Up the Past, Publishing for the Future

This book is published as part of the Sustainable History Monograph Pilot. With the generous support of the Andrew W. Mellon Foundation, the Pilot uses cutting-edge publishing technology to produce open access digital editions of high-quality, peer-reviewed monographs from leading university presses. Free digital editions can be downloaded from: Books at JSTOR, EBSCO, Internet Archive, OAPEN, Project MUSE, ScienceOpen, and many other open repositories.

While the digital edition is free to download, read, and share, the book is under copyright and covered by the following Creative Commons License: CC BY-NC-ND 4.0. Please consult www.creativecommons.org if you have questions about your rights to reuse the material in this book.

When you cite the book, please include the following URL for its Digital Object Identifier (DOI): https://doi.org/10.52156/m.5678

> We are eager to learn more about how you discovered this title and how you are using it. We hope you will spend a few minutes answering a couple of questions at this URL: https://www.longleafservices.org/shmp-survey/

More information about the Sustainable History Monograph Pilot can be found at https://www.longleafservices.org.

For my grandmother

CONTENTS

List of Illustrations xi
Preface xiii

Introduction 1

CHAPTER 1
Mount Vernon Ladies' Association of the Union 17

CHAPTER 2
Ladies' Defense Association 35

CHAPTER 3
The Richmond Bread Riot 54

CHAPTER 4
Confederate Women and Britain 74

CHAPTER 5
The Home for Needy Confederate Women 99

Epilogue 119

Notes 125
Bibliography 163
Index 179

ILLUSTRATIONS

FIGURE 1. Captain Sally Louisa Tompkins memorial window 3

FIGURE 2. Plans for Statue of Sally Tompkins 4

FIGURE 3. "Jeff. Davis! 'As Women and Children'" 41

FIGURE 4. Alfred Waud, "The Rebel Iron-Clad Fleet Forcing the Obstruction in James River" 52

FIGURE 5. "Sowing and Reaping" 59

FIGURE 6. Virginia Women's Monument in October 2019 122

PREFACE

This book examines white women who supported the Confederacy from middle- and planter-class families. Most of these women came from slaveholding families and their wartime actions and relationships show how class functioned as a gendered political concept at the top of the racial hierarchy of the Confederate South.[1] Such a study puts social history into dialogue with political and intellectual history, and the source material consulted reflects this approach: first-person narratives and the records of women's organizations are juxtaposed with political speeches, military orders, and legislative records.[2] In doing so, it becomes clear that women's and gender history is a significant constituent of political and intellectual history.[3] This methodology draws connections between the abstract ideology and the tangible lived reality of nationalism. It bridges the gap between intellectual and social history, between the political elites and the people: How did the people experience nationalism in their everyday lives? In this way, ideologies must be understood as more than intellectual history, but how they were represented in first-person experiences of war.

At the same time, generalizations cannot be made about wartime gendered lived experience. Women's accounts and experiences of the war underpin this study, and some women joined together and formed organizations to pursue common aspirations in support of the Confederacy. This methodological focus on women's voices reveals the lack of uniformity between their experiences of and ideas surrounding the Confederacy; women had a variety of concerns and varying levels of investment in the Confederate republic throughout the war. Adopting an approach that weds individual women's voices in the private sphere, collective organizations in civic society, and political ideology and policy in the political sphere reveals the ways in which women's wartime experiences shaped Confederate political culture and not simply the ways in which Confederate political culture shaped women's wartime experiences.

Particular to the context of the Civil War, the hardships and conditions of war often meant that these women had to prioritize their physical safety and survival over documenting the war or contributing to civic organizations. Often, the level of women's activity—as individuals writing first-person accounts or as a collective organization lobbying for a set goal—was dependent upon their proximity to the severity and frequency of military action. The Mount Vernon Ladies' Association of the Union was unable to organize a meeting of its state vice regents from 1860 to 1864 given the war. Furthermore, during and in the immediate aftermath of the First Battle of Bull Run in July 1861, the activities and writings of the organization came to a virtual standstill. Sarah Tracy, the personal secretary to the founding regent, Ann Pamela Cunningham, and the representative of the organization at Mount Vernon during the war, was eager to monitor the first major land battle of the war and guard her own safety from the violence less than thirty miles away. The ideological aims of the organization were subjugated to the lived realities of war. Participation in these wartime organizations required a level of privilege.[4] Women needed to be removed from the physical dangers of war to some extent in order to focus on more abstract and less immediate concerns. Individual physical survival needed to be secured before collective institutional survival could be pursued.

Likewise, with Union occupation, communication networks were compromised. Even if letters and dispatches were written, there was no guarantee these writings would reach their intended audience. Communications between the founding regent of the Mount Vernon Ladies' Association of the Union, Cunningham in Rosemont, South Carolina, and Tracey at Mount Vernon were limited after South Carolina's secession in December 1860. Communications between the Ladies' Defense Association in Richmond and auxiliary organizations in Virginia were also limited and often faced the arduous hurdle of traveling across Union lines. In addition, the Union blockade severely restricted communication between the South and the rest of the world. It was difficult to export not only goods but Confederate propaganda to the British and French markets. Commanding general of the Union army General Winfield Scott's Anaconda Plan not only strangled the South into a sense of economic isolation but to some degree a sense of ideological isolation. As discussed in chapter 4, the difficulty in transporting the case for Confederate recognition, in term of both physical emissaries (like James Murray Mason and John Slidell) as well as ideological propaganda, made the Confederate cause more reliant on European surrogates and sympathizers to craft, circulate, and lobby the cause abroad.

The hardships of war also manifested in a shortage of essential materials for survival on the home front; the amount of women's writings can also be understood as a response to this scarcity of physical materials. Living in Richmond during the war, Clara Minor Lynn recalled, "in many Southern libraries the curious visitor will notice the fly leaves in some of the old books are missing. If he is of an inquiring turn of mind, he will be told 'they were torn out and used for paper during the war.'"[5] On June 11, 1863, Emily Noble wrote to her brother Richard stationed in Richmond: "I have not got paper to write you a long letter. Brother you will not think hard of me for such a short letter. Times is hard here but crops is good."[6] Simply put, documentation of the war required the necessary physical materials to do so. These materials, and the privilege of time to write and the education to do so, were often restricted to the upper classes. Women were also selective in the topics they wrote about in their wartime diaries and letters. Most women did not discuss slavery outside of Suzanne Lebsock's definition of personalism. According to Lebsock, slaveholding women fleetingly discussed their personal relationships with individual enslaved persons rather than offer political commentaries on the institution of slavery. Using this personal frame of reference to engage with slavery, these women were keen to showcase how they treated their enslaved persons as members of the family.[7] This relative silence in the archive should not be read as ambivalence or opposition to slavery. Recent historiography has shown, through elite white women's actions and through Works Progress Administration (WPA) interviews with former enslaved persons, elite white women were actively engaged with the administration of the plantation household and slavery, and its attendant processes of violence.[8] These women may not have written about their roles in slavery in detail as they may have considered it too mundane to record.[9] These women's wartime writings are an incomplete record of their wartime activities and concerns, but they still reveal important information in their changing relationship to the state, and in doing so, the greater context of war.

This book was a long journey, and I am indebted to many in its completion. This project developed as a PhD dissertation under the supervision of Betty Wood. Betty passed away as this book went to press. Her work ethic, brilliance, and, most of all, her kindness will be admired by scholars for years to come. Michael O'Brien also generously supported this project from the start and also sadly passed away far too soon. Michael always pushed me to consider the intellectual history of gender history; I hope he would be (reservedly) pleased with this book. Catherine Clinton has been a fatigueless supporter of my work and I am grateful to have her in my corner. Sarah Meer, Paul Quigley, and Andrew O'Shaughnessy have consistently offered their time and expertise to develop this project into its best and final version, as seen in the forthcoming pages.

The series editors, Liz Varon and Orville Vernon Burton, offered unwavering support of this project from the start. My editor, Nadine Zimmerli, has been a tireless champion of this work and has consistently provided sharp and helpful feedback. I am lucky to have her as an editor. The anonymous readers, particularly reader 2, pushed me to refine my arguments and make this a better book.

Several organizations generously funded this research: Fred W. Smith National Library for the Study of George Washington; Robert H. Smith International Center for Jefferson Studies at Monticello; Virginia Center for Civil War Studies at Virginia Tech; U.S. Embassy/British Association of American Studies Small Grant Fund; College of Charleston Pearlstine/Lipov Center for Southern Jewish Culture; Virginia Museum of History and Culture Andrew W. Mellon Fund; Association of British American Nineteenth Century Historians Peter J. Parish Memorial Fund; German Historical Institute in Washington, D.C.; Cambridge Overseas Trust; and Sara Norton Fund at Cambridge.

This work has benefited from the expertise of archivists across Virginia, especially in extended trips to the Library of Virginia and Virginia Museum of History and Culture. Rebecca Baird and Mary Thompson at the Washington Library went above and beyond to help me pull together my work on the Mount Vernon Ladies' Association of the Union (MVLA).

Colleagues at Keele University—especially Kate Cushing, Siobhan Talbott, Alannah Tomkins, Nick Seager, and Oliver Harris—have offered timely guidance and support. Friends and loved ones on both sides of the Atlantic have supported me over the course of this project and made life outside of this book much more enjoyable: Joe Boyle, Clare Walker Gore, Melissa Yates, Lara Talverdian, Natalie Thomlinson, Florence Sutcliffe-Braithwaite, Laura Kounine, James Lawlor, Jasper Heinzen, Laura Crombie, Cara and Bradley Maitland, Arddun Arwyn, Matt Phillips, Bjorn Weiler, Sadie Royal Collins, Rachel Williams, Erin Baugher, Susan Royal, Udeni Salmon, and Ignatius.

The last debt is to my family. Betsy Hansen has been one of my favorite people from my earliest memories. Martin's love is the best thing about my life; I'm lucky to share a life with him. My grandmother raised me with unconditional love and selfless generosity. She was the best person I have ever known. This book is dedicated to her.

THE WEAKER SEX IN WAR

Introduction

SALLY LOUISA TOMPKINS WAS born into a slave-owning Virginia family at Poplar Grove, about thirty miles west of Richmond on the Pamunkey River, in 1833. She attended the Norfolk Female Institute for one year and moved to Richmond in 1854. At the outbreak of the American Civil War, she opened the Robertson Hospital in the prewar home of Judge John Robertson in an affluent part of the new Confederate capital. Even in the first few months of the war, women's work in wartime medical care was a salient issue for Confederates to rally around to support the newborn republic.[1] Mary Chesnut visited the Robertson Hospital in August 1861 and admired Tompkins's efforts: "The men under Miss Sallie's care looked so clean and comfortable. Cheerful, one might say."[2] The hospital received glowing praise from the Southern press throughout the war: "The hospital is often in [the] charge of a solitary young lady, who reads prayers to the men every morning... their [the soldiers'] gratitude for the kind treatment they receive is frequently very touching."[3]

A few months into the conflict, the Confederate Army Department surgeon general Samuel Preston Moore ordered the closure of all private hospitals in the Confederacy. In response, on September 9, 1861, under guidance from Confederate president Jefferson Davis, the first secretary of war, LeRoy Pope Walker, commissioned Sally Tompkins as an unassigned captain in the Confederate army so her hospital could remain open under military leadership.[4] Given the Robertson Hospital's low death rate—of over 1,300 patients over the course of the war, only seventy-three died—the Confederate government recognized the success of Tompkins's work.[5] Of course, smaller hospitals such as hers did not usually care for the most seriously injured soldiers, who often immediately went to the nearby Chimborazo Hospital.[6] Still, Tompkins was the only woman to be a commissioned officer in the Confederate army. In accepting the commission, Tompkins stipulated that she "would not allow my name to be placed upon the pay roll of the army."[7] In a clear expression of the wartime culture of self-sacrifice, Tompkins would only serve the Confederacy without financial recompense.

It is important to recognize that Sally Tompkins was a slaveholder; enslaved persons, including five of her own, labored in the Robertson Hospital, as they did in hospitals throughout the South.[8] One of her enslaved persons, William, was arrested for burglary in November 1864. He had stolen a jar of brandy peaches and ten pounds of chewing tobacco from a confectionary behind St. Paul's Church.[9] This incident was reported in the local press; the report did not focus on Tompkins's exemplary record at the Robertson Hospital, but it did describe Tompkins as a slaveholder. Just as the physical and ideological survival of the Confederacy relied on slavery, so, too, did the work of the Robertson Hospital.[10]

Sally Tompkins, "the Florence Nightingale of the Confederacy," and the Robertson Hospital continued to receive praise and support from the Confederate government, the Richmond press, and Confederate citizens until its closure in 1865. After the war, Tompkins worked in charity and nursing efforts around Richmond. In 1905, after exhausting her own financial resources, she moved to the Home for Needy Confederate Women, where she died in July 1916 and was given a military burial.[11] Tompkins became a prominent feature of Confederate memory and Lost Cause ideology in the last years of her life and after her death. In May 1889, a portrait of Tompkins was presented to the Confederate Literary Memorial Society at the Confederate Museum in Richmond.[12] In December 1910, the Robert E. Lee Camp, Sons of Confederate Veterans, erected a bronze tablet at the site of the former Robertson Hospital commemorating its work.[13] Tompkins unveiled the tablet at the ceremony. In the centennial of the Civil War, the St. James Episcopal Church in Richmond (Tompkins's church), installed a stained-glass window depicting Tompkins with an angel evoking her nickname, "Angel of the Confederacy" (see figure 1).

In 1966, the Women of the Confederacy Memorial Committee sought to erect a statue of Tompkins on Monument Avenue in Richmond to sit alongside the likes of Stonewall Jackson and Robert E. Lee.[14] The famed Spanish surrealist artist Salvador Dalí submitted a proposal, sketched by Richmond artist Bill Wynne, for the design of the statue: Dalí's Tompkins was an adaptation of St. George as a Grecian goddess slaying a dragon while standing on a mushroom pedestal held up by Dalí's finger (see figure 2). Just like the male military heroes of the Confederacy went to battle against the Union on the front lines, Tompkins went to battle against the dragon of disease on the home front. However, the Richmond public found Dalí's proposal to be too radical for the traditionalism of Monument Avenue and too focused on the artist. As General Edwin P. Conquest queried, "Are we erecting a Sali or a Dalí?"[15] Following this outcry, the Women of the Confederacy Memorial Committee soon withdrew their plans for a Tompkins statue on Monument Avenue.

FIGURE 1. Captain Sally Louisa Tompkins memorial window, design drawing, installed September 10, 1961, St. James Episcopal Church, Richmond, Virginia. Library of Congress Prints and Photographs Division.

The narrative of Sally Tompkins's gendered service to the Confederacy is a familiar one: she supported the Confederate cause through work consistent with the cult of womanhood and the domestic sphere. However, what is less familiar are the ways in which male leaders in government and civic society used her gendered work to strengthen Confederate nationalism. When the Davis administration made her a captain, it was not simply ensuring the continued operation of her hospital under military command, it was molding Tompkins into a symbol for the Confederate cause. The government's militaristic endorsement afforded an increased legitimacy to Tompkins's work, and, at the same time, the government harnessed Tompkins's unrivaled track record in patient care to strengthen the perceived efficacy and strength of the Confederate medical effort and the Confederacy writ large.

FIGURE 2. Plans for Statue of Sally Tompkins, design by Salvador Dalí and sketch by Bill Wynne. Virginia Museum of History and Culture. Richmond, Virginia.

Moreover, when the Richmond press fastidiously reported on the establishment and work of the Robertson Hospital, especially Tompkins's leading role in its progress and success, the press was not just reporting the news, it was making Tompkins a household name in Richmond and throughout the region. Circulated through print culture, Tompkins became a touchstone for the reading public to process the significance of individual wartime service to the Confederacy. Officials in government and civic society shaped, projected, and circulated Tompkins, and her work with the Robertson Hospital, as an evocative symbol of Confederate nationalism predicated on her womanhood. Sally Tompkins served the Confederacy as a nurse and she served the Confederacy as a nationalist symbol; she engaged with Confederate nationalism in tangible actions during the war and was projected as a symbol of the Confederate cause both during and after the war. Like the other women discussed in this book, she was both an actor for and a symbol of the Confederate cause; she became intertwined with both Confederate political culture and Confederate nationalism.

The rich and abundant body of scholarship exploring Confederate womanhood has shown how Southern women experienced the Civil War in different ways according to a number of interlocking factors. Race and class status defined a woman's position in the antebellum social hierarchy and would continue to do so throughout the Civil War period. Race and class privilege insulated some women at the top of the social hierarchy from the worst horrors of war and exacerbated it for those at the bottom of the hierarchy.[16] Women's age and kinship networks, particularly marriage and motherhood, worked to shape their expected contributions to the war effort.[17] An individual woman's loyalty to the culture of self-sacrifice was defined through what she herself could sacrifice to the cause, whether it be a husband, a son, or simply her personal devotion under previously unimaginable dire circumstances.[18] Women in the North not only experienced the war differently than those in the South, but within the Confederacy, women's experiences of war varied according to state and region. Those in the Upper South were often forced to confront the advancing Union army and the prospect of occupation earlier than most, though not all, women in the Lower South.[19] Some women, often those who were educated and literate, left written accounts of their experiences of war, in diaries, letters, or even published fiction based on loosely veiled versions of their own lives; others did not.[20] Regardless of these differences, Southern women did share some significant commonalities across their wartime experiences. Women had to grapple with new physical dangers on the home front; they had to negotiate new catalysts of family separation; and, crucially for this book, the most important commonality shared by all women inside the Confederacy was that each individual had to decide, sometimes to others and sometimes just for herself, would she support the Confederacy?

At its core, this book explores the relationship between middle-and planter-class white Southern women who supported the Confederacy and the emerging ideology of Confederate nationalism, and it argues that Confederate leaders used these women to advance the Southern cause. This is not to say that women were passive in this process: women were in control of their contributions to national devotion and were knowing and keen participants in shaping and circulating a gendered nationalist narrative.

Older histories on Southern women and nationalism tend to focus on the fluctuations in women's commitment to Confederate nationalism over the course of the war: Did women's commitment to Confederate nationalism wane over the course of the war? If so, when and why did it do so?[21] This book moves this conversation forward by using women in Virginia to explore how, precisely, Confederate leaders recognized, mediated, and amplified middle-and planter-class women's devotion to the Confederacy to strengthen national sentiment and to recover women's active and decisive roles in fortifying this relationship between gender and nationalism.

Through their contributions to Confederate nationalism, these women forged new relationships with the state. This book uses the term "state" to denote the Davis administration and central government structure of the Confederacy. This emerging Confederate state recognized the power of middle-and planter-class white women in a new and different way than had the United States during the antebellum years; Confederate leaders harnessed women's gendered work of national devotion and projected it to a regional audience to strengthen nationalist sentiment. These women were engaged not only in making symbols of the new republic, like Confederate flags and Confederate soldier uniforms; rather, they themselves were made into symbols of the new republic.[22] These women might not have had, or even sought, a role in the political sphere, but the Confederate political sphere recognized women's value to strengthen nationalist sentiment across both civic and political society.

This book will not examine all Confederate women, only middle-and planter-class white women who supported the Confederacy, because, as the story of Sally Tompkins exemplifies, these were the women the Confederate leadership used to advance its agenda. It will explore the triangulated relationship between gender, political culture, and nationalism to complicate current understandings of the roles of women on the Confederate home front: In what ways did women's actions support or undermine Confederate identity and political policies? How did women themselves negotiate the process of the construction of national identity and their relationship to the Confederacy? How did the Confederate government use women to help build its nationalist mission, both inside and outside the Confederacy?

"The weaker sex in war" of this book's title is taken from the Ladies' Defense Association's mission statement (as discussed in chapter 2) and also draws on the familiar rallying cry across war cultures that men are dutifully bound to the physical protection of women as the weaker sex: men's wartime service is (at least partially) motivated by safeguarding their vulnerable wives and daughters.[23] While the Confederacy certainly deployed this trope, it pushed it further. In the Confederacy, the state used middle-and planter-class white women to advance its cause. This was not just about individual men fighting for their households, this was the collective Confederate state marshalling the symbolism of middle-and planter-class white womanhood to strengthen Confederate nationalism.²⁴ While certainly not a goal of male Confederate leaders, this strategy challenged nineteenth-century notions of women's weakness and the ideal of the Southern lady.²⁵ In using them to advance their own cause, intertwining women with political culture and nationalist discourse, the Confederate state implicitly recognized the potential strength of women on the ideological battlefield for hearts and minds.²⁶

For frequent readers of gender and Civil War history, the cast of characters presented in this book will be familiar. What will be less familiar is the analytical frame through which these women are presented: Confederate nationalism was shaped and projected to wider audiences through women's bodies and gendered politics. With few exceptions, the women discussed in this book played active roles in shaping their symbolism. They were not merely manipulated as passive pawns by Confederate leaders; these women frequently decided when and how they would contribute to their performance of national devotion, in terms of both rhetoric and action. While male leaders then co-opted and circulated this performance to a wider audience, these women defined and controlled much of this nationalist narrative. In this way, women inextricably tied themselves to the creation and circulation of Confederate nationalism.

Historians have continued to challenge the mythology of the Southern lady to examine the active, and often eager, roles elite white women played in sustaining slavery in the nineteenth-century South.²⁷ This book contributes significantly to this historiography by showing the ways in which these women built and strengthened Confederate nationalism, an ideology that justified the establishment of a republic based on slaveholding. These women were not only socially and economically invested in slaveholding as individuals, they were also ideologically invested in the idea of a slaveholding republic. This is not to suggest that all middle- and planter-class white Southern women played crucial roles in this process. Rather, the following chapters examine the activities and actions of individuals and organizations that did play important roles in the production of Confederate nationalism, and in doing so, this book offers a new lens through which to consider women's relationship to the Confederate state.

Both the Union and the Confederacy were aware of the ways in which Southern women could undermine their respective causes.²⁸ For the Union, Confederate female spies, like Rose Greenhow and Belle Boyd, threatened military operations. Also, unruly Confederate women in Union-occupied areas, like General Benjamin Butler's New Orleans, undermined the Union's social and civic control.²⁹ For the Confederacy, some of its women became an "enemy from within," contributing to networks of unionism or desertion and undermining the collective commitment to the Confederate cause.³⁰ Furthermore, some lower-class white women in the South challenged traditional domestic policy to advance more radical social and welfare reforms in their own interests. Stephanie McCurry focuses on the ways in which both the Union and Confederacy recognized the potential of Southern women across class (and race) lines to disrupt and weaken their respective causes, whereas this study examines how the Confederacy recognized some middle-and planter-class white Southern women's potential to strengthen their cause. White Southern women held political capital that could be used to either embrace nonprogressive or progressive agendas, or more specifically, to either support or undermine Confederate nationalism.

Gender and Nationalism

As an ideology, Confederate nationalism needed to grapple with the relationship between change and continuity, and, at the same time, "be at once elitist in purpose yet popular in appeal."³¹ Uniting Southerners across the socioeconomic spectrum under one nationalist ideology was a challenge for the Confederacy throughout the war. Positioning itself in the legacy of divinely sanctioned American movements, particularly the Puritans' journey to New England and the American Revolution of 1776, the Confederacy portrayed secession as an act of purification from the ungodly and sinful North. Both political and clerical leaders adhered to this doctrine of the South as "God's chosen people."³² The Confederacy not only looked back inwardly to the American past, but outwardly to European struggles for revolution in order to contextualize and legitimize its own radical conservatism.³³ Both the home front and front lines looked to military leaders, especially Robert E. Lee and the Army of Northern Virginia, as instruments of Confederate nationalism in which to take pride and unite understandings and symbolisms of nationhood and identity.³⁴ The cultural maintenance of the Southern way of life as well as the Old South's social hierarchy; the perpetuation of the institution of slavery; the political doctrine of states' rights and republicanism; and the rejection of the free labor market economy (as seen in the urban North) were all key ideological constituents of the definition of Confederate nationalism. In this way, Confederate nationalism must be conceptualized as both political and cultural, as both a movement of political legitimacy and a republic forged through shared culture.³⁵

However, Confederate nationalism was defined not only through ideas but also circumstances.³⁶ While historians have debated the strength of Confederate nationalism over the course of the war and its role in the Confederate defeat, it is clear that it did face structural challenges.³⁷ Desertion, class antagonisms, struggles over centralization, and political conflicts over slavery were all tangible realities that posed a threat to Confederate nationalism as an ideology. Furthermore, lower literacy rates and a weaker printing industry compared to the North, compromised the Confederate state's ability to produce and circulate nationalist messages through print capitalist structures.³⁸ This is why the Confederacy's engagement with supportive women was so important; it allowed leaders to circulate a nationalist message through women's bodies and actions.

Two analytical frameworks, one applied inside the household and one applied outside of it, are particularly useful in interrogating the relationship between middle-and planter-class white women, power, and nationalism. First, inside the household, Thavolia Glymph argues that historians can better understand the power of planter white women by not just comparing them to elite white men or to Northern white women, but to the power of enslaved women over time. With the breakdown of the planation household during and after the Civil War, as planter white women's power waned, former enslaved women gained power: "the transformation of the plantation household—that space where the ideology of southern white womanhood was constructed and reproduced through the denigration of black women—came to be viewed by slaves as central to the redefinition of freedom, citizenship and womanhood."³⁹ Glymph reveals the growing precarity and insecurity of white women's position within the household over time. Dependent upon the violent brutalization of enslaved women, white women's power in the household was conditional and, under threat with the advent of war, gradually eroded. However, looking outward, their power outside the household strengthened in terms of their new relationship with the state as individuals in their own right.

Second, bridging the domestic and the public spheres, Linda Kerber argues that as women received more rights from the state, they received less rights through their husbands.⁴⁰ In the early republic and antebellum America's constructs of coverture, obligations were gendered, rights were restricted according to gender, and most white women's relationship to the state was mediated through their husbands.⁴¹ After the American Revolution, the legal relationship between husband and wife based on the British model of coverture remained intact: "married women's obligations to their husbands and families overrode their obligations to the state [. . .] married women owe[d] their primary civic obligation to their husbands."⁴² The Confederacy knowingly disputed the early republic's understanding of federalism, and it also unwittingly challenged the foundations of coverture, not on legal terms but on social terms. With the advent of war, Confederate women were able to forge unmediated relationships with male political and military leaders as individuals in their own right without their husbands. The Civil War not only reformatted Southern family and gender roles, it reformatted women's relationship to the Confederate state.

In both the Union and the Confederacy, the Civil War strengthened the ties between military service and citizenship.[43] Excluded from military service, Confederate-supporting women found new ways to meaningfully contribute not only to the wartime cause outside of bearing arms but also outside of their husbands' oversight. With the withdrawal of men from the plantation household and home front, consistent with most wartime societies, Confederate women adopted new roles out of necessity to ensure societal survival in an immediate and tangible context.[44] At the same time, Confederate women also contributed to the ideological drivers of the republic; they helped build and strengthen Confederate nationalism. In order to do this, the women discussed in this book forged new relationships with Confederate leaders outside of their households. They became more outward-looking and engaged with issues that were less focused on their family's lived experiences and more focused on issues affecting the entire Confederate republic. These women shifted their focus from their families to the state. They shifted their lobbying efforts from their husbands to Confederate leaders. They shifted their location of activity from inside the plantation household to outside the plantation household.[45]

This is not to say these women completely turned away from their husbands, they did not. Rather, with the advent of war, women constructed a new relationship with the state that was not mediated through their husbands. Women had direct, and sometimes impactful, relationships with Confederate leaders that were oriented around issues that affected the Confederacy as a whole, and not just issues that affected women as individuals or family matriarchs. While Kerber's thesis is focused on rights and citizenship, it does hold a wider valence of power relations and women's changing relationship to the state relevant to this book. The women discussed in this book were not concerned with the expansion of their individual rights in a liberal tradition and the attainment of the full rights of citizenship, as seen in the Northern women's rights movement. In the Confederacy, these conservative women's new relationship with the state was centered on collective interests, and the ways in which women could give to the state through their devotion to the Confederate cause.[46] These women were concerned with strengthening collective nationalism for the Confederate republic as opposed to expanding individual rights for themselves as citizens.

Given this new relationship with the state, outside of the political sphere, and often framed through civic duty, Confederate women were informed and engaged with wartime political and social issues in decisive ways. An exclusion from political rights did not translate as women's exclusion from political culture. Kerber's notion of Republican Motherhood defines women's service to the newly formed late eighteenth-century American republic in terms of civic duty. Women were responsible for educating their sons in civic virtue as the next generation of leaders as well as supporting their husbands as the current generation of leaders.[47] An educated citizenry was a prerequisite for a healthy democracy, and women played an instrumental role in ensuring the sustainability of the American experiment in democracy. Restricted to the domestic sphere, women did not have direct access to the electoral political sphere; their access was mediated through their husbands (and, again, their civic obligation was to their husbands rather than to the state). Decades later, Confederate women were still excluded from the electoral political sphere, but they now contributed to political culture and civic duty as individuals rather than merely through their sons and husbands. Confederate women were the daughters and granddaughters of the Republican mothers who emerged from the American Revolution, but the advent of the Civil War allowed them to foster more direct relationships with the state and political sphere. As such, and consistent with recent works in Southern women's history, this book adopts a more capacious and inclusive definition of political culture.[48] Political culture is not restricted to the electoral political sphere but permeates civic society in both the public and private spheres.[49] While historians have examined conservative Virginia women's antebellum and postwar relationship to political culture, this book addresses this temporal gap in the historiography to examine conservative Virginia women's wartime engagement with political culture.[50]

The political culture of the Confederacy unfolded on the back porch of Mount Vernon and in the pews of the Methodist Church on Broad Street in Richmond. Southern women lobbied Union military as well as Confederate military and political officials at varying levels for various causes. These Confederate women had definite political effects, inside and outside of the Confederacy, even if the women themselves would not identify these ideas or actions as "political."[51] Moreover, these women held power in civic society. As Glymph shows, white women were intrinsic to the management of plantation slavery and were actively engaged in the required systemic violence of the institution.[52] Stephanie E. Jones-Rogers expands on Glymph's work to show how white women gained economic power from slavery: white women bought, sold, and perpetuated violence against enslaved persons, and in doing so, worked to shape the domestic slave market economy.[53] Both Glymph and Jones-Rogers reveal that Southern white women might not have had access to the electoral political sphere, but they did have social and economic power in civic society through slaveholding. Building on this work, with the advent of war, this book shows how white slaveholding women extended this power in civic society, as both actors and symbols of the Confederate cause, through their engagement with Confederate nationalism.

Virginia

The Weaker Sex in War uses Virginia as a lens to examine overarching issues addressing gender and nationalism across the Confederacy given the state's central role in Confederate social and political history. Moreover, Virginia offers a diverse demography consisting of both urban and rural communities as well as a geography consisting of coastal, mountain, and piedmont regions. In terms of urban studies, Virginia was home to the capital of the Confederacy; Richmond and its environs were at the vanguard of Confederate political, economic, and military life. The capital attracted Southerners from across the region, bringing a constant flow of visitors to Richmond. In 1860, Richmond was home to about 38,000 residents; by 1863, the Confederate capital's population was estimated to be approximately 100,000 people.[54] Such fluctuations in migration to the capital led to serious issues for civic authorities to remedy, including food and housing shortages as well as the struggle to control and regulate crime and labor.[55]

Virginia became an unrelenting battleground: From the First Battle of Bull Run, the first major land battle of the Civil War, in July 1861, to the surrender at Appomattox in April 1865, the state was a central site of battles and troop movements throughout the war.[56] Virginia suffered more than 120 battles throughout the war, over three times the number of the next highest state, Tennessee, and far fewer than Georgia, Louisiana, North Carolina, and South Carolina.[57] Virginia was at the heart of Southern civilian and military life, as well as Confederate political culture during the war. Virginia was the most populous state of the Confederacy; in 1860, the year before the war, nearly 1.6 million residents lived in the state. With almost 500,000 enslaved persons within its borders, Virginia also had the highest enslaved population. According to the 1860 Virginia census, 52,128 people were slaveholders out of a total population of 1,596,318 people: approximately 32 percent of Virginians owned enslaved persons on the eve of the Civil War. However, only 25,355 people owned five or more enslaved persons, placing them in the top 15.8 percent of the total population.[58]

Virginia was not quick to embrace secession. In the 1860 presidential election, Virginia did not vote for the Southern Democratic candidate John C. Breckinridge, but was one of three states that voted for John Bell of the short-lived Constitutional Union Party. Virginia was one of the last states to secede, and its convention voted against secession on April 4, 1861. In her diary, Samuella Hart Curd described the Union sentiment in Virginia in early 1861, "Virginia convention in session, strong by Union, but I fear, there can be no compromise."[59]

Less than two weeks later, on April 17, the convention voted to secede after the Battle of Fort Sumter and Lincoln's call for 75,000 volunteers.[60] On May 23, Virginians voted to support secession. Not all convention delegates or Virginia voters supported secession. Unionism was particularly strong in the western counties, with lower levels of slaveholding and a tighter economic relationship to the neighboring Union states of Ohio and Pennsylvania. Indeed, West Virginia broke off from Virginia and was admitted to the Union as a state in June 1863.[61] There were also collectives in Union-occupied areas of the state from early in conflict. Like other states in the Confederate South, there were Unionists scattered across the state of Virginia.[62]

The state of Virginia eventually joined the Confederacy, but not all Virginians pledged themselves to the Confederacy, including its women. Southern women's loyalty to the Union (or disloyalty to the Confederacy) could be shaped by a variety of issues, including moral imperatives on the slavery question and/or if they were enslaved, economic survival, opposition to Confederate policies as well as family and cultural ties. Some women, like Richmond-based Union spy Elizabeth Van Lew, actively supported the Union and tried to undermine the Confederate cause.[63] Other women were ambivalent and uncertain about the future of the Confederate cause, like the First Lady of the Confederacy and wartime Richmond resident Varina Howell Davis.[64] Enslaved women engaged in various strategies of resistance throughout the war undermining not only plantation mistresses in their individual plantation households but the foundations of both slavery as an institution and slavery as "the cornerstone" of the Confederate republic.[65] While this book examines Virginian women who supported the Confederacy, not all women in Virginia supported the Confederacy; these other women contributed to the war culture of the Confederacy in significant ways, though the Confederate state did not use these women as symbols to strengthen its nationalist agenda.

The Virginian organizations and women discussed herein held wider links to the Confederacy beyond the state of Virginia. While the Mount Vernon Ladies' Association of the Union was based in Mount Vernon, the organization sought vice regents to run auxiliary state organizations and to represent state interests in its central organizational structure. During the war, the organization had Southern state vice regents from Virginia, Georgia, Alabama, Mississippi, Louisiana, Tennessee, North Carolina, South Carolina, Arkansas, and Florida. The Ladies' Defense Association in Richmond was established in March 1862 to support the capital in a highly publicized campaign, but other ladies' gunboat associations sprung up across the South in the spring of 1862, including in Louisiana, Georgia, and South Carolina. The Richmond bread riot was not an isolated event. In the spring of 1863, a series of food riots took place across the South, including in Atlanta, Georgia; Salisbury, North Carolina; Mobile, Alabama; and Petersburg, Virginia. As the final chapter considers, the establishment of the Home for Needy Confederate Women in Richmond in 1898 served as a model for the construction of Confederate women's homes across the South in the early decades of the twentieth century, homes such as the Confederate Women's Home in Fayetteville, North Carolina, in 1915. The organizations and causes discussed in this book may have originated and/or had the largest following in Virginia, but these ideas had a greater valence and presence across the South. The book's focus on Virginia provides a prism to consider these local and state issues on a regional level in terms of their greater impact on Confederate nationalism and political culture.[66]

The following chapters interrogate the relationship between gender and nationalism on the Confederate home front to show how conservative middle-and planter-class white women actively worked to build nationalism in both their tangible works for the cause and their abstract symbolism of the cause. Each of these chapters reveals how the state recognized the power of women as both wartime actors and symbols, and responded in different ways and to different ends, to women's wartime activities. Women's wartime activities were not monolithic and women supported different initiatives across the war, but these activities helped to shape women's relationship to the state. Likewise, women's relationship to the state was not static, but it was central to building and strengthening Confederate nationalism. These women may not have had power in the political sphere, but the political sphere recognized their power to shape nationalist engagement and discourses.

Chapter 1 examines how women in the Mount Vernon Ladies' Association of the Union (MVLA) tried to adopt a posture of "neutrality" during the secession crisis and early war to leverage women's roles as symbols of virtue and as social mediators. The chapter shows that this neutrality was a sign of their antebellum politicization and was a strategy for intervening in public life, but that such a stance became deeply contested. As founding regent Ann Pamela Cunningham's exchange with Massachusetts politician Edward Everett dramatizes, for the "ladies" who worked on behalf of the MLVA and various Confederate causes, so-called neutrality was both a rejection of the Union and an assertion of the legitimacy, as a belligerent power whose citizens deserved access to American symbols, of the Confederacy.

Chapter 2 shows how pretenses of neutrality fell away in the Confederate capital in the spring of 1862 as Confederates faced the spectre of "invasion" from Union general George McClellan's army and of Union occupation. The Ladies Defense Association (LDA) both asserted women's right to intervene in military matters and provided a useful symbol, for Confederate culture more broadly, of women's patriotism.

Chapter 3 discusses the Richmond bread riot and class conflict among whites to show that the Confederate government sought to protect elite women against the unruliness of the "unworthy" poor. In its connection of the conscription laws and the draft riot, this chapter argues that elites displayed not just insensitivity but outright animosity to those deemed unworthy.

Chapter 4 interjects women and gender into the historiography on foreign recognition of the Confederacy. This discussion uses the examples of Rose Greenhow and other emissaries and propagandists to show that advocates of foreign recognition framed their case in gendered terms, with an emphasis on women's victimization designed to demonize the Union and undercut its claims to humanitarianism.

Chapter 5 shows how women attempted to render female descendants of soldiers' families as "living monuments" to the Confederacy, who deserved the literal support of the government; the chapter thus shows that Confederate memorialization was not about mourning but about keeping the Confederacy "alive" in lineage and in spirit.

The epilogue comments on the controversies over including Sally Tompkins in the Virginia Women's Monument and illustrates that Tompkins should be regarded, in light of women's centrality to the construction of Confederate nationalism, as a political symbol, and not just as an apolitical caregiver.

Overall, *The Weaker Sex in War: Gender and Nationalism in Civil War Virginia* highlights the centrality of gender to Confederate identity and nationhood, both for its (mostly female) population on the home front and its (mostly male) governmental policy architects and influencers. Conservative women played crucial roles in creating, and, at times, problematizing, the idea of the Confederate republic. Middle- and planter-class white Southern women who supported the Confederacy were central to these processes not only as individual actors with agency but also in their projection and circulation as potent symbols reinforcing foundational principles of the Confederate republic. These women were not concerned with expanding their individual rights as citizens nor were they passive in political culture; rather, they actively defined the terms of their engagement through performance of national devotion. Confederate male elites may have mobilized these women as archetypes to advance a Confederate agenda, but conservative women were complicit in this process. Seen in this way, Confederate nationalism was more dependent on gender than has been previously argued. This fundamental relationship between the Confederacy and the conservative middle-and planter-class women on its home front eludes a simple, uniform narrative. In offering a more layered and interdisciplinary account of this relationship, this book aims to come to terms with the fraught reality between the government and its people, between the construction and reception of nationalism, and between the possibility and impossibility of a Confederate victory.

CHAPTER 1

Mount Vernon Ladies' Association of the Union

WRITING TO THE MARQUIS de Lafayette in February 1784, George Washington confessed his "heartfelt satisfaction" upon returning to his beloved Mount Vernon after the War of Independence,

> I am become a private citizen on the banks of the Potomac, and under the shadow of my own Vine and own Fig-tree, free from the bustle of camp and the busy scenes of public life, I am solacing myself with those tranquil enjoyments, of which the Soldier who is ever in pursuit of fame, the Statesman whose watchful days and sleepless nights are spent in devising schemes to promote the welfare of his own, perhaps the ruin of other countries ... can have very little conception.[1]

Washington could have hardly predicted that far from being his refuge from the American Revolution, Mount Vernon would lie on the front lines of the American Civil War: not only as a physically vulnerable site just across the Potomac River and Union forces in Washington, D.C., but as an unwitting ideological battleground to assert and maintain an official position of neutrality against allegations of Confederate loyalty. With the advent of the Civil War, Mount Vernon became a nexus of military and political debates surrounding claims to neutrality, debates that encompassed soldiers and statesmen alike, from the enlisted Confederate to the commanding general of the Union army: Who were the rightful heirs to the country's revolutionary legacy, the Union or the Confederacy?

George Washington played a crucial role in forging the collective identity of the Confederacy through memory. The official Confederate seal depicted Washington on horseback, and Jefferson Davis's second inauguration took place on Washington's 130th birthday, at the foot of a statue of Washington in the Confederacy's new capital in Richmond. Davis began his address: "On this the birthday of the man most identified with the establishment of American independence, and beneath the monument erected to commemorate his heroic virtues and those of his compatriots, we have assembled to usher into existence the Permanent Government of the Confederate States."[2] This identification and reverence of Washington as a means to build a cohesive Confederate national identity was not restricted in its usage to Confederate elites. Significantly, women on the home front often called the celebrated generals Robert E. Lee, Stonewall Jackson, and P. G. T. Beauregard "second Washingtons" in their letters and diaries; these Southern women also undertook new wartime roles through organizations such as the Mount Vernon Ladies' Association, which forms the focal point of this chapter.

The legacy of the American Revolution and the Founding Fathers were central to definitions of Confederate nationalism. Depicting themselves as the rightful inheritors of 1776 was one of the core ways in which the Confederate elites tried to coalesce the lower classes around the Confederate cause. To compel nonslaveholding whites to support a war and economic policies that did not benefit them as individuals, the Confederacy portrayed itself as more than just a union of slaveholders but as the legitimate successors of the American revolutionary tradition, safeguarding core American ideas that had emerged at the end of the eighteenth century.[3] The memory of the American Revolution was an inclusive exercise all white Southerners across gender and class lines could engage with and feel a sense of shared belonging in a collective identity. In terms of defining Confederate nationalism through an invention of tradition and shared culture *ideologically* embodied in Washington, the Confederacy crafted a message with the potential to resonate with and hold real meaning for the masses.

This is not to say that the legacy of Washington was not important to the Union. Lincoln issued a presidential proclamation on February 19, 1862, the same month as Davis's second inauguration, to celebrate Washington's birthday; the tableaux, *Columbia at Washington's Tomb*, was popular in the Union during the Civil War years; and Union soldiers frequently diverted their journeys for the opportunity to visit Mount Vernon and Washington's tomb throughout the war. While the Confederacy was forceful and prolific in its use of the memory of Washington to bolster its nationalist cause, the Union also valued Washington's legacy in the Civil War.

Given the significance of Washington to both sides of the conflict, who held the right to safeguard Washington's legacy during this tumultuous chapter in American history? Or, more specifically, as this chapter addresses, was the Mount Vernon Ladies' Association (MVLA) capable of preserving the memory and integrity of the Father of the Nation in the context of the American

Civil War? Wartime Mount Vernon offers a nuanced lens to examine issues surrounding the gendered politics of loyalty, neutrality, and nationalism. While the MVLA physically occupied the mansion throughout the duration of the war, it had to defend itself against claims of Confederate loyalty. These rumors of Confederate loyalty became more frequent and more scandalous in the spring of 1861. Mount Vernon was in a militarily strategic position on the Potomac River south of Washington, D.C. Indeed, a steamer service had connected Georgetown and Mount Vernon in the antebellum years. During the war, U.S. secretary of war Edwin Stanton terminated the steamer service citing its potential security threats. Had the Confederate military or Confederate sympathizers in the region been given access to the Potomac River in such close proximity to the nation's capital, civilians as well as government officials in Washington, D.C., would have been physically threatened – and Mount Vernon could have been used to bring the war to the Union capital.

Mount Vernon's geographic position also held an emotional symbolic meaning: This was the Father of the Nation's home. According to Thavolia Glymph, Southern white womanhood was defined and created in the plantation household.[4] Washington's plantation household magnified this construction of Southern womanhood and gave it a national audience. The women of the MLVA were not just campaigning for Washington's legacy, they were performing the conventions of good Southern womanhood through a familiar framework of the household, but to a new audience far beyond their own family and enslaved persons. Furthermore, within individual plantation households, white women's pursuit of domesticity was often reliant upon yet always "greatly complicated" by slavery and slave labor.[5] Likewise, in their work to preserve and cultivate Washington's home along mid-nineteenth-century standards of civilization, the MVLA contended with Washington's and Mount Vernon's historic ties to slavery, as well as individual organizational members' ties to slavery, making issues of home and slavery deeply intertwined for Southern white planter women in the antebellum and wartime South.[6]

Given this geographic and symbolic importance of Mount Vernon, visible and outspoken Confederate supporters occupying George Washington's home would have given a great deal of credence to the Confederacy. Such an acquisition would have illustrated Confederate claims to be the rightful inheritors of the American revolutionary tradition, and in doing so, strengthened Confederate nationalism. If the MLVA were to have shown such partisanship, Confederate leaders would likely have harnessed their words and actions to support the Southern wartime agenda; the organization and its women members could easily have become a symbol of Confederate nationalism, like other women discussed in this book. However, the organization meticulously avoided its appropriation as a symbol for the Confederate cause. On a highly visible stage, brimming with emotion and tradition and projected to a national audience, the women of the MVLA actively championed and performed the neutrality of the nascent organization. This performance of neutrality was necessary to appeal to the entire nation and to ensure the organization's postwar survival, even if individual members were not wholeheartedly committed to neutrality and many likely supported secession. The MVLA's civic actions held political meaning and the organization became a symbol of not only the preservation of George Washington's legacy but also of wartime neutrality. The women of the MVLA controlled their contributions to and performance of this campaign for neutrality and played active and eager roles to intervene and help determine the wartime status of Washington's estate.

Historians have examined the early years of the MVLA (1856–59) and its role as a mediator in the late 1850s sectional crisis before the outbreak of war. Chronologically, this chapter picks up where this scholarship concludes to provide the first comprehensive analysis of the role of the MVLA in the Civil War. Available studies do not include an engagement with the MVLA during the war years other than a brief reference that the MVLA "remained neutral" during the war.[7] Indeed, as Prince Napoléon Joseph Charles Paul Bonaparte reflected on his visit in August 1861, Mount Vernon was "removed from the scenes of conflict, yet surrounded by them. . . . this little corner of the earth was kept sacred, neutral ground! . . . it was a fact by itself in the history of the World, and the wars of the world."[8] As the prince's reflections show, by August 1861, after General Order 13 was issued by the commanding general of the Union army Winfield Scott on July 31 establishing the estate's nonpartisan status, neutrality was the defining feature of wartime Mount Vernon for both contemporary observers as well as historians.

But what about the early months of the conflict, from South Carolina's secession in December 1860 to the issuance of Scott's order on July 31, 1861? In order to chart the MVLA's path to neutrality, this chapter offers the first examination of the MVLA during the first few months of the war, when the organization faced allegations of Confederate loyalty. This was a time when Northern recognition of its self-declared neutrality and the avoidance of Union occupation seemed unlikely. To simply state that Mount Vernon was neutral during the war obscures the fraught realities this organization grappled with in the first months of the conflict. The MVLA understood the significance of neutrality in terms not only of military engagement (i.e., the physical safety of Mount Vernon) but also of wider civic sentiment (i.e., the ideological battle for hearts and minds on the home fronts). To promote organizational neutrality, the women of the MVLA forged new relationships with and lobbied their cases to Union leaders, for example, the veteran Massachusetts Whig politician and the 1860 vice presidential candidate for the Constitutional Union Party, Edward Everett. In these ways, these women adopted new and expanded roles in civic society to petition leaders in the political sphere for neutrality.

As an organization, the MVLA understood that it needed to appear neutral, even if many of its individual Southern members may have supported the Confederacy. Neutrality was a realpolitik strategy for the organization to survive the war and not necessarily a reflection of the individual convictions of its members. Such a distinction testifies to these women's growing consciousness of political culture and their eagerness to engage with broader issues than they had in the antebellum period. These women did not enjoy full rights of citizenship, nor did they seek them, but in the wartime context they forged more direct and less mediated relationships and exchanges with male leaders in the political and military sphere.

It is important to recognize that, unlike the rest of the women in this book, the women of the MVLA did not champion Confederate nationalism. However, the strategies and partnerships pursued by the conservative women of the MVLA in the secession crisis and first three months of the war are similar to the efforts undertaken by nationalist women during the war. Beginning this book by exploring the MVLA in the secession crisis from December 1860, before Confederate women's wartime organizations and causes were established (as discussed in chapters 2 through 5), shows the trajectory of conservative Virginian women's agency and engagement with political culture from secession to the Lost Cause.

Acquisition of Mount Vernon

In 1853, Louisa Bird Cunningham, upon seeing the ruinous state of George Washington's Mount Vernon estate from a steamer traveling on the Potomac River, wrote to her daughter, Ann Pamela, that if the men of the country could not keep Mount Vernon in repair, it was up to the women to do so. Accordingly, Ann Pamela soon began a fundraising effort to save Mount Vernon. Writing under the name "A Southern Matron," Cunningham published a patriotic and gendered appeal addressed to "The Ladies of the South" in the December 2, 1853, edition of the *Charleston Mercury*:

> Ladies of the South, can you still be with closed souls and purses, while the world cries "Shame upon America," and suffer Mount Vernon, with all its sacred associations, to become, as it is spoken and probable, the seat of manufactures and manufactories; noise and smoke, and the "busy hum of men," destroying all sanctity and repose around the tomb of your own "world's wonder?"[9]

The fundraising effort soon spread to a national scale and Cunningham erected an organizational structure to reflect its geographic scope. At the head of the national organization would be a regent and each state organization would be directed by a vice regent: a federalist division of power applied to a civic organization. Sarah Agnes Rice Pryor described an early meeting of the Virginia chapter of the MVLA as "'a meeting of ladies—yes, *ladies*! Making speeches and passing resolutions like men.'"[10] In 1856, the Mount Vernon Ladies Association of the Union charter was accepted and incorporated by the state of Virginia. Initially, the women selected "Mount Vernon Association" as its name. However, their advisors, led by Charleston lawyer James Louis Petigru, suggested the insertion of "Union" in the title to highlight their commitment to unionism in the context of the sectional crisis. It is likely that "Ladies" was also added in order to highlight the apolitical agenda of the organization and its abstention from sectional political affairs. In addition, the inclusion of "Ladies" could also dissuade possible critiques of the MVLA as an infringement on public sphere masculine affairs.[11] Women's work in civic society could not been seen as overshadowing men's work in the public sphere.

Nominally, Mount Vernon had been in the hands of John Augustine Washington III since 1841, when his mother gave him managerial control of the estate. He became the estate's legal owner upon his mother's death in 1855 and unsuccessfully tried to sell it to both the U.S. Congress and the state of Virginia. In 1858, the MVLA bought the estate from Washington with a $18,000 down payment on the $200,000 (with interest) agreed sale price for 200 acres of the Mount Vernon estate, including the house and tomb. The MVLA paid Washington four more equal installments over the next four years to complete the sale. Three years later, in 1861, the Civil War broke out with its founding regent, Ann Pamela Cunningham, at the MVLA's helm.

While she came from a distinguished slaveholding South Carolina family, Ann Pamela Cunningham, founding regent of the MVLA, was far from the ideal of elite antebellum Southern womanhood of wifely and maternal domestic duty, as discussed in the introduction. Following a horseback riding accident, she was a semi-invalid and often debilitated by various health issues. In fact, in the first MVLA fundraising lectures in Richmond delivered by Washington scholar and MVLA surrogate Edward Everett, Cunningham was too ill to sit in the audience. Pryor recalled that "At the last moment a small sofa—chaise lounge—was pushed on the platform, and upon this the devoted woman [Cunningham] was laid, and forgot all her weakness."[12] Furthermore, she never married, her prominent paternal ancestors were Loyalists in the American Revolution, and she strayed from the domain of female civic duty into more male politically charged issues several times over the course of her life. John C. Calhoun had tutored her father Robert Cunningham in the study of law. However, during the Nullification Crisis of 1832, they came to a public disagreement when Cunningham advocated a staunch Unionist position.[13] This disagreement filtered down to their daughters in early 1832 when Ann Pamela Cunningham and Anna Maria Calhoun were roommates at Barhamville, an elite female academy near Columbia. In letters to his daughter, Calhoun was dismayed at the selection of her roommate, and he told her to abstain from political debates with Ms. Cunningham.[14]

Cunningham was aware of the importance of eliding sectional strife prior to the outbreak of war and ensuring the MVLA's claims to neutrality after the outbreak of war in April 1861 with the Battle of Fort Sumter. Cunningham had planned to stay at Mount Vernon during the war to oversee its renovation. However, after the recent death of her father, the family was struggling to manage their Rosemont plantation in South Carolina. Obliging her mother's wishes, Cunningham returned home in December 1860 after only living at Mount Vernon for a few weeks. In her absence, Cunningham selected Sarah Tracy, her personal secretary from New York, and Upton Herbert, a distant cousin of the Washington family from Virginia, to occupy the estate during the war: a Northern woman and a Southern man to safeguard the neutrality of Mount Vernon. Mary McMakin of Philadelphia joined Tracy at Mount Vernon as a companion for propriety's sake. Tracy wrote to Cunningham in early 1861 that an association surrogate advised, "the presence of ladies there [Mount Vernon] would be its greatest protection."[15] Indeed, in several of the letters exchanged between Tracy and Cunningham during the war, the term "the presence of a lady" was used to imply the ways in which gender—namely, the social construction of women as physically weak and ideologically apolitical—could be showcased to physically protect and ideologically preserve Mount Vernon during the tumultuous context of war. As such, "the weaker sex in war" warranted physical and ideological protection. These three wartime guardians of Mount Vernon slept in bedchambers on upper floors and used Washington's study as a dining room, endeavoring to keep as much as the house open to visitors as possible.[16]

While it is debatable whether Cunningham herself was a secessionist in the months leading up to Fort Sumter, from her secret work with the Ladies' Confederate Naval Association it is clear that she held conservative beliefs and supported the Confederacy after the outbreak of war.[17] However, Cunningham concealed from the public her involvement with the new organization so that it would not undermine the ideological neutrality of Mount Vernon. The founding regent of the MVLA could not be seen to publicly endorse the Confederate cause; her personal convictions, if made public, could compromise the collective objectives of the organization. There is no record of the Northern press critiquing her role in the Ladies' Confederate Naval Association, though newspapers critiqued her partisanship, as explored below.

One day after Virginians voted to support secession, on May 24, 1861, Union forces entered Alexandria, a location close to the United States capital of Washington, D.C., with strong transport networks that would prove advantageous in the conflict. Union forces would occupy Alexandria for the rest of the war. Before the Union presence in Alexandria, Upton Herbert rejected several offers to join the Confederate army. According to Tracy, "Both his brothers, and every friend he has, have done so, and they wonder much that he has refused the command of every company offered. He says very little about it, but has, I know, made a sacrifice for Mount Vernon."[18] Or to put it another way, he sacrificed his Confederate allegiance for Mount Vernon's neutrality.

In addition to Tracy, Herbert, and McMakin, free Blacks were present in daily life at wartime Mount Vernon. After the organization bought Mount Vernon from John Augustine Washington in 1858, the women decided not to use enslaved labor as its previous owner had (and he had been virulently criticized by William Lloyd Garrison in the Northern press for doing so). Instead, they hired the free children and grandchildren of one of George Washington's former enslaved persons, and later free carpenter, West Ford.[19] Again, the organization attempted to elide a loaded sectional issue in the name of civic duty. The employment of free Black laborers at Mount Vernon was a stratagem of the MVLA to dim the slavery issue.

However, this narrative obscures the fraught and more complicated relationship between the MVLA and slavery. While the MVLA may have averted direct financial support of slavery, it nevertheless indirectly financed the institution. Washington used his payments from the MVLA to purchase another plantation, Waveland, in Fauquier County and eight male enslaved persons to labor on this new plantation. Furthermore, while Washington sold the organization one-sixth of his ownership of the Mount Vernon estate, he retained the remaining five-sixths for farm use.[20] This farmland relied on an extensive network of enslaved labor to render it profitable. An inventory dated June 8, 1861, details the property, including sixteen enslaved persons with a cumulative reported value of $16,600. Two of these enslaved persons, Jim Mitchell and Edmund Parker, would go on to work for the MVLA.[21] While the MVLA removed enslaved labor from one-fifth of Washington's holdings, enslaved labor remained on the vast majority of his original landholdings.

Furthermore, Cunningham as founding regent of the MVLA had been born into an elite slaveholding family. When Cunningham left Mount Vernon to return to her family in December 1860, she did so to help manage the plantation, and its 138 enslaved persons, in the wake of her father's death. In this way, Cunningham prioritized her familial obligations, and implicitly her family's obligation to plantation culture and slavery, over her obligations to the MVLA. Unsurprisingly, the Cunningham family's slaveholdings, as well as the slaveholdings of the Southern state vice regents, was never publicized by the MLVA. Through selective presentation, the MVLA showcased a narrative that precluded the organization from any involvement or complicity with the institution of slavery. Again, the use of "ladies" in the organization's name highlighted the ideal of the Southern lady and not the lived reality of the violence and social as well as economic power of slaveholding women.[22]

However, this strategy of selective memory and omission was not universally convincing. Women's rights and abolitionist campaigners Elizabeth Chace and Elizabeth Cady Stanton were both invited by the MVLA to serve as state vice regents. Both rejected these offers as they felt their work for their reform movements was of far greater importance. They both published their refusal letters in the December 31, 1858, edition of William Lloyd Garrison's abolitionist newspaper, *The Liberator*. Stanton proclaimed, "She labors hard to restore Mount Vernon and forgets that the good old Revolutionary Fathers, in declaring that 'All men are created equal' lost together all sight of the negro and the woman.... Until we give the world freedom, and a new type of womanhood, we have no energies to expend elsewhere."[23] Chase concurred, "How can the women of this nation talk of commemorating that struggle [American Revolution], when, with their consent, and approval and aid, every sixth woman in the land is liable to be sold on the auction-block, and is often so sold, for the vilest purposes?"[24] For these leaders of the fight for women's rights and abolition, saving Mount Vernon was a frivolous cause and distracted from the urgent issues of gender and race reform in the mid-nineteenth century. Unlike the conservative women of the MLVA, Stanton and Chase lobbied for progressive reforms to secure the full rights of citizenship across race and gender lines.

On the other end of the spectrum, the women from the South who did accept positions of vice regents were also associated with other causes outside of Mount Vernon. These Southern women often held close associations to the Confederate republic, either through their families or their own actions as individuals. For example, Octavia Walton Le Vert, vice regent of Alabama (1858–77), was a socialite, published a book *Souvenirs of Travel* in 1857, and two years earlier traveled to Europe to represent Alabama at the Paris Exhibition. While she was not an ardent secessionist, she supported Alabama at the outbreak of war and nursed wounded Confederate soldiers. Mary Middleton Rutledge Fogg, vice regent of Tennessee (1858–72), worked for Felicia Grundy Porter's Soldiers' Aid Society to support Confederate soldiers during the war. A 1908 obituary of Letitia Harper Morehead Walker, vice regent of North Carolina (1859–1908), praised her service to the Confederacy: "Her life was spent with enthusiastic devotion to the Confederate cause—providing for sick and wounded soldiers, making clothes and comforts and blankets for their camps, and welcoming and entertaining them in the beautiful old home Blendwood." The obituary went on to claim she sheltered "President Davis and family and Cabinet [,] Vice President Stephens, Generals Beauregard, Magruder, and other weary officers passing through Greensboro."[25] Catherine Willis Grey Murat, vice regent of Florida (1858–67) and great grandniece of George Washington, bought the Bellevue plantation in 1854 after the death of her husband Prince Achille Murat in 1847. As a widow, Murat owned enslaved persons and actively supported the Confederacy; she is even believed to have fired a cannon on the grounds of the state capitol celebrating Florida's secession from the Union.[26]

Some vice regents were associated with the Confederacy in their marriage to Southern Democrats and later Confederate leaders. Catherine Morris Anderson McWillie, vice regent of Mississippi (1858–73), was married to the antebellum Democratic governor of Mississippi William McWillie (1857–59). As governor, McWillie supported slavery and states' rights. He later supported the Confederacy. Sarah Frances Smith Johnson, vice regent of Arkansas (1859–62), was married to the antebellum Arkansas Democratic senator and congressman Robert Ward Johnson. Johnson was a staunch advocate of slavery, served in the Confederate Congress, and was a strong supporter of Jefferson Davis. Mary Cox Chesnut, vice regent of South Carolina from 1860 until her death in 1864, was married to one of the wealthiest planters in South Carolina. Her son James Chesnut Jr. was a leading antebellum Democratic politician and served as senator from South Carolina from 1858 until the state's secession and later brigadier general in the Confederacy. His wife, and Mary's daughter-in-law, was the famed wartime diarist and Confederate supporter Mary Boykin Chesnut. Mary Cox Chesnut wrote an affectionate letter to Cunningham expressing her "admiration" for her "wonderful efforts" with the MVLA as its founding regent.[27] This is not to say all of these women were steadfastly committed to Confederate nationalism. Yet in terms of optics to their wider communities, region, and even fractured nation, their voluntary work and/or visibility of family members as prominent supporters of the Confederacy associated them with the Confederate cause. Such actual or perceived associations of Confederate loyalty from its individual members could undermine the neutrality of the organization.

From the start of the war, Cunningham was concerned about the visibility of neutrality at the estate. She required that soldiers shroud any physical appearance of loyalty to either the Union or the Confederacy to be admitted to George Washington's home. Within the first few weeks of the war, Tracy relayed an update to Cunningham on her instructions, "They have behaved very well about it. Many of them come from a great distance and have never been here, and have no clothes but their uniforms. They borrow shawls and cover up their buttons and leave their arms outside the enclosures, and never come but two or three at a time."[28] Despite these new measures, soldiers still seemed to take pleasure in visiting Mount Vernon and seeing the preservation of Washington's estate. For example, in his diary, Private James A. Minish of the 105th Pennsylvania Regiment provided a detailed account of his 1861 trip to the estate, "we seen the [saddle] holster of Washington & several of the knapsacks used in the revolutionary war. . . . we were in the setting room of the general. . . . the building and grounds were kept in the same manner as they were during the life of Washington. . . . I will never forget the sights of Mt. Vernon."[29]

Mount Vernon's neutrality was also vulnerable to manipulation by some opportunistic civilians. In July 1861, Tracy learned that her Northern friends with Southern loyalties were trying to smuggle intelligence to Confederate general P. G. T. Beauregard via Mount Vernon. She wrote to the vice regent of Delaware of the betrayal, "The only correspondence from Mount Vernon to the South are letters to Miss Cunningham, and a very neutral place it would be, if the Regent cannot be permitted to hear what is going on here!"[30] Tracy's "friends" sought to exploit Mount Vernon's quest for neutrality for their own gain.

The "Theft" of Washington's Body and General Order 13

One episode in particular illustrates this broad and multidimensional struggle for Mount Vernon's neutrality: claims that George Washington's body had been removed from Mount Vernon at the outbreak of war. After the secession of South Carolina and the departure of Cunningham, the MVLA was forced to respond to allegations of its secessionist sympathies. Tracy lamented, "I am constantly asked by people from every direction whether it is true that this Ms Cunningham is a 'Secessionist?' . . . I was told the other day that it would break up the Association."[31] Codifying these rumors in print, a January 25, 1861, article in the local *Alexandria Gazette* boldly claimed, "the Southern matron, is now at Barhamville. We are informed that her patriotic heart beats in ardent response to the great Southern movement, and that her only regret is that she cannot bring the tomb of Washington with the South."[32] While the article stopped short of accusing the MVLA of stealing Washington's body, it did plant the seed of a rumor that would plague the association for the next few months and lay the blame squarely with Cunningham, the imperfect Southern lady.

These rumors soon spread to a national scale, and that spring several Northern newspapers raised the likelihood that Washington's body had actually been removed on the MVLA's watch. As stated on the front page of the *New York Herald* on May 18, 1861, following up on its previous front page story about the removal of Washington's remains, from May 15, 1861, "a guard of honor, some three hundred strong, under the command of Captain Maury, was formed with a view to remove the entire sarcophagus of Washington and to transfer it to Lexington, Virginia." The article went on to speculate on the likelihood of the theft, "If it has not been accomplished it will be strange, for it was the intention of many influential persons not to leave these precious ashes to the hazards or war."[33]

In response to these mounting allegations in the Northern press, the organization likewise responded in the court of public opinion, and vice regents wrote to their local newspapers to dispute these virulent claims. In a letter to the *Philadelphia Evening News* in response to a May 15 article that reported John Augustine Washington III had taken Washington's remains and joined the Confederate army, vice regent of Delaware Margaret Comegys expressed indignation that the body of Washington could have been moved from Mount Vernon. She even copied the relevant clauses from the contract between Washington and the MVLA to prove that there was no legal basis to the claims.[34]

Similarly, Tracy responded to the *New York Herald* in a letter to the *National Intelligencer*, "the public, the owners of this noble possession, need for no molestation of this one national spot belonging alike to North and South. Over it there can be no dispute!" Tracy went on to praise the work of the MVLA, "The Ladies have taken every necessary precaution for the preservation of the place, and their earnest desire is, that the public should feel confidence in their faithfulness to trust, and believe that Mount Vernon is safe under the guardianship of the Ladies of the Mount Vernon Association of the Union."[35] Validating these claims, the *New York Times* reported a Union army expedition was dispatched less than a week later to investigate these rumors. On May 26, 1861, the newspaper published an article aptly titled, "A Visit to Mount Vernon. The Tomb of Washington Unmolested." According to the newspaper, Union general Daniel Sickles, who less than two years earlier had become the first person to use temporary insanity as a defense in U.S. legal history for the murder of his wife's lover, sent three emissaries to investigate the whereabouts of Washington's remains, "They found it [the tomb] had never been molested; cobwebs were on the bars of the gate, weeds had grown up from the ground in the interior of the vault."[36] While confirming the security and location of Washington's remains, the entrance of the Union army into this rumor mill only fed fuel to the growing fire over both the vulnerability of Mount Vernon as a geographic location as well as the weakness of the MVLA as a newly established organization to safeguard Washington's body. According to two leading New York newspapers, in articles published within one week of each other, both the Confederate and Union armies had visited Mount Vernon for very different reasons: theft and reconnaissance, respectively. Regardless of their accuracy, these journalistic representations introduced Mount Vernon as a site ripe for military intervention into the Northern public imagination.

This episode of the alleged theft of Washington's physical body also reveals the deep structural weaknesses in disseminating Confederate nationalism to non-elites as early as the spring of 1861.[37] Although this episode was a discrete snapshot of the aspirational ideological drive of Confederate nationalism—to take the legacy of American Revolution, in the physical form of Washington's body, and transplant it in the South—other than the local *Alexandria Gazette*, this rumor did not appear in the Southern press.[38] While this rumor was soon proved to be false in the May 26, 1861, *New York Times* article mentioned above, it was printed in several Northern newspapers earlier that month. While this rumor was widely circulated in the Northern press, before this episode was discounted as false, the Southern press did not mention or reprint this story that spoke to the core tenets of Confederate nationalism.

Benedict Anderson's theory of nationalism emphasizes the circulation of a shared print culture in the formation of national identity. This shared print culture, and newspapers in particular, offered a crucial structural means to disseminate the Confederate nationalist message to the masses. However, most of the nation's printing presses were in the North and transportation and communication networks were compromised in northern Virginia from May 1861 with the Union occupation. No matter how culturally connective and politically inspiring Confederate nationalism could be in its abstract definition and rhetoric (as an ideology), its failure to physically reach the masses severely compromised its efficacy (as a tangible lived reality). This was a missed opportunity for the Confederacy to make their abstract definition of nationalism more tangible to the masses; the South's alleged repossession of Washington's body for their cause would have been a touchstone for all Southerners to come together and meet on common ground across class lines.

From South Carolina, Cunningham was so vexed by these recent newspaper rumors she wrote to Edward Everett, a champion of the MVLA and its most successful fundraiser, to ask him to reconsider his wartime support of the Union and publicly assert his own personal neutrality to safeguard the Mount Vernon mission, given his well-known association with the project. Everett politely refused the request, "I felt that my relations with the community in which I live, perhaps I may venture to say with the country, forbade my standing neutral."[39] While Cunningham publicly prioritized organizational neutrality over her personal loyalty to the Confederacy, Everett could not commit to such a position. Women in civic society could lobby for neutrality after 1860, but Everett, the former vice presidential candidate of the Constitutional Union Party in the 1860 presidential election, felt the relationship with his local community was more important in May 1861. Nevertheless, Everett advocated privately for the neutrality of Mount Vernon and wrote to commanding general of the Union army, Winfield Scott. Scott was already familiar with the potential military significance of Mount Vernon. In 1851, Scott had joined President Millard Fillmore and other officials to evaluate whether Mount Vernon could be used as a hospital for soldiers.[40] The U.S. government declined to buy Mount Vernon, leaving the estate available for purchase by the MVLA five years later. Everett wrote to Scott about the prospect of Mount Vernon's neutrality in May 1861:

> I hope you will not think me too impertinent if I suggest the expediency of a General Order directing that special care should be taken to prevent injury by fire or otherwise to Arlington House where many articles of furniture and other personal relics of Washington are preserved and also ordering extra precautions for the preservation intact of Mount Vernon and its sacred precincts.[41]

In a postscript, Everett urged that in addition to the General Order 13 being issued by Scott, it also be published to the country. Now a national memorial to Robert E. Lee, Arlington House held strong links to both the Washington and Lee families. Lee married his distant cousin and the great-granddaughter of Martha Washington, Mary Custis, at Arlington House in 1831. Six of their children were born at Arlington House and this was their family home until the outbreak of war. Given the house's vulnerable position on the Potomac River, the Lee family left Arlington House at the start of the war and the Union seized the house and grounds.[42] Not only would Everett's proposal target the Lee family, it would prove the case for Mount Vernon's neutrality in the court of public opinion. This General Order was not just about soldiers respecting the physical objects of Arlington House and grounds of Mount Vernon, but also about the American people respecting the ideological stance of the MVLA. Cunningham, a conservative Southern woman, directly lobbied a Northern politician, who then presented her case to the commanding general of the Union military. In the context of war, Cunningham had more direct access to male leaders and was able to forge strategic relationships to further her own agenda.

In response to these ongoing rumors that did not seem to be nearing a resolution in civic society, General Winfield Scott issued General Order 13 on July 31 to assert Mount Vernon's neutral status. As per Everett's request, the order was widely publicized in the North. However, much to the MVLA's dismay, in his order, Scott shamed Confederate forces and identified the Confederates as belligerents prompting government intervention:

> Mount Vernon, so recently consecrated to the Immortal Washington by the Ladies of America, has been overrun by bands of rebels, who having trampled under the foot of the Constitution of the United Sates, the ark of our freedom and prosperity, are prepared to tramp on the ashes of him to whom we are all mainly indebted for these mighty blessings.[43]

Once again, Tracy resorted to the organization's modus operandi and quickly penned a letter to the *National Intelligencer* stating that Scott was "misinformed" and no Confederate soldiers had even visited Mount Vernon since the occupation of Alexandria. She ended the letter underlining the importance of both the estate's and organization's neutrality, "The Regent is earnest and decided in her direction and request to those she has made responsible for the preservation of order and neutrality at Mount Vernon."[44] Tracy acted as an individual in her own right and took on a more public role to lobby for the interests of the MVLA in newspaper culture; she directly addressed the newspaper, and the newspaper printed her claims to its audience.

From the July 31, 1861, issuance of Scott's order, there was little further debate as to the Confederate loyalty of the MVLA. The neutrality of Mount Vernon was respected and guaranteed with little incident from the first summer of the war onward.[45] However, the issuance of General Order 13 was not the beginning of the narrative of Mount Vernon's neutrality, rather it was the ending point. Preceding it were months of writing letters to regional and national newspapers; building partnerships with leading politicians like Everett; and preserving and managing the estate for the recognition of Mount Vernon's neutrality. This valence of neutrality was not just applicable in a military sense to soldiers who would come into physical contact with the estate during the war, but also, and perhaps more important, to a sense of civic duty the MVLA fulfilled to the American people that transcended regional loyalties, even during the Civil War.

After the War

The Civil War was an early test for the young organization and the stakes were high. If the neutrality of Mount Vernon had not been recognized, not only would its legacy and preservation have been compromised, but the longevity of the organization would have been thrown into jeopardy. This appearance of neutrality was not just about surviving the present war, it was also about ensuring the future success of the organization. The organization recognized the need to perform neutrality for its livelihood, regardless of the individual convictions of its members.

After the war, the MVLA used their track record of striving for neutrality in the war years as proof of their steadfast, unparalleled commitment to civic duty and rejection of regional allegiances. As a result of promoting their wartime history, the MVLA developed a far more extensive and far more Northern network of donors. In 1869, Cunningham successfully petitioned Congress for an indemnity claim of $7,000 for loss of income during the war; a claim that may not have been successful if the MVLA had not made neutrality the cornerstone of its wartime agenda. The organization was able to pay off its wartime debts by the end of the 1860s; this was an unexpected feat that would not have been possible without this new sprawling web of donors and indemnity claim.

More broadly, the organization solidified its standing as nonpartisan in the Northern court of public opinion in the years following the war. Even though some members were active in the Lost Cause and the United Daughters of the Confederacy, these issues rarely penetrated official organization business. For instance, Georgia Page King Smith Wilder, vice regent of Georgia, 1891–1914, was an early member of the United Daughters of the Confederacy in Georgia. The organization expected a separation between the interests of the individual member and the interests of the collective organization, just as it had during the sectional crisis and Civil War. In an aberrational appearance of Confederate memory in the records of the MVLA, in the 1900 annual meeting, Margaret Sweat, vice regent of Maine, memorialized former vice regent of South Carolina Lucy Holcombe Pickens, wife of South Carolina governor Francis Pickens, after her death in 1899, "After a brief dream of empire, to add a pathetic agony over the 'Lost Cause' to the many trials and sorrows that strewed her path for the rest of her life. The imaginary kingdom, which to many was only an ill-considered political experiment, was to her a glorious reality, a faith, a religion, and she gave it a loyalty that only strengthened as it became hopeless."[46] While the Lost Cause shaped Pickens's postwar public and personal lives, it did not shape her work in the organization. Like George Washington himself, the organization strove to transcend political divisiveness in another postwar era. In other words, General Order 13 ensured the physical safety of Mount Vernon during the war, but the MVLA and its conservative women members' performance of wartime neutrality secured its nonpartisan ideological status afterward.

This chapter illustrated how wartime Mount Vernon provided a new opportunity to interrogate the gendered relationship between neutrality and civic society on the Confederate home front. These women established new relationships and dialogues with Union journalists, politicians, and military officers, ushering the women of the MVLA into urgent Northern public sphere debates of loyalty and allegiance. As active agents, these women exercised a voice in civic society and helped to shape discourses surrounding the future of Mount Vernon's neutrality. In the secession crisis and early months of the war, these women forged new partnerships with male leaders to advance their agenda; and they knowingly offered not only the physical site of Mount Vernon, but their organization, as a representation of nonpartisanship. While most of its individual Southern women members held strong political and/or cultural associations to the Confederate republic and the Confederate elite, the organization itself professed neutrality. As stated earlier, although these women did not hold or lobby for the full rights of citizenship, they made a distinction between their associations with the Confederacy as individuals and their performance of neutrality as organizational members.

Like the rest of the women discussed in this book, these conservative women had a multifaceted and evolving relationship to the Confederate cause. Women, such as Maria Clopton, navigated new realities and opportunities posed by war. Maria Clopton was the founder and president of the Ladies' Defense Association (LDA) in Richmond from 1862 to 1863. As discussed in chapter 2, the LDA was an ardent nationalist organization committed to supporting the Confederate military and raising funds to buy a gunboat. From 1864, Clopton appears to have lent her services to another cause: the MVLA. In her account book of household expenses from 1864, Clopton collected subscription fees to Mount Vernon from twenty-four individuals totaling $2,500.[47] Just a year earlier, Clopton had spearheaded one of the most nationalistic causes in the Confederate war effort, but by 1864 she was volunteering for an explicitly nonpartisan, antinationalistic cause. Such a transition testifies to the agency of some women as individual actors in this narrative of gender and political capital; women could commit themselves to diverse, or even conflicting, causes. Crucially, these women brokered new relationships with male political and military leaders and held the capacity to change over time and shape Confederate society in different ways.

CHAPTER 2

Ladies' Defense Association

BEFORE SHE WAS A fundraiser for the Mount Vernon Ladies' Association in Virginia as discussed in chapter 1, Maria Clopton served as the president of the Ladies' Defense Association. In the spring of 1862, several ladies' gunboat associations emerged across the South. These organizations sought to raise money for the construction of ironclads to aid the Confederate naval effort. The Battle of the Ironclads (or Battle of Hampton Roads) over two days in March 1862, off the coast of southern Virginia near Norfolk, was the first battle of ironclad warships. While the battle was a draw, this was a landmark battle in naval history and it held the power to galvanize and intensify national sentiment on both home fronts of the conflict.[1] Furthermore, the battle received international attention. Europe's imperial powers closely watched this development in modern warfare and its potential to transform mid-nineteenth-century naval fleets. Within the Confederacy, the construction of ironclads gave naval officials the opportunity to diversify and strengthen their naval power to combat the Union's Anaconda plan to strangle the Confederacy with a naval blockade.

At the same time, in terms of their fundraising efforts, it gave the Confederate home front, and women like Clopton, a new outlet to participate in the Confederate military cause. Historians of ladies' gunboat associations tend to use these associations as barometers to measure women's commitment to Confederate nationalism.[2] However, as this chapter demonstrates, a more multidimensional approach shows that women garnered political capital for the Confederacy through their work in the gunboat associations. Women's wartime actions constitute more than social history, they contribute to political and intellectual history. These women, and the women discussed in the subsequent chapters of this book, not only engaged with political culture as actors, but they also became willing and eager Confederate nationalist symbols. These women carved out new roles for themselves in the Confederate republic and expanded their power in civic society through work in organizations such as the Ladies' Defense

Association (LDA). In turn, such efforts translated into an expanded influence in the political sphere as male leaders praised and used the LDA's works as one way to bolster Confederate nationalism.

It is important to note here that these conservative women did not use their new relationship with the wartime state and their power in civic society to pursue a progressive agenda focused on the expansion of their own rights as individual citizens. Instead, they turned to strengthening the collective ideological drive of Confederate nationalism. The conservative women of the LDA used their power in civic society to lobby for the collective interests of the Confederacy and in so doing shored up a government committed to restricting the full rights of citizenship across gendered, racial, and classed lines. With the advent of war, these women brokered new relationships and exchanges with male political and military leaders to champion the Confederate cause and perform national devotion.

Tracking women's participation in gunboat associations is not just a way to assess women's commitment to Confederate nationalism, as other historians have done; this involvement meant women helped build Confederate nationalism. Women were active agents in fashioning a narrative of Confederate strength that observers inside and outside of the Confederacy noted. Middle-and planter-class white women permeating the traditionally masculine sphere of military affairs in their work with the Ladies' Defense Association carried such symbolic value that the LDA became a dynamic source of political capital and nationalist fervor for the Confederate mission.

In terms of its impact and effect on Confederate military and political affairs, the Confederate state's projection and circulation of the work of the LDA was in many ways more significant than the actions of the LDA. Confederate leaders recognized the potential power of the work of the LDA to strengthen national identity, and they in turn used the work of the LDA to advance this agenda. Through their publicity and fundraising campaigns, the women of the LDA actively collaborated with these leaders and strove to strengthen nationalism. These women forged a new relationship with the state through their active participation in and performance of nationalist devotion.

Women's Defense of the Capital

Following the establishment of ladies' gunboat associations across the South, including in Charleston, South Carolina and Savannah, Georgia, the Ladies' Defense Association in Richmond was founded in late March 1862, and Maria

Gaitskell Clopton served as its president. Under Clopton's leadership, the LDA quickly established its organizational structure and mandate that adopted ideals and actions of antebellum Southern womanhood to the exigencies of the wartime context. In early 1862, Clopton turned her townhouse on Franklin Street between Third and Fourth Street into a hospital for Confederate soldiers. Her hospital was lauded for its low mortality rate; of course, such smaller hospitals did not usually care for the most seriously injured soldiers, who often immediately went to the nearby Chimborazo Hospital.[3] Clopton's daughter Adelaide wrote to her sister Namie (Clopton) Nicholls in July 1862, "Ma works, works, works all the time at the hospital."[4] After Surgeon-in-Charge Henry Augustus Tatum died, accompanied by mounting complaints from neighbors about the suitability of Maria Clopton's private residence as a hospital, the Clopton Hospital closed in October 1862.[5] Clopton's second-in-command, vice president of the Ladies' Defense Association Wilhelmina Henningsen, also ran a wartime hospital in Richmond until 1863. The hospital work of Clopton and Henningsen fits well into antebellum conventions of Southern womanhood: care and nurturing within the home. Likewise, antebellum Southern women were engaged in fundraising efforts throughout the first half of the nineteenth century, but this was a narrow scope of interests mainly restricted to the support of benevolent societies focused on temperance and religious charity.[6] The purpose of the LDA's fundraising project, a gunboat for the military defense of the capital city, was markedly different from earlier antebellum pursuits and represents a decisive shift in the parameters of appropriate public sphere interests and activities for women. At the end of March 1862, the LDA rapidly set up its structure and procedures of operation: it assigned collectors for each ward as well as leadership positions, set membership dues ($1 for women and $2 for men's honorary membership), and installed a decentralized network for collecting contributions.[7] The new organization also codified its aims, passed resolutions, and issued its founding mission statement.[8]

In molding its mission statement, the LDA leadership was mindful of its entrance into issues traditionally associated with men. They were explicit in their intentions to support men's work and how women as the "weaker sex" would shape their activities: "That we, as the weaker sex, being unable to actively join in the defense of our country, will encourage the hearts and strengthen the hands of our husbands, brothers, fathers and friends by all means within our power."[9] For women to enter this realm in a socially acceptable way, they needed to uphold cultures of honor and shame as well as standards of Southern masculinity.[10] The LDA's resolution professed not only organizational strength but also female weakness; women might be entering into new issues and activities, but they would only be doing so as "the weaker sex in war."

The inclusion of "ladies" in the organization name itself highlights how ideas surrounding class, gender, and race structured notions of elite white women's weakness. In the antebellum and Confederate South, there was a disconnect between the ideal of the powerless yet civilized and refined Southern "lady" and the lived experiences of white slaveholding women.[11] Slaveholding women were instrumental in the management of plantations, including the supervision and discipline of enslaved persons.[12] They also engaged in the broader economic landscape of the plantation; they routinely bought and sold enslaved persons and were influential financial agents in the domestic slave market.[13] As these women were foundational to the managerial and economic operation of the plantation, they wielded power. This notion of power was dependent upon the use of violence against enslaved persons; in turn, elite white women's exercise of violence was essential to the functioning of the slave regime.[14] Such sustained and systemic engagement with violence stood in stark contrast to perceptions of women's weakness and gentility. When the LDA included "lady" in its name, it obfuscated white women's social and economic power derived through violence against enslaved persons. Instead, the LDA invoked the ideal of elite white women's subservience, passivity, and weakness to their elite white male relations. Framing their contributions in terms of gendered limitations neutralized the threat of the LDA's work to Southern masculinity and upheld Southern honor.

Given Jacqueline Glass Campbell's argument that men and women shared common values, motivations, and goals in their commitments to Confederate nationalism and waging war, it is not surprising that these women were keen to engage with military affairs, albeit in a circumscribed way, to uphold Southern cultures of honor and masculinity.[15] Campbell applies James McPherson's ideas of "hearth and home" as a motivation for Confederate men to support the Confederacy to Confederate women.[16] Confederate women on the home front were often left to defend their homes from Union occupation and destruction through individual encounters and interactions with Union soldiers. Women civilians had to defend their actual homes, and not just the idea of home, particularly in Union general William Tecumseh Sherman's "geographic and psychological" campaigns in the final year of the war in Georgia, South Carolina, and North Carolina.[17] For some women, the defense of home was necessary for the physical survival of themselves as individuals and their families. In this sense, women's collective engagement with military and defense issues in the LDA can be seen as an extension of their defense of individual households. In both instances, women engaged with military culture and worked to more closely tie the home front and front lines in their individual and collective activities of defense. Moreover, the Civil War strengthened the relationship between military service and citizenship, and women were excluded from traditional understandings and definitions of military service. The LDA was one way in which women could engage with military culture, at a time when citizenship was dependent on military service.[18]

After proclaiming the weakness of their sex within the organization's name and meeting minutes to uphold Southern cultures of honor and masculinity, Clopton used gender to shame Richmond's wealthy gentleman to contribute more money to the gunboat association. In an April 1862 letter published in the *Richmond Dispatch*, after praising the culture of sacrifice of Southern women contributing to the drive, "All honor to the women of the South! No fairer page of history will be written than that recording their labors of love in this struggle of independence; the ladies need no urging to do their duty," Clopton immediately indicted Southern men to meet the standard set by their women counterparts. She chastised, "What shall we say to the gentlemen? Especially to those of large possessions and ample means. May we not feel certain that they, too, will come out nobly—not with their hundreds but with their thousands."[19] Questioning how "noble" Richmond men were, particularly those of "ample means," implicitly drew on the dueling notions of honor and shame that underpinned Southern culture. Contributing to the gunboat association was not solely to support the ladies' collective mission but also to prove individual Southern men's honor.

Furthermore, in one of its first acts as an organization, the LDA passed a resolution to ask Richmond newspapers to print the names of individuals donating one hundred dollars or more to the cause.[20] On April 21, 1862, Confederate printer and political organizer Blanton Duncan wrote to Clopton that local newspapers would agree to publish the names of large donors in order to publicize the work of the LDA.[21] This strategy was two-fold: the work of the LDA and its prominent donors not only would be widely circulated and celebrated but would also expose those in the community of means not contributing to the cause. Moreover, Clopton and Vice President Henningsen ran a committee devoted to "gentlemen" offering at least $1,000 subscriptions.[22] The organization created a threshold of elite donors. In this way, Clopton used newspaper culture to shame men who did not contribute to the cause and honor those who did.[23]

These ideas surrounding the culture of honor and shame were not only important to LDA fundraising initiatives but also to overarching understandings of Southern masculinity. The Civil War created a crisis of masculinity in which the expectations of manhood from the antebellum South proved to be unachievable in the lived reality of the Confederacy. Training in honor, avoidance of shame, and ambitious desire were inculcated in the younger generation of planters from an early age within their patriarchal families, social institutions, and wider communities.[24] The protection of women, as "the weaker sex," was essential to notions of Southern masculinity.[25] Alongside its reverence of white planter women, the denigration and domination of enslaved persons was also essential to Southern masculinity.[26] Men considered their duties to protect their family, including a patrilineal slaveholding legacy, as paramount.[27] The outbreak of the Civil War provided the opportunity for the younger generation, namely those who had not fought in the Mexican-American War in 1846–48, to apply the abstractions of their formal and informal educations to the practicalities of war. The Confederacy and the next generation of the plantocracy would try to prove their nationhood and manhood together. The LDA's appropriation of this culture of honor to strengthen fundraising efforts reveals the organization's sharp awareness of the power of masculinity to Southern society and the Confederate cause; the desire to prove and uphold masculinity could be used, or even manipulated, to galvanize individual and/or societal action.

At the same time, this failure to uphold these standards of masculinity could be used, or even manipulated, to shame men and the Confederacy, perhaps seen most clearly in the capture of Jefferson Davis after the fall of the Confederacy. After the fall of Richmond in April 1865, Davis fled the capital and moved south accompanied by a small group of advisors. They temporarily set up a governing body in Danville, Virginia, but were quickly forced to move farther south by the advancing Union army. On May 10, just over a month after the fall of Richmond and Lee's surrender at Appomattox, Davis was captured outside of Irwinville, Georgia, wearing his wife's cloak and shawl. This led to reports that Davis tried to escape Union capture by dressing as a woman. In the spring of 1865, in the Northern states, Jefferson Davis was routinely depicted as wearing woman's clothes while fleeing Union capture; the president of the Confederacy, the pinnacle of Southern political power, was presented as a frightened and weak Southern woman (see figure 3). As Nina Silber has shown, these images were a condemnation of Confederate men and the Confederacy as a whole; Davis can be read as a metaphor for both the weaknesses of Confederate masculinity and the Confederate republic.[28] Davis and Confederate men had been stripped of their masculinity and honor, shamed, and themselves became "the weaker sex in war."[29]

FIGURE 3. "Jeff. Davis! 'As Women and Children'," Scattergood, engraving, Philadelphia, 1865. Library of Congress Prints and Photographs Division.

While pursuing a bold strategy in embedding masculine cultures of honor and shame into campaigns for subscriptions, the LDA also pursued more conventional means to raise money and raise the organization's profile. These traditional fundraising activities, such as organizing bazaars and performances, were consistent with Southern women's antebellum societal roles and reveal the ways in which some Confederate women adopted and reconfigured established antebellum conventions to accommodate the wartime context. In one of its first meetings, Vernon, who would serve at the LDA's secretary until her death in May 1862, put forth a resolution to set up a bazaar to collect donations in Richmond.[30] She, in turn, was named chair of the committee to oversee the establishment and operation of the bazaar.[31] The April 19 and 21 editions of the *Richmond*

Dispatch printed notices of a performance to raise money for the LDA, and news of the performance was widespread across Richmond society. As Eliza Oswald Hill, a prolific chronicler of wartime events in the capital, wrote in her diary on April 18, "the young ladies intend giving next week a concert for the Gun Boat fund."[32] This participation of the younger generation of white middle-and planter-class women shows the wide appeal of the organization's aims and the eagerness of this younger generation to contribute not just to the Confederate cause but to the work of the LDA. In total, the LDA raised over $20,000 for the construction of the gunboat.[33]

Similar to strategies deployed in the antebellum era, the women members utilized the power and influence of their male relations to advance their organization's agenda. Maria Clopton was the widow of Judge John Bacon Clopton and held considerable reverence in Richmond society. The wife of General Charles Frederick Henningsen, Wilhelmina Henningsen, was vice president. The wife of the chief of ordnance Josiah Gorgas, Amelia Gaye Gorgas, was an active member. Martha Maury, cousin of Betty Herndon Maury of the famed naval family, served as treasurer and likely ensured that former superintendent of the U.S. Naval Observatory and Confederate navy commander Matthew Fontaine Maury acted as the LDA's greatest champion.[34] Matthew Fontaine Maury frequently addressed or hosted the meetings; he also acted on behalf of the organization in some negotiations with the Confederate government. The LDA was so appreciative of Maury's patronage they passed a resolution to publish a pamphlet celebrating his service to the LDA and the Confederate cause.[35] In this way, the LDA was not simply a barometer for women's commitment to nationalism as some historians have argued, but rather how the LDA sought to produce nationalist materials (other than the gunboat) themselves.

These familial relations did afford the LDA a greater familiarity with Confederate political and military leaders in the public sphere. For instance, the LDA meeting minutes on the afternoon of April 3, 1862, describe Maury urging the LDA to arrange to meet with Jefferson Davis to discuss their plans to fund a gunboat.[36] The minutes for April 4 detail that the meeting with Davis took place the previous evening and Davis offered them the opportunity to fund the next gunboat the Confederate government constructed.[37] On April 5, 1862, the *Richmond Dispatch* reported that a delegation from the LDA met with President Jefferson Davis and Secretary of the Navy Stephen R. Mallory. The meeting was productive and at its close these two Confederate political and military leaders "tendered to the Association the gunboat now in process by the Government, which will facilitate the consummation of their project very much, and enable the ladies to afford the Confederate capital a most formidable defence."[38] Davis and Mallory personally met with the LDA and offered them a gunboat to lend the organization's name hours after Maury had suggested this to the organization, and one month after the organization was founded. Simply put, without the influence and aid of their prominent male relations, the LDA probably would not have been as successful in such a short amount of time in securing its aims. This also illustrates that class was central to the LDA's success. As E. Susan Barber's work has shown, lower-class white women in Richmond were given opportunities to contribute to the Confederate military effort through their work in ammunitions factories. However, as the March 13, 1863 explosion at the Confederate Ordnance Laboratory on Brown's Island in Richmond that left at least forty dead, mostly women and children, shows, this was dangerous work done mainly out of economic necessity as opposed to ideological impetus.[39]

It should also be noted that it is unlikely that Maury considered his work with the LDA to be an exclusively altruistic endeavor. The work of the LDA celebrated the Confederate navy and showcased the ways in which the home front should support not just soldiers' relief efforts but the navy as an institution as well. After the Battle of the Ironclads, the Confederate navy found itself the focus of attention both inside and outside of the Confederacy. The efforts of the conservative women of the LDA provided an opportunity to extend this interest and support of the Confederate navy to benefit the Southern military effort. The LDA and male Confederate leaders worked together to construct and circulate a narrative of nationalist devotion focused on this single gunboat for the capital.

When the gunboat, CSS *Virginia II*, was finally completed and launched on the James River in June 1863, newspapers across the entire state from the *Staunton Spectator* to the *Alexandria Gazette* reported on its baptism and focused on its important contribution to the Confederate navy. The *Richmond Enquirer* reported on June 30, 1863, "The Richmond fleet will now soon be big enough to do the enemy a good turn in the way of sinking some of his ships, driving his troops out of the way, and damaging his prospects in lower Virginia generally."[40] The LDA's fundraising drive had a real impact on the development of Confederate naval strength and technology. These women inserted themselves into the traditionally male sphere of military affairs and helped fund the construction of a gunboat infused with Confederate nationalism in fundraising campaigns and in its use. These conservative women harnessed their new relationship with the wartime state and their expanded roles in civic society to advocate for the defense of the republic. While not enjoying, or even desiring, the rights of full citizenship, these women were able to influence individuals, like

Davis, and ideas, like nationalism, in the political sphere. In comparison to the work and legacy of the LDA, the impact of the gunboat itself was short-lived. Three years later, in April 1865 when the Union invaded Richmond, the gunboat was annihilated.

Although the LDA projected a unified and strong façade to Richmond society, there is evidence of some internal conflict within the organization. Namely, some members and subscribers became divided as to how the newly raised funds should be spent. On May 27, 1862, Anna Logan wrote to Clopton expressing her concern and disapprobation that she had heard that plans to fund a gunboat had been abandoned and the organization now planned to donate the money to sick soldiers.[41] Also symptomatic of these rumors, a letter addressed to Clopton signed only by "A Member" asked for a meeting to be called so the organization could listen to all members' wishes regarding the expenditure of funds.[42] From Lynchburg, Catherine Speed wrote to the LDA to confirm whether they were still raising money for a gunboat "as it was reported the government would prefer building the Boats without the aid of the ladies."[43] Speed went on to tell the LDA her auxiliary organization had raised three thousand dollars and would like to contribute some of these funds to the LDA, but only if they could confirm they were still committed to building a gunboat as opposed to another cause. From the organization records, it is clear that most surrogates and members did not support giving money to sick soldiers through the LDA. This money, and this organization, should be allocated to and represent military support for the Confederate capital, not medical support for individual soldiers.[44]

The very name of the organization, Ladies' Defense Association, suggests an outlook concerned with militaristic affairs and policy. This represents a stark shift from antebellum notions of the purpose of women's work; the LDA explicitly rejected the prescription of a role to care for sick soldiers and embraced a role to fundraise for military structure and operations. This is not to say that individual members of the LDA did not support caring for sick soldiers; its very own president, Clopton, ran a Richmond hospital, after all. However, and as seen in chapter 1's discussion of the MVLA, the organizational aims were different from individual members' aims. Women could support the LDA and support caring for sick soldiers outside of the organization; these commitments were not mutually exclusive. On April 11, 1862, the Confederate Congress, in one of its references to women on the legislative record over the course of the war, issued a joint resolution to commend "the patriotic women of the Confederacy for the energy, zeal and untiring devotion which they have manifested in furnishing voluntary contributions to our soldiers in the field, and in the various military hospitals throughout the country."⁴⁵ Soldier's relief and hospital care was acceptable and praiseworthy work for wartime Southern women. However, the LDA would be different. The LDA was clear in its intentions and aims; it would not nurture soldiers, it would strengthen the Confederate navy. This was not a soldiers' aid society; this was a defense association. This was not about alleviating the pain and suffering of individuals; this was about strengthening the collective defense of the republic.

While there was a growing network of ladies' gunboat associations across the South in early 1862, the LDA in Richmond was exceptional given its location. Operating in the capital of the Confederacy gave the women unparalleled access to Confederate political and military figures, like Davis and Mallory. This was an advantage not shared by women's organizations in the lower South. Furthermore, Richmond offered the symbolism of the Confederate capital. The protection of the capital was of paramount importance to subscribers to the LDA. Writing on behalf of Mrs. Col Strange on April 27, 1862, Philip de Catesby Jones informed the LDA that Mrs. Strange wished to donate a large quantity of iron "for defence of our capital."⁴⁶ Given the hardships within the overcrowded and under resourced city, particularly after the Battle of Seven Pines (May 31–June 1, 1862), organization surrogates were eager to praise the people of Richmond. Logan wrote to Clopton, "I am very proud of the citizens of Richmond that they have determined to burn the beautiful city rather than surrender—It required very brave hearts to decide such a question."⁴⁷ Its location in Richmond served as a motivation for some to contribute to the LDA.

Women's aid societies across Virginia closely monitored and praised the work of the Ladies' Defense Association. In addition to the above testament of support from Speed and the women of Lynchburg, the Prince Edward Ladies' Aid Association offered financial support to the LDA. Its president, Cornelia A. Berkeley, wrote to Clopton of their "wish to aid you in this noble enterprise" and offered $150 and several luxury items for the cause.⁴⁸ Not only does this demonstrate a network of women's associations across the state of Virginia working in concert, it shows that Virginia women outside of the capital looked to Richmond and the LDA for guidance and leadership. Many observers both inside and outside the Confederacy were looking to the Confederate capital to help assess the sustainability of this new republic. The LDA's drive was not simply to fund a gunboat in the city where it was founded, but rather, crucially, to capture the symbolism of greater protection for the Confederate capital, in terms of both military structure and civilian support. As LDA secretary Vernon, a Georgia native, said in an address at one of the organization's early meetings that was printed by the *Richmond Enquirer*, "I cannot withhold any effort on my part to which conduces to the defence and safety of the Confederate Capitol, since it becomes the common interest of all Confederate states. The efforts of the best years of my life have been given to the South—the whole South—and I have to rejoice to know that they have not been in vain."[49]

The LDA's efforts must be conceptualized not only for their tangible actions in Richmond, but also, and perhaps more important, for the meaning of their actions to a wider audience in dedication to this common interest. Both the conservative women of the LDA and male Confederate leaders worked together, in actions and rhetoric, to present the acquisition of a gunboat as a nationalist triumph. The women of the LDA used their new relationship with the state and their new roles in wartime society to advance the interests of the Confederacy. Neither the Confederate leadership nor its conservative women, like the women of the LDA, were interested in women using their new societal roles to argue for their own full rights of citizenship. Instead, both male leaders and these women were concerned with advancing the ideological drives of Confederate nationalism, an ideology dependent upon race, gender, and class inequality.

Spartan Motherhood

The mission of the LDA and the work of its individual members draws parallels to a common trope that captures the fraught relationship between women, gender, and wartime society: Spartan motherhood. Spartan motherhood is a prevalent metaphor in wartime societies across history serving a nationalistic function in its sacrifice of the personal for the political; the sacrifice of the relationship between mother and son for the relationship between citizen and the state. Recognizing the emotive power of the rhetoric of Spartan motherhood, the LDA explicitly compared itself to Spartan mothers of the Confederate capital. On March 28, 1862, the *Richmond Enquirer* published the minutes of one of the first meetings of the LDA. This included an address given by LDA secretary Vernon that outlined the mission of the new organization in terms of women's sacrifice on the home front to complement men's sacrifice on the front lines. In a high neoclassical style, she concluded her address:

> The battle fields of the South are drenched in blood of her best and bravest men, and watered with the tears of mothers, whose names will descend to the future in such illuminous chivalrous pages, as consigns to the myth of traditional lore, the best characters of Sparta.

She bends over the lifeless form of her heroic son who lies wrapt in the swathing robes of his country's glory, and the bloody sword of his valor lies broken and unsheathed beside him. A pang cleaves her heart at the first fearful sight as she feels the song of his milk-teeth on her tender breast, and the voice of his infant prattling falls on her ear.

But hark! The ring of the shrill bugle in the distance, and the canon's loud roar, reminds her that a ruthless foe is trampling upon the sanctified dust of her slumbering fathers in the genial South land. She turns in her indignant pride from the pale warriors, whose blood-stains have been washed with the tears of his mother, and gathering up the fragments of her broken heart in the folds of her chivalrous mantle, exclaims: Go hence, my darling boy, to your destiny; for what is a son to a mother who has no country! . . . The birth-pangs of nations, as well as individuals, at last are for women to suffer.[50]

This speech was central to not only the establishment of the LDA, but it was one of the milestones of Vernon's life. Vernon's May 19, 1862, obituary in the *Richmond Whig* details this address, "Mrs. Vernon read an address, prepared by herself, which displayed her ability as a writer, and attested, her devotion to the Southern cause."[51]

The closing lines of this address are crucial to the stated objectives of the LDA in two ways. First, it shows that the LDA clearly perceived and positioned itself within the lexicon of Spartan mothers' sacrifice to the military cause. Second, it shows the LDA envisioned its service to the Confederate military as more than individual sacrifice. After the Southern woman mourned the loss of the young boy on the battlefield, she rose with "indignant pride" to tackle the next hardship because "the birth-pangs of nations, as well as individuals, at last are for women to suffer." In this speech, women's wartime contributions to the military effort expanded from a mother's individual biological sacrifice of her son to a collective social drive to aid and support the Confederate military as an institution. The LDA situated its work within the legacy of Spartan motherhood; its work was a step of progress from the individual to the collective, from the biological to the social, from emotional support to political support. With the founding of the LDA, women organized to support the military as an institution while maintaining the ideological drives of Spartan motherhood. In sum, the LDA used the tenets of Spartan motherhood to support and justify its organizational structure.

The LDA did not hold a monopoly on the usage of Spartan motherhood as a way to frame women's wartime service and its significance to Confederate nationalism. Augusta Jane Evans, the celebrated writer and ardent supporter of the Confederate cause, often used classical allusions, like references to the women of Sparta, to articulate women's roles in the Southern war effort in her canon of published and unpublished wartime writings. In a letter to Confederate general P. G. T. Beauregard dated August 1862, Evans situated the story of Confederate women within a much longer narrative of the relationships between women and war across time and place: "[I] lament the role assigned to us [women] in the mightiest drama that ever riveted the gaze of the civilized world; and to envy the obsolete privileges of the young Hungarian Adjutant, the heroine of Comorn."[52] Yet, not satisfied to cast women in such powerless roles, Evans continued, "though debarred from the 'tented field,' the cause of our beloved, struggling Confederacy may yet be advanced through the agency of its daughters.... King Agis found himself unable to accomplish his scheme of redeeming his degenerate country from avarice and corruption, until the Ladies of Sparta gave their support to his plan of reform."[53] The ladies of Sparta were essential to King Agis's efforts to strengthen his country, just as conservative white planter women were essential to strengthen the Confederate republic.

Evans is best known for her best-selling Confederate novel that was banned by Union generals, *Macaria; or, Altars of Sacrifice* (1864). The novel portrays Southern women's self-sacrifice and unwavering devotion to the Confederate cause. It integrates a wide array of classical allusions to romanticize women's relationship to the Confederacy, but Evans continued to recognize the power of, but perhaps overused, Sparta metaphor to capture the gravity of Southern women's lives: "Another adjective than 'Spartan' must fleck with glory the pages of future historians, for all the stern resolution and self-abnegation of Rome and Lacedæmon had entered the souls of Southern women."[54] In one of the early and frequent discussions about women's roles in Southern society, one of the characters, Irene, tells another character, Elektra, "'Have you forgotten that, when Sparta forsook the stern and sublime simplicity of her ancient manners, King Agis found himself unable to accomplish his scheme of redeeming his degenerate country from avarice and corruption, until the ladies of Sparta gave their consent and support to the plan of reform?'"[55] This is the same passage Evans wrote to Beauregard two years earlier to convey Southern women's roles in the Confederate cause. Evans used the same language and allusion from her unpublished personal letter to Beauregard and recycled it in her published novel. In her use of Spartan womanhood, Evans identified a powerful frame to present her ideas related to gender, war, and sacrifice first to Beauregard, and then to a wider commercial audience.

As a seasoned writer, Evans's wartime use of Spartan womanhood highlights the ways in which this trope included *all* Confederate women, even if they were single and/or childless; women across the Confederacy could read this novel and include themselves in Evans's definition of Spartan motherhood.[56] The two protagonists of *Macaria*, Elektra and Irene, never marry or have children. Yet, they devoted their lives to the Southern cause. In this more inclusive social construction, the badge of honor of Spartan motherhood was extended to all Confederate women rather than just those women who gave birth to sons; motherhood was socially as opposed to biologically defined. Still, this new definition of motherhood was restrictive in terms of race and class and only applied to white middle-and planter-class women. Yet for these women at the top of the Southern social hierarchy, this was a more inclusive, accommodating frame to present their contribution to the cause and their new relationship to the Confederate state. This was a collective social construction of motherhood and service, not an individualistic biological function of reproduction. Such claims to the redefinition of motherhood along lines of collective service dictated a new relationship between women and the state. In this relationship, women could offer their services to the state as individuals, and not only through their male relations or the sacrifice of a son. Again, with the advent of war, conservative, middle-and planter-class white women assumed more power in civic society and redefined a more direct relationship with the wartime state.

These parallels between Confederate womanhood and Spartan motherhood were not manipulative distortions of the historical narrative. Some Confederate women's actions were similar to those of Spartan women; this rhetoric accurately reflects tangible, material actions of a select group of Confederate women. Sarah Pomeroy, using Drew Gilpin Faust's research in *Mothers of Invention*, finds that some Confederate women acted in a similar fashion as Spartan women in the sacrifice of their sons to war and state. As one mother wrote in the *Winchester Virginian*, "I am ready to offer you up in the defense of your country's rights and honor and I now offer you, a beardless boy of 17 summers,—not with grief, but thanking God that I have a son to offer."[57]

Just as the LDA framed their mission in 1862, some women selected Sparta as an easily recognizable, emotionally connective lexicon to portray their service to the Confederate cause. This relationship between women and military culture was important not only during the war to Confederate nationalism but also after the war to Lost Cause ideology. Confederate women, writing and speaking about themselves after the war for a mass audience, often articulated the Spartan motherhood metaphor and identified themselves as Spartan mothers of the Confederacy.⁵⁸ The imagery of women's self-sacrifice within a militaristic context was an emotive message to Southern sympathizers at the turn of the twentieth century.⁵⁹ Presenting this gendered devotion through a framework of militaristic contributions, the early twentieth-century memory of Spartan motherhood celebrated and advanced the Lost Cause, just as mid-nineteenth-century articulations of the LDA and Spartan motherhood celebrated and advanced Confederate nationalism.

The rhetoric of Spartan motherhood was used by the Confederate president and also alludes to a longer narrative of American women's association with the classical tradition. In one of his few references to Southern women in his wartime speeches, on September 23, 1864, Davis evoked the metaphor of Spartan motherhood in rallying Georgians to defeat Sherman on his March to the Sea: "To the women no appeal is necessary. They are like the Spartan mothers of old. I know of one who had lost all her sons, except one of eight years. She wrote me that she wanted me to reserve a place for him in the ranks."⁶⁰ While this Sparta allusion was common in wartime societies, Caroline Winterer has shown that American women beginning in the eighteenth century more broadly associated themselves with the classical tradition, often with goals of social reform. Most notably, American women described themselves as Roman matrons at the end of the eighteenth century and the establishment of the new republic.⁶¹ In a similar vein, creating broad, generalized associations with Sparta, perhaps the most iconic and celebrated military society in history, Southern women accentuated the military prowess of the Confederacy. In describing themselves as Spartan mothers, women created a role for themselves in the masculine military affairs of the Confederacy. This was a rhetorical stratagem employed by women to glorify the region as well as their own roles in the war effort. In this way, the Spartan mother during the Civil War echoed the figure of the Roman matron in the eighteenth century. Both inserted women into the masculine tradition of war and the construction of nation and nationalism.⁶²

Members of the LDA were not sacrificing their individual sons to the Confederate war effort, they were collectively engaging with military issues in new ways to serve the Confederate wartime state. The physical space in which the organization operated suggests a sense of conflation between military affairs and women's work. The LDA held their meetings in the office of Matthew Fontaine Maury just as often as in the Methodist Church on Broad Street. The LDA was entering the physical space of the public sphere of masculine military affairs in measured ways. Just like Spartan mothers, the LDA channeled gender conventions to blur the distinction between private and public spheres, between social and military causes, between female and male authority. Just like Spartan mothers, the LDA assumed a new role to address the gap between the needs of the Confederate military and the limitations of the Confederate government. Just like Spartan mothers, the actions of the LDA helped shape military affairs from outside of the formal governing sphere. On the outside pushing in, the LDA negotiated a new capacity in which women could contribute to the military effort. This was a more inclusive and less intimate means by which women could contribute to the military success of the republic; Confederate women did not require a biological son to sacrifice to military service. In their work, the LDA extended the roles in which women could have an impact on military affairs beyond the realm of reproductive service. Again, these women did not advocate for roles in the political sphere as individuals and expanded rights as citizens. Instead, they used their work in civic society to show how women could contribute to the war effort and nationalism beyond biological reproduction. These women did not see themselves as full citizens, but they did see themselves as more than mothers.[63]

CSS *Virginia II*

The work of the ladies' gunboat associations, and the Ladies' Defense Association in particular, testifies to the agency of at least some Confederate women in molding and showcasing their nationalist devotion. These women played active roles in the construction of the narrative of their commitment to the Confederate cause. The service and self-sacrifice of women to support the Confederate military was a source of political capital to build and strengthen Confederate nationalism. These women knowingly inserted themselves into a lexicon of rhetoric and actions that would bolster Confederate support. They knew their work would be harnessed for the Confederate nationalist mission and they were proud to serve the cause, in terms of both their actual work and the symbolism surrounding it. In many ways, the representation of women on the home front organizing en masse and collectively committing themselves to the military effort on the front lines was the model, paradigmatic image of wartime nationalism. Such an image obscured internal conflicts on the home front, or any sense of a fractious relationship between the government and its people and fraught communication between the home front and the front lines. Instead, the Confederate government and journalistic accounts projected a homogenizing and simplistic account of the Confederacy; women on the home front supported the Confederate war effort.

FIGURE 4. Alfred Waud, "The Rebel Iron-Clad Fleet Forcing the Obstruction in James River," *Harper's Weekly*, February 11, 1865. NH 59187, Naval History and Heritage Command. This image depicts the CSS *Virginia II*, CSS *Richmond* and CSS *Fredericksburg* at Trent's Reach, where the CSS *Virginia II* would suffer major damage.

This abstract representation of Southern women's work for the Confederate navy proved to be more valuable to the Confederacy than the actual work itself. The LDA raised over $20,000 to fund a gunboat, the CSS *Virginia II*, but it did not live up to the fame or glory of its namesake, the CSS *Virginia I*. The LDA-sponsored vessel saw its first action in June 1864 and its final action in January 1865 at Trent's Reach where it suffered severe damage (see figure 4). The CSS *Virginia II* was destroyed by the Confederates upon evacuating Richmond in April 1865. In sum, the CSS *Virginia II*'s track record in battle could hardly be appropriated to strengthen Confederate nationalism.

However, the LDA's track record could be used to strengthen Confederate nationalism. This was not just about the tangible gains of their work—raising funds for the construction of the CSS *Virginia II*—this was about the powerful political capital garnered from women's visible support of the Confederate cause. Richmond newspapers frequently reported on the activities of the LDA, with three important emphases: their productive meeting with President Davis and other Confederate political and military leaders; their valorizations and celebrations of the Confederate military efforts in their printed meeting minutes and meeting speeches; and LDA president Maria Clopton's tireless championing of women's steadfast devotion to the organization's mission. Women's involvement in the LDA was not just a measure of their own individual commitment to Confederate nationalism, it was used by Confederate newspaper and political culture to build and strengthen Confederate nationalism. The work of the LDA highlighted the resolve and strength of the Confederate people, not just the Confederate state.

The women of the LDA were cognizant actors throughout this process. These women were active participants in the shaping and projecting of their works and experiences to a wider audience for a nationalist agenda. Confederate leaders recognized the emotive power of these women and deployed them to strengthen their wartime cause. These women claimed a military contribution to and relationship with the state that went beyond the sacrifice of sons to the war effort. With the advent of war, the women of the LDA claimed more expansive roles in civic society that were not dependent on biological motherhood, and these actions in civic society had significant effects in the political sphere. Even though these women did not want to be recognized as individuals with the full rights of citizenship in the political sphere, their work was recognized and valued in the political sphere by male leaders. The LDA may not have been progressive, but it was effective in advancing its conservative agenda through its performance of national devotion.

In April 1863, two months before the CSS *Virginia II* was launched on the James River, the Confederate government became acutely aware of an episode of white lower-class Southern women undermining Confederate nationalism: the Richmond bread riot. In its response to the Richmond bread riot, the government acted, at least in part, to safeguard the physical security and ideological symbolism of middle-and planter-class white Southern women on the home front, women like those active in the MVLA and LDA.

CHAPTER 3

The Richmond Bread Riot

O**N THE MORNING OF** April 2, 1863, Confederate War Department clerk J. B. Jones encountered the swelling crowd that would soon descend on the Confederacy's capital city and hold its government officials accountable to their demands for lower food prices. This was the beginning of the Richmond bread riot:

> This morning early a few hundred women and boys met as by concert in the Capitol Square, saying they were hungry, and must have food. The number continued to swell until there were more than a thousand.... Not knowing the meaning of such a procession, I asked a pale boy where they were going. A young woman, seemingly emaciated, but yet with a smile, answered that they were going to find something to eat. I could not, for the life of me, refrain from expressing the hope that they might be successful; and I remarked they were going in the right direction to find plenty in the hands of the extortioners.[1]

The women were successful. Not only did they ravage the local "extortioners" for food until the government called the public guard, but they set into motion a chain of events, instigated from the bottom-up, that forced the Confederate government to come to terms with the increasing plight of their capital city's poorest, and often women, residents. As visceral and cataclysmic of an event as the Richmond bread riot was on the day of April 2, the governmental response, in practice and rhetoric, in the days following proved to be just as, if not more so, significant in the life span of the Confederacy.

Stephanie McCurry has convincingly argued that lower-class white women's actions as soldiers' wives in the 1863 Confederate food riots led to an expansion of welfare policy, at the state level, across the South. This is the legacy of the Southern food riots in governmental practice.[2] Going further than McCurry, this chapter shows that while it was lower-class white women who pushed the government to intervene, the Confederate leaders often rationalized this intervention by insisting that it protected the home front and middle-and planter-class white womanhood. This is another legacy of the food riot—in the end, leaders utilized this form of protest to shore up Confederate nationalism. In other words, McCurry argued that lower-class women were political actors in the Richmond bread riot, but that story is far from complete. In the riot's aftermath, middle-and planter-class white women came to be seen as custodians of Confederate nationalism and as such potent symbols required government protection from internal threats.

Whereas the first two chapters of this book examined how governments responded to middle-and planter-class white Southern women's engagement with political culture through newly formed organizations, this chapter examines how the Richmond City Council and Confederate leaders responded to lower-class white women's engagement with political culture. It considers the political and intellectual history of the riot beyond the formation of a new welfare system and posits that the riot was central to understandings of the relationship between gender and nationalism for both planter-and lower-class white women. In doing so, this chapter illustrates Richmond's investment in protecting middle-and planter-class white women from class and race threats—the same threats faced by the Confederate republic on a more collective level.

The chapter opens with an examination of the official rhetoric that justified and rationalized this new welfare policy in Richmond, at the institutional and individual levels, in the aftermath of the riot. As argued by Mary A. DeCredico, the city's poor were divided into two separate and discrete classes: the "unworthy poor" and the "worthy poor."[3] From mid-April 1863, the Richmond City Council redistributed resources to the worthy poor and protected them from the violent unworthy poor. In creating these two classes, the council deflected responsibility for their role in creating the conditions that caused the riot.

First, in socially constructing these identities, the city council drew clear and concrete borders of admittance into the Confederate body politic. These were not simply naturalized categories of gender and class from the Old South that the Confederacy struggled to marry. These were new socially constructed categories, molded, shaped, and further divided by the Confederacy to protect the middle and planter classes as well as Confederate nationalism. Furthermore, in fetishizing this binary, the council and Confederate leaders conveyed the illusion of a more inclusive Confederate nationalist ideology and a more effective Confederate system of governance. Acutely cognizant of its ongoing struggle to achieve a populist following for its nationalist cause, the council and

Confederate leaders' rhetorical response to the riot projected an image in which the Confederate elites had not alienated *all* members of the lower classes, just the *unworthy* ones.

Second, this chapter examines the ways in which the protection of middle-and planter-class white women became a driving force behind Confederate politics at the central and local levels in the first half of the war. Two of the domestic political issues on the Confederate home front that garnered the most attention from both inside and outside of the Confederacy were responses to the April 1862 Conscription Act and the April 1863 Richmond bread riot. While these issues were divergent in their initial aims and parties involved, they converged in the governmental responses to these issues. Although the government was motivated by a variety of factors, the protection of middle-and planter-class white women on the home front was a crucial concern that underpinned both governmental interventions. As laid out in previous chapters, these women—now cast as requiring government protection—did not have, or desire, the full rights of citizenship. Rather, the gendered inequity and wider perceptions surrounding middle-and planter-class white, conservative women as "the weaker sex in war" made them fitting—and willing—beneficiaries of government intervention to secure and protect their position at the top of the wartime race and class hierarchy. In governmental rhetoric and policy, these women were weak and needed government protection. The subsequent government intervention to safeguard the "weaker sex in war" was framed to showcase both government efficacy and to strengthen Confederate nationalism by neutralizing related class and race threats to the republic.

At the same time, these middle-and planter-class women used their new relationship with the Confederate state to emulate welfare policy in the political sphere in civic society. In doing so, they replicated the category of the soldier's wife as a deserving beneficiary of aid in informal neighborhood and family networks of support. Women's actions in civic society reinforced male government leaders' actions in the political sphere. In this way, conservative middle-and planter-class women became active participants in supporting Confederate government policy.

As this chapter argues, middle-and planter-class white women, physically safe and committed to the war effort, showcased Confederate strength. The protection of these women was not just about securing the material needs of the wives, mothers, and daughters of the Confederacy's wealthiest citizens, it was about projecting a strong image of middle-and planter-class white womanhood to audiences inside and outside of the Confederacy. Safeguarding this model of conservative white womanhood as a symbol of the Confederacy reified the nascent state's nationalist doctrine and testified to the efficacy of its government in political practice.

Representations and Rhetoric of the Bread Riot

In the spring of 1863, a succession of bread riots erupted across the South.[4] On April 2, 1863, six days after Jefferson Davis issued a national day of fasting, the largest uprising of the Southern springtime food riots took place in the capital city of Richmond.[5] That April, the Confederate economy was in dire straits; the government passed impressment and tax-in-kind laws to combat food shortages, and exorbitant migration to the capital city led to overcrowding and a strain on already scarce resources. In the 1860 census, Richmond was reported to have about 38,000 residents, and by 1863 conservative estimates placed the city's population at 100,000. Furthermore, the winter of 1862–63 was exceptionally harsh; at least nine inches of snow had fallen at the end of March, severely limiting transportation networks. Speculation, hoarding, and, of course, inflation were rampant in the Confederate capital on the eve of the bread riot. The *Richmond Dispatch* found that by January 1863 a family's food bill had increased roughly tenfold from the beginning of the war.[6] Six months after the enactment of the October 1862 Twenty Slave Law, which released one white man on a plantation owning twenty or more enslaved persons from military service, class conflict had been embedded even deeper in the Confederate body politic, heightening the stakes of existing economic debates and class divides across the South.

Women planned the Richmond riot for at least ten days ahead of April 2.[7] Mary Jackson, a soldier's mother and market seller, was its leader. Utilizing her established networks within the city's market culture, from March 22, Jackson started spreading the word there would be a meeting of local women to discuss the high prices of food. While its life span was a mere ten days and its structure was informal and unofficial, this group of lower-class Richmond women still united together to successfully pursue a common goal; this was a wartime women's organization. The meeting was held on April 1 and the following day's riot was planned. The route was determined (head first to Capitol Square) and the use of violence was expected (Jackson entered Capital Square armed with a six-barreled pistol).[8] They planned to first request an audience with the governor to present their concerns and then, if unsuccessful, to make offers of government prices for items that they would then take from speculators in the city.

The next day, the women marched on the capitol and their plans to discuss matters with political leaders were unsuccessful. The rioters pillaged and looted stores, and eventually the public guard was dispatched to neutralize the women rioters. In total, there were up to three hundred women rioters, comprised mostly of soldiers' wives, but also some men. Male eyewitness accounts of the riots often exaggerated the number of women and their mayhem. Hal Tutwiler, a Confederate signal corps officer working in Richmond, wrote to his sister Netta in Alabama the day after the riot, "Almost every one of them was armed. Some had a belt on with a pistol stuck in each side, others had a large knife, while some were only armed with a hatchet, axe or hammer.... It was the most horrible sight I ever saw."[9] Tutwiler's account is representative of many local men's accounts of the riot: a mob of women overtook the capital to partake in mindless violence without cause. Similarly, John Lancaster Waring wrote to his brother, Warner, on the day of the riot, "[the women] went down on main street and broke in all the stores that they could get in."[10]

Forty-four women and twenty-nine men were arrested in the aftermath of the riot. Only twelve women were convicted of any charge. As E. Susan Barber and others have shown, local newspapers reported on the physical appearance of the women rioters at their trials, drawing implicit comparisons between the women rioters and prostitutes.[11] By these accounts, they were not good citizens of the Confederacy, but sexual deviants on the margins that required regulation. Despite these sensational descriptions, only one known prostitute was actually arrested in the riots: Lucy Palmeter.[12]

The Northern pictorial press rarely included images of Confederate women.[13] However, an engraving of Southern women's food riots appeared in the May 23, 1863, edition of *Frank Leslie's Illustrated Newspaper*, a diptych entitled "Sowing and Reaping." This title draws on Paul's teachings in his epistle to the Galatians: "Do not be deceived; God is not mocked, for you reap whatever you sow" (see figure 5).[14] Considering the diptych as two images in a series, as they first appeared in the May 23, 1863, edition, allows a reading of a sequential cause-and-effect relationship. Planter-class women first "sow" the seeds of rebellion in urging their husbands off to war and lower-class women "reap" the consequences of planter-class women's actions in their starvation. In the second diptych, the lower-class women are depicted as masculine and crass; they have rejected the gender conventions of good womanhood and civic duty in a similar way as the above representations of prostitutes in the Southern press.[15]

Regardless of these sensational eyewitness and journalistic accounts, the representation of severely impoverished women's participation in the riots posed a threat to Confederate interests.[16] This was clear evidence that the Confederacy could not secure one of the most fundamental responsibilities to its citizenry: it

FIGURE 5. "Sowing and Reaping," *Frank Leslie's Illustrated News*, May 23, 1863. Library of Congress Prints and Photographs Division.

could not feed its people. As such, the Confederacy and its leading representatives portrayed the women rioters as holding a visceral penchant for mayhem and debauchery. This was violence without rationale carried out by the undeserving poor. These women were not starving; they were just violent and required social control to safeguard the rest of Confederate society.

The Richmond City Council held a meeting on April 2 to address the day's riots. Mayor Joseph Mayo and Governor John Letcher attended the special meeting, where the council dismissed the genuineness of the women's plight; these women had acted "ostensibly for want of provisions, but in reality instigated by devilish and selfish motives."[17] The council went on to praise municipal and private efforts in supporting their most vulnerable residents before the riot: "the Council of the City of Richmond have heretofore appropriated liberally for the support of the poor, and the citizens generally have freely contributed to their necessities on all occasions when applied to," and, in any event, "no recent application have been made by the poor to the Council or to the citizens."[18] The government had secured its obligation to the people and upheld its end of the social contract; the rioters had failed to uphold their end. Considering this self-aggrandized municipal legislative track record and the generosity of its citizens, alongside the misguided "devilish and selfish motives" of the women rioters, the council resolved, "the said mob or riot was uncalled for and did not come from those who are really needy, but from base and unworthy women instigated by worthless men who are a disgrace to the City and the community."[19] The government did not deem itself responsible for the riot; unworthy women and worthless men were to blame and government intervention was required to protect the Confederate home front.

Despite the council's claim that there was not a real problem related to famine and starvation, that this was only an imagined threat instigated by the unworthy poor with a penchant for violence, the council held another meeting two days later. This meeting called for the establishment of a special committee to investigate the "relief of the meritorious poor of the City."[20] Then, on April 9, the mayor requested another council meeting in order to address the needs of the worthy poor, defined as "the destitute poor of the City as well as of the families of soldiers in the field from this City."[21] By mid-April, the city had allocated $20,000 to the relief of the poor, with the opportunity for additional funding as needed.

Furthermore, former Confederate secretary of war, Confederate brigadier general, and grandson of Thomas Jefferson, Councilman George Wythe Randolph presented the "Ordinance For the Relief of Poor Persons Not in the Poor House." This new ordinance set up the Richmond Free Market. An application system accompanied the new market: a board would meet once a week to determine the merit of the applications for relief and any "person who has participated in a riot, rout, or unlawful assembly" would not be eligible to receive aid. Randolph drew lines of inclusion and exclusion into the benefits system of the new Confederate welfare system. The final section of the ordinance stated, in another ominous reference to the events earlier in the month, that "the agent and his assistant when attending the Free Market or at the depots of fuel shall be vested with the powers of policemen and may arrest and commit all persons breaking the peace or guilty of riotous conduct."[22] The ways in which the physical space of the market would be policed and socially controlled was made clear. The Richmond Free Market, both as an abstract concept and as a physical space, was defined through the groups it regulated and excluded.

Before his service on the Richmond City Council and during his tenure as Davis's secretary of war (March to November 1862), Randolph had been an architect of the first conscription act in American history: the April 1862 Confederate Conscription Act. He modeled this act after the Virginia conscription law he helped draft on the military committee of the Virginia Convention of 1861. He also saw the congressional passage of an amendment to his conscription policy, the Twenty Slave Law, the month before he resigned his post in October 1862.[23] These actions show Randolph's commitment to collective responsibility on both the front lines and home front. He applied the same ideological principles of shared duty and centralization to both men in battle and women at home. This was collective service from below to ensure elitist aspirations from above.

Randolph's conscription and welfare plans were both, at least partly, designed as gendered mechanisms of social control to harness lower-class whites to the Confederate mission.

Randolph's dualistic obligation to both "the people" and the elites in the political sphere shared similarities with his wife's work in civic society. Mary Randolph was committed to wartime hospital work. Yet, while she was devoted to collective service, she also embraced elite culture. The Randolphs socialized in the most elite circles of Richmond society, and Mary Randolph was a renowned hostess who threw memorable and ornate parties. Mary Chesnut was enchanted with Mary Randolph's beauty: "The men rave over Mrs. Randolph's beauty; called her a magnificent specimen of the finest type of dark-eyed, rich, and glowing Southern woman-kind."[24] Like her husband, Mary Randolph tried to reimagine and widen definitions of the common good and mutual benefit during the war. In her hospital work, Randolph advocated for sharing provisions and medical care between Union and Confederate soldiers. Chesnut recalled the conflict, "Mrs. Randolph proposed to divide everything sent on equally with the Yankee wounded and sick prisoners. Some were enthusiastic from a Christian point of view; some shrieked in wrath at the bare idea of putting our noble soldiers on a par with Yankees, living, dying, or dead."[25] Ultimately, Randolph's proposal was rejected by the Ladies' Aid Association of Richmond. In a similar vein, as secretary of war, George Wythe Randolph designed and campaigned for a new program to supply Confederate soldiers by exchanging cotton with the Union for food. This proposal was ultimately rejected by Davis and the rest of his cabinet. Both Mary and George Wythe Randolph saw the advantage in strategic and mutually beneficial interactions with the Union for what today would be called humanitarian relief; this proved, however, to be unpopular in both political and civic society in wartime Richmond.

Through his wife's work and elite social circle, Randolph was exposed to the concerns and anxieties of both middle-and planter-class women (directly from his wife) as well as the lower classes (indirectly through his wife's work). He would also have to balance and negotiate the concerns of Richmond's lower-class women, as seen in his response to the Richmond bread riot. Randolph's response to the Richmond bread riot dominated the city council agenda. The council held five meetings throughout the month of April, and, of these meetings, only one did not discuss the bread riot. Moreover, women's food riots in the spring of 1863 across the South forced the Confederacy to construct a new welfare system for its most vulnerable citizens; the rioting women engaged with political culture and were responsible for the creation of the Confederate welfare state in the second half of the war.²⁶ While the April 1863 Richmond City Council records show that the claims of the rioting women were responsible for the organization of a new welfare system and the council recognized the social and political legitimacy of the women's claims, the council went to great effort to show that it was not responsible for the riot itself. Even though the council distanced itself from explicitly accepting responsibility for the causation of the riot, within forty-eight hours it had set up a new organizational structure to investigate how to better meet the needs of the impoverished.

Some political leaders were not as empathetic to the needs of the lower classes. Not only did the Richmond City Council, as a collective body on the legislative public record, reject the economic validity of women's claims, individual central government leaders in their private writings also attacked the women's self-identification as "famine-stricken." Nearly twenty-five years after the end of the war, a letter from the Beauvoir Estate to the *Richmond Dispatch* appeared in the *New York Times* on April 30, 1889: "Richmond's Bread Riot: Jefferson Davis Describes a Wartime Event." This is the same verbatim account as presented in Varina Howell Davis's 1890 memoir of Jefferson Davis's life: "Though the mob claimed that they were starving and wanted bread, they had not confined their operations to food-supplies, but had passed by, without any effort to attack, several provision stores and bakeries, while they had completely emptied one jewelry store, and had also 'looted' some clothing stores in the vicinity." The letter summarized, "the fact was conclusive to the President's mind that it was not bread they wanted, but that they were bent on nothing but plunder and wholesale robbery."²⁷ Looking back through the prism of memory and time, this account still upheld ideas surrounding the unworthiness and unjustified violence of the April 1863 Richmond bread riot.

Moreover, according to one eyewitness, in addressing the crowd on April 2, Jefferson Davis did not simply address the riot itself but also the economic underpinnings of food shortages in the Confederacy, "He told them that such acts would bring *famine* upon them in the only form which could not be provided against, as it would deter people from bringing food into the city."²⁸ Davis displaced the blame from the Confederate government. Individual food sellers were to blame, not the Confederate government.

The chief of ordnance for the Confederacy, Josiah Gorgas, provided a similar displacement of governmental blame on the following day, April 3: "Their pretence was bread; but their motive really was license. Few of them have really felt want.... It was a real women's riot, but as yet there is really little cause for one—there is scarcity, but little want." Gorgas continued his economic justification,

"Laborers earn $2.50 to $3.00 per day, and women and children can earn $1.50 to $2.50. With such wages and flour at even $30 they cannot starve."[29] Gorgas made it clear that the Richmond women did not understand the basic law of supply and demand. Their actions were not driven by economic need; "their motive was license." In stark contrast, in the very next sentence, he praised Davis's sophisticated understanding of the politics of inflation. He met with the president on the day of the riot for one hour, to talk "over various matters": "He understands the geography and resources of the country very well. He spoke of the high prices, and said that large as his salary appeared, and altho' he lived just as he did as a Senator in Washington, he found it took all of it to defray his expenses."[30]

The Richmond City Council and individual central government leaders fastidiously created a representation of women rioters as void of economic need, caricaturing them as the unworthy poor. The government did not simply condemn their violence but also their lack of rationale. In this representation, the Confederate government was not flawed; instead, the women were unjust and required government intervention to regulate their roles in Confederate society. In accepting responsibility for alleviating the plight of the poor in the aftermath of the riot, the Confederacy attempted to project an image of governmental strength and efficacy. Its protection of the worthy poor and punishment of the unworthy poor tried to showcase the Confederacy's ability to deliver justice, address inequality, instill law and order, and safeguard its citizens on the home front. In other words, Confederate leaders tried to make clear that they oversaw an effective wartime government, not only capable of fighting a war on the front lines but also of maintaining the peace on the home front.

In rejecting responsibility for the riot itself, the Confederacy tried to create a more inclusive image of Confederate national support. From the outset, the Confederacy needed to unite white Southerners across the economic spectrum behind its cause. With the passage of the October 1862 Twenty Slave Law, class relations in the Confederacy descended to a nadir; this was a "rich man's war, but a poor man's fight."[31] In castigating blame for the riot on the unworthy poor, as opposed to "the poor" as a whole, the Confederacy fashioned a narrative where at least some of the poor stood in unison with the Confederate nationalist message and were in turn protected by the Confederate government. The Confederacy had not failed to unite all of the poor behind its mission, just the unworthy poor who were marginal and delinquent members of society.

However, the government's scorn for the rioters was not always shared and expressed by all Confederate people. Namely, the will of the government was not always in sync with the needs of its middle-and planter-class white women. Women inside and outside of Richmond quickly learned about the riot. Some witnessed it firsthand, others through word of mouth or written circulations. By April 7, the *New York Times* featured an article on the riot titled, "Bread Riot in Richmond: Three Thousand Hungry Women in the Streets. Government and Private Stores Broke Open."[32] Even though middle-and planter-class women wholeheartedly rejected the use of violence, some women did express sympathy for the motives and plight of the rioters. Middle-and planter-class women could not be dismissed as prostitutes on the margins of society. Rather, they constituted a crucial demographic in trying to maintain stability on the home front and were salient touchstones of the strength of the Confederate cause. Their sympathy for the rioters posed a threat to state interests as it lent credibility to the rioting women's concerns and, in doing so, undermined the government's narrative of rioters' unworthiness. While middle-and planter-class white women did not engage with the political culture of the riots themselves on April 2, they did engage with the political culture of responses to the riot in its aftermath.

Sarah Agnes Rice Pryor, wife of former Virginia congressman and Confederate brigadier general, Roger Atkinson Pryor, received a letter from a friend in Richmond shortly after the riot. The letter described the riot and began with the following statement: "Something very sad has just happened in Richmond—something that makes me ashamed of all my jeremiads over the loss of the petty comforts and conveniences of life."[33] Pryor's friend recognized the differences in white women's experiences of wartime sacrifice across class lines. Margaret Wight lived in Richmond and its environs from the 1830s through the Civil War. The 1840 census listed her husband's occupation as commerce and the family held four enslaved persons. The day of the riot she wrote in her diary, "This has been a memorable day for our capital of the Southern Confederacy and one that will injure us more in the eyes of the Yankees than anything that has occurred." She went on to absolve the "worthy poor" from blame in these events, "The worthy women among our poorest classes had no concern in it. This is but one of the disgraceful attendants upon this unholy and in my opinion unnecessary war."[34] While Wight identified a worthy faction among the poor and did not condone the actions of the rioters, she did see the riot as constitutive of the overall shortcomings of the wartime Confederacy. The "unnecessary" war was to blame, not the rioting women.

Judith White McGuire was the daughter of a Virginia Supreme Court justice and was the wife of John McGuire. From early 1861, she was forced to leave her home in Alexandria and work in various administrative capacities for the Confederate government in Richmond to support her family in such dire economic conditions. On the day of the riot—"the first time that such a thing has ever darkened Richmond"—she identified the Richmond bread rioters as the victims in this wartime society: "I fear that the poor suffer very much; meal was selling to-day at $16 per bushel. It has been bought up by speculators. Oh that these hard-hearted creatures could be made to suffer. Strange that men with human hearts can, in these dreadful times, thus grind the poor."[35] However, two days later McGuire reframed her commentary of the riot. On April 2, she had referred to "the poor" as one homogenous group victimized by the conditions of war and deserving of her sympathy. By April 4, she divided the poor into two groups, the rioters and the "industrious" poor, just as the Richmond City Council had: "The riot, it is ascertained, was not caused by want; it was no doubt set on foot by Union influences . . . the industrious poor are supplied with work by the Government, and regularly paid for it."[36] McGuire's change of rhetoric on April 4 was strikingly similar to the rhetoric expounded by the council on the evening of April 2.

Visible sympathy from the middle and planter classes for the actions of the lower-class bread rioters was met with a swift and harsh response from the state. According to Michael Chesson, in one instance, Mrs. Lane and Mrs. Isabella Ould, by all accounts respected, middle-class women, were heard expressing approval for the actions of the rioters outside of Richmond City Hall after the first day of hearings. They were promptly arrested and charged with incendiary language (although eventually discharged).[37] In this incident, the Confederate state issued a strong, unequivocal message to other potential sympathizers and its citizens more broadly: public sphere articulations of solidarity with the rioters would not be tolerated. While not all middle-and planter-class white women supported the rioters, these instances of sympathy worked in two powerful ways. First, privately voiced as well as publicly declared support strengthened the idea that the rioting women were rational actors with a reasonable agenda. Some middle-and planter-class women, as "respectable" members of Confederate society, identified with their cause. Second, these instances showcased the Confederacy as struggling to maintain popular support; these women defended the rioters, not the government. In defending the rioters, middle-and planter-class white women not only negotiated issues surrounding the social and political legitimacy of the riot, but they also delivered an implicit critique of the Confederate war effort that led to these circumstances.

The Protection of Planter Women

The spring 1863 bread riots were not the only instance of Southern women's critique of Confederate policy. Women's class-based protest against the Confederate government can be seen in an earlier, albeit less sensational wartime episode: planter-class white women's resistance to Randolph's conscription plan. In both instances, women from opposite ends of the socioeconomic spectrum forced the government to respond to their demands; and in both instances, the government intervened, at least partly, to protect middle-and planter-class white women on the home front from internal threats. On April 16, 1862, formulated by Randolph, the Confederacy passed the first draft act in American history, conscripting all white men aged eighteen to thirty-five for military service.[38] Six months later, an exemption to Randolph's conscription act was passed: the Twenty Slave Law.

As Drew Gilpin Faust has shown, the exemption was at least partly a response to impassioned lobbying efforts from the planter class, including planter women's letters to the Confederate government to request exemptions for their male relatives in order to help manage their enslaved population and prevent insurrection.[39] However, while Faust argues women framed their opposition to the Conscription Act in terms of threats to their physical safety, Stephanie E. Jones-Rogers shows how women's requests for exemptions for their male relatives were economically motivated. According to Jones-Rogers, women's letters to government leaders expressed concern over their enslaved persons running away, the loss of their property, and its impact on their economic standing.[40] Women recognized conscription as a serious threat, albeit more to their economic than physical survival.

As both Jones-Rogers and Thavolia Glymph argue, the outbreak of war redefined slaveholding white women's relationship to slavery and the power dynamics in the plantation household. With the prospect of emancipation, enslaved women resisted the conditions of their bondage and ran away from plantations with greater frequency than in the antebellum period.[41] This increased power of enslaved women correlated to a decrease in power for their white mistresses; white women's plantation management became more difficult and tenuous, and, as a result, their authority was more vulnerable.[42] In the context of this resistance, planter women desperately sought to retain their power and their property. Some mistresses left their homes and relocated with their enslaved persons to avoid the Union military (often referred to as "refugeeing"), while others took out runaway slave advertisements.[43] Some held their enslaved persons captive in their homes so they would not flee. When this failed, and enslaved persons were able to flee, some mistresses would keep their children.[44] Such actions undertaken by plantation mistresses do not reveal a fear for their physical safety from their enslaved population but rather a determination to retain their economic property. Requests for exemptions for male relatives may not have exercised direct violence on enslaved persons, but such actions nevertheless amounted to a campaign calling for structural violence: men exempt from service could help safeguard women's economic status and property holdings.

The October 1862 exemption, also known as the Twenty Slave Law, can also be read as a response to Abraham Lincoln's issuance of the preliminary Emancipation Proclamation the previous month. The language used in the exemption reveals its central aim of social control and regulation of the home front from its very first words, "to secure the proper *police* of the country."[45] This measure became a specter of class warfare. The planter class was given the option to "police" the home front and the lower classes were forced to fight on the front lines.[46]

Seven months later, on May 1, 1863, after nearly a month of setting up Randolph's new welfare system in the wake of the riot and navigating the rhetoric of class in the Richmond City Council, the Confederate Congress, also meeting in Richmond, amended the Twenty Slave Law. This military service exemption would only extend to *overseers* on plantations with twenty or more enslaved persons, and where "a minor, a person of unsound mind, a femme sole, or a person absent from home in the military or naval service of the Confederacy" claimed ownership.[47] Women on the home front would still be protected, albeit by their overseers, but planter men would have to serve in the military effort. The exemption aimed to curtail the privilege of planter men showcased in the October 1862 Twenty Slave Law; a performance of privilege that was similar to the inequality of wealth that was put on prominent display in the Richmond bread riot less than a month earlier.[48] Again, just as in the aftermath of the Richmond bread riot, the Confederate government shifted its lines of inclusion and exclusion in the Confederate body politic to ensure that the home front was protected from internal threats.

Although planter women concerned with the Twenty Slave Law and lower-class women rioting in the streets of Richmond both confronted the government for increased economic protection of their households, planter women writing letters to the government was a far different form of protest than lower-class women rioting in the streets. Planter women were at the top of the economic hierarchy, did not exercise violence, did not intentionally act as a group, and were not solely responsible for the actualization of their desired outcome. (Planter men's lobbying efforts and the imminent enactment of the Emancipation Proclamation played greater roles in the passage of the Twenty Slave Law than women's letters.) Still, these two forms of protest share significant similarities that hold resonance for the wider context of Confederate governance. Namely, these two episodes highlight the omnipresent and powerful threat of internal enemies within the Confederacy and the necessity of government intervention, as seen in the passage of the Twenty Slave Law and the Richmond City Council's swift allocation of aid following the bread riot, to safeguard middle-and planter-class white women from these threats. The Confederacy was not just fighting a war against its external enemy on the front lines, but its internal enemies on the home front. In the case of the Twenty Slave Law, the Confederate government intervened partly to protect the home front, namely planter-class white women, from the internal threat of a slave insurrection. Southern women chronicled the threat of slave insurrection; this was an issue at the forefront of their daily lives. Mary Caperton of Blacksburg wrote to her husband, George, a surgeon in the Confederate army, on May 9 1861, "There seems to be some uneasiness in the county about the negros. Mrs. Mary Preston told me that Mr. Hoge who lives four miles from here had put 4 or 5 of his negros in confinement." She went on to tell him of an African American preacher in the neighborhood who told his brethren, "'Lincoln was a second Christ and that all that the white people said about Lincoln was a lie from beginning to end.'"[49]

Possible slave insurrection and violence was not just a threat inside Virginia but across the South. On April 8, 1861, days before the outbreak of war, Mary Chesnut recalled a meeting with Charlotte Wigfall where they discussed the external enemy of the Union and internal enemy of the enslaved population, "we had a right to expect with Yankees in front and negroes in the rear. 'The slave-owners must expect a servile insurrection, of course.'"[50] On one night in the winter of 1861 at the beginning of the war, Mary Norcott Bryan of New Bern, North Carolina, believed her death to be imminent, "My mother came from her room above and said there were strange noises in the yard, the negroes were singing 'Hurrah! Hurrah! We are free! We are free!' We sprang out of bed very much frightened.... Our feelings cannot be described."[51] The family made it through the night safely; Bryan had misidentified a party on a neighboring plantation as a violent insurrection. While this is a comical episode, it testifies to white Southerners' deep-seated fears and anxieties surrounding the potential for enslaved violence and the urgency to regulate this threat.[52] Sarah Morgan described an apocalyptic scene in Baton Rouge when the city dwellers lost control of enslaved persons in the aftermath of the city's August 1862 fall to Union forces, "the town being pillaged by negroes and the rest of the Yankees.... They also bragged of having stopped ladies on the street, cut their necklaces from their necks, and stripped the rings from their fingers, without hesitation."[53] According to Morgan, the physical safety of "ladies" was endangered by former enslaved persons and the Union forces.

In a similar vein, in the case of the Richmond City Council's response to the April 1863 Richmond bread riot, the government intervened to protect the middle-and planter-class white home front from another internal threat: the untrustworthy and rebellious poor. Middle-and planter-class white women were acutely aware of the potential danger the lower classes posed to them in wartime. In April 1862, Margaret Pennybacker's wounded Confederate soldier brother was receiving clandestine medical care in her friend's home in a Union-occupied area of Virginia's Shenandoah Valley. When this news spread throughout the local area and the Union army learned of her brother's location, Pennybacker seethed that "of course some of the 'poor white trash' as the Negroes called them, reported him [to the Union military]."[54] The communication networks of the "poor white trash" threatened the safety and security of Pennybacker's brother and the family home of her friend.

Again, this was an issue that extended beyond the Virginia home front. Such instances support Glymph's claims that with the advent of war interactions between elite white women and poor white women became more volatile with an increased potential for conflict, and elite white women regularly documented animosity for poor white women in their personal writings.[55] Eugenia Phillips described the riotous response of the New Orleans lower classes to Union general Butler's invasion and his May 1862 General Order No. 28, an order allowing Union soldiers to treat New Orleans women as prostitutes if they undermined Union authority: "LOW WOMEN took advantage of the situation to insult the foreign foe. So of course the respectable portion of the citizens suffered for this."[56] According to Phillips, lower-class women were at least partly responsible for the persecution of middle-and planter-class women under Butler's order. Also from New Orleans, Louise Clack was most concerned with unruly lower-class Southerners, not the invading Union military, "there was a fear in every household of the mobs that were collecting—made up of our own lowest classes. Fire and robbing was anticipated ... had not anticipated such an out-break as a mob of our own people."[57] For these middle-and planter-class white Southern women, the introduction of the Union army to the Southern home front intensified fears surrounding the internal threat of lower-class whites.[58] Lower-class whites, bolstered by the Union military presence, posed a serious physical and ideological threat to the Confederacy, both for safeguarding the home front and for crafting government policy.

While the Confederate government had limited influence in Union-occupied areas, it could still determine policy in its capital. The response to the Richmond bread riot must be considered in a wider conceptual framework beyond welfare reform for lower-class women; the government's intervention was also to shore up security, including the protection of middle-and planter-class white women, and neutralize class divisions on the home front. Middle-and planter-class white women as well as male Confederate leaders were cognizant of the threats facing their cause, both internally in terms of lower-class whites and the prospect of a slave insurrection, as well externally from the Union. While Confederate leaders were unable to effectively address all threats facing the new republic, they did respond swiftly and decisively in the wake of the Richmond bread riot. Lower-class white women could not be seen as weakening the new republic; the government needed to showcase its strength and preserve established class categories that presented the national devotion of middle-and planter-class white women as eager symbols of the Confederate cause.

This class conflict could be seen as not only threatening the new republic but also the physical safety and abstract symbolism of middle-and planter-class white women. The very evening of the riot, the Richmond City Council recognized the importance of assuring and protecting middle-and planter-class white women. After castigating the "unworthy poor," the council resolved:

> That the people of the surrounding country may be assured that all provisions sent by them to this City, if seized by a mob will be paid for by the City, and that every power possessed by the authorities will be exercised to the utmost limit to prevent any repetition of the riot which has broken hitherto uninterrupted order and quiet of this City.[59]

To be clear, before the city council set up plans to assist the "worthy poor," they reassured the planter class on the home front around Richmond of their economic and physical safety. Of course, the wartime planter-class home front was largely women. The council recognized that the support of such women would benefit the government's agenda and help neutralize class conflict. This recognition of the importance of support and symbolism of planter-class white women can also be seen the following month in the council's May 11, 1863, discussion of the death of General Thomas "Stonewall" Jackson. The council asked the "citizens of the republic to share in her [his widow's] grief for a loss irreparable to her and to the country."[60] The council framed the death of Jackson through his planter-class white widow, Mary Anna Jackson, as a more emotive and powerful lens to gain strength for the Confederate cause. While such a recognition is intertwined with issues of widowhood and gendered mourning, the council still linked her personhood to the republic to create an evocative symbol of gendered nationalism. The council both understood the necessity to protect middle-and planter-class white women and used them to advance its own objectives.

In contrast to these two episodes of animosity between classes seen in the Richmond bread riot and challenges to conscription, there is evidence of some solidarity across class stratifications through informal networks of support between white women. Yet these instances can hardly be qualified as apolitical acts of altruism from middle-and planter-class women to help lower-class women. Middle-and planter-class white women in civic society adopted the same strategy as political society: to socially control poor whites to neutralize their internal threat to the Confederate war effort. Aiding lower-class women was not just to alleviate their suffering, it was to maintain the social status of middle-and planter-class white women and the social hierarchy of the Confederate state. Middle-and planter-class white women did not have the full rights of citizens in the political sphere, but they could still emulate welfare policies of the political sphere in civic society.

With the advent of war, more informal conservative women-led networks of support emerged in local Southern communities to address the needs of the local area, including the needs of poor white women.[61] Clara Minor Lynn of the Richmond area detailed the financial and emotional support that plantation owners, exempted from military service, provided to impoverished local women: "Old planters who staid at home often agreed to support the families of their poorer neighbors, who had gone to the front." Lynn went on to describe the specifications of this interclass support structure, "Their wives came down from the mountain or out of the piney woods, often carrying hand carts to get corn, and never went back empty handed. When the husbands were killed they came to get the young ladies to give them some kind of mourning."[62] Lynn detailed an interclass dependence network in which the wealthy families financially subsidized poorer families, and poorer families militarily supported wealthy families.[63] Elite charity to lower-class whites was not a nascent development coinciding with the Civil War, but it became increasingly important in the dire economic context of wartime society.

Putting forth a similar interclass support structure, Bessie Callender of Prince George County, Virginia, served as treasurer of a charity association that she established with other local wealthy women to support lower-class white women whose husbands served in the military: "We received orders from the quarter master in Richmond, then we had a tailor to cut drawers and shirts ... every Saturday morning was pay day; it was hard work.... We paid good prices; often the pay roll amounted to $1000, of course in Confederate money, a week." Callender reflected on the broader class encounters in her work, "In this way I became well acquainted with a class of women I had not known before."[64]

Both Lynn and Callender presented programs to improve the conditions of poor women, but these programs were exclusively limited to wives of Confederate soldiers.[65] This created a triangulated network of assistance: poor families provided military service to the state and, in turn, wealthy families (often represented by the plantation mistress) provided financial assistance to those poor families. Proving their husbands' service to the Confederate military would be the foundational requirement for women to claim Confederate pensions as widows at the state level in the late nineteenth and early twentieth centuries.[66] In the antebellum South, such projects of elite private charity for lower-class whites were often politicized. Not only did whites want to reform those who were seen as a societal burden to create a more productive and safer community, they also wanted to ensure their own superiority in the Southern social hierarchy.[67] As such, these wartime incidents of middle-and planter-class women's charity to lower-class women must be read with a critical eye and considered dualistically as both benevolent and as a self-serving mechanism of social control, consistent with both prewar antecedents and wartime government measures.

Interclass encounters were a reality on the Southern home front and they put into sharp relief the real and imminent threat lower-class whites posed to its security. In response to the Richmond bread riot, the city council created a welfare system not just to alleviate the economic plight of lower-class women but also to reinforce social control on the Confederate home front and regulate the internal threat of potentially violent lower-class whites. Likewise, mirroring state efforts in political society, middle-and planter-class women often provided informal networks of support to local women. This assistance not only provided immediate material relief, it also supported one overarching goal of Confederate leaders: to neutralize the threat of lower-class whites. While not holding the full rights of citizenship, conservative middle-and planter-class white women, like Lynn and Callender, reproduced political categories in civic society, as seen in the soldier's wife as a deserving recipient of aid. Male leaders in political society and conservative middle-and planter-class white women in civic society thus acted in concert to simultaneously control lower-class white women and protect upper-class white women.

In the Richmond bread riot, lower-class white women were political actors affecting real policy change, but middle-and planter-class white women also held a role in this process. The Confederate government, at least partially, intervened to protect middle-and planter-class white womanhood and maintain the Southern social hierarchy from internal class threats. One of the core critiques of Confederate governance was its inability to respond to the needs of its citizens in a quick and effective capacity. However, in the two most visible instances of middle-and planter-class white women en masse under threat from domestic issues other than Union occupation, the April 1862 Conscription Act and the Richmond bread riot, the Confederate government responded both quickly and effectively. For all their shortcomings, Confederate leaders, at both the central and local levels, recognized the political capital in protecting middle-and planter-class white women. This was an emotionally charged and visceral frame to present Confederate strength. If the Confederacy was too weak to protect the wives, mothers, and daughters of its ruling class, the republic would be seen to be doomed.

As this chapter has shown, the government adroitly intervened and implemented new policies to safeguard middle-and planter-class white women; the physical security of these women was central to this projection of the idea of strength. These middle-and planter-class women were situated in broader debates surrounding Confederate nationalism and governance. Crucially, Confederate leaders not only needed the peaceful subservience of lower-class Southern women on the home front as a tangible lived reality, they also needed the conviction of middle-and planter-class white women on the home front as an ideological abstract to project to domestic, Northern, and global observers.

Across the Atlantic, observers in Europe took a keen interest in the affairs of the Confederacy, and European political leaders were confronted with the issue as to whether their governments would formally recognize the Confederacy. Inside the Confederacy, some middle-and planter-class white Southern women engaged with transatlantic political culture and fastidiously monitored political developments in Europe. Outside of the Confederacy in Britain, Confederate surrogates and some Confederate women themselves invoked middle-and planter-class Southern women to appeal to the British people and lobby the British government for recognition. Middle-and planter-class white women not only looked inward to contend with domestic threats, but they also looked outward to negotiate global threats to the collective security of the Confederacy.

CHAPTER 4

Confederate Women and Britain

THE AMERICAN CIVIL WAR was a global event. For a brief window in the mid-nineteenth century, the young republic's Civil War fundamentally reconfigured the terrain of international trade networks and economic relationships between nation-states as well as empires; political theories related to federalism and the right to secession; and the overarching global balance of power. The Confederacy recognized the importance of the Old World in this New World conflict and lobbied Britain and France for recognition from early 1861. The Confederacy was particularly keen to appeal to its former Mother Country for recognition and assistance, given Britain's unmatched naval and industrial resources in the mid-nineteenth century as well as its economic reserves and potential to lend capital. On May 13, 1861, one month and one day after the bombardment of Fort Sumter, Queen Victoria issued Britain's proclamation of neutrality in the American Civil War. Despite this swift and decisive response to the conflict across the Atlantic, the prospect of British intervention became an enduring issue throughout the American Civil War. This was not just top-down foreign relations restricted to formal diplomatic channels and state governments; this was a bottom-up social issue that permeated public discourse on both sides of the Atlantic.

Both the British political leaders and the populace were active participants and invested parties in the wide-ranging economic, political, and moral debates surrounding the possibility of formal British support for the Confederate cause. Likewise, both Confederate leaders and the Confederate people held a vested political interest as to whether their cause would be recognized by Britain. This chapter examines the specter of recognition, for both political elites and the people, from both sides of the Atlantic, through a gendered lens of analysis.

First, this chapter explores how middle-and planter-class white women perceived Britain and examines these women's broadening political consciousness in terms of their interest in and commentary on the Confederacy's diplomatic relationship to Europe. Middle-and planter-class white women widened their frame of discourse on Europe from social and cultural knowledge and capital in the antebellum years to political recognition in the wartime years. With the advent of war and their new relationship with the state, these women engaged with political culture in new ways and became invested in issues outside of their local areas and networks. These conservative women were steadfastly committed to the agenda of Confederate recognition abroad; they recognized the importance of the Confederacy's standing in not just a national but a global context. Middle-and planter-class white women were concerned with strengthening and advancing the Confederate mission and monitored international issues that could affect the trajectory of the Confederacy.

Second, this chapter interrogates how Confederate sympathizers in Britain perceived Southern women as "the weaker sex in war." It shows the ways in which the case for recognition was fashioned according to these women's victimization and suffering at the hands of the Union military: Southern women, without reference to their class or race, were used as nationalist symbols to lobby the British government for intervention. Pro-Confederate lobbyists obscured distinctions in both class and race to advocate for "Southern women" as a monolithic and victimized group in need of protection.

An examination of the ways in which gender became central to the rhetoric of Confederate recognition in Britain after 1862, as well as an analysis of how this rhetoric changed over the course of the war, has not been explored in the existing historiography.[1] Within this new frame of analysis, gender and politics worked in two ways.[2] First, middle-and planter-class white women demonstrated a growing political consciousness on an international scale. Second, the international community recognized the power of Confederate women as nationalist symbols to advance the Confederate agenda. Some women, like Rose Greenhow and Belle Boyd, were cognizant of their power in the international arena and actively shaped themselves into nationalist symbols to strengthen pro-Confederacy sentiment in Britain. Greenhow and Boyd forged new relationships with the Confederate state as well as with British political and civic leaders in their roles as Confederate emissaries to Britain. While Greenhow and Boyd held real political capital and derived celebrity status from their diplomatic efforts, they did not then apply this experience and status to advance other causes that affected their lives, such as lobbying for women's full rights as citizens. In this way, their actions and types of engagement in the political sphere closely resembled that of conservative women active in the Mount Vernon Ladies' Association and the Ladies' Defense Association. Women such as Rose Greenhow and Belle Boyd negotiated their exchanges and relationships with male leaders in the Confederacy and in

Europe as individuals. They were not concerned with rights for themselves but rather with the recognition of the Confederacy, and they harnessed their conservative sociopolitical consciousness to publicize—and humanize—the Confederate cause abroad. After all, it was precisely the idea of "the weaker sex in war" that made such women palpable emissaries of the Confederacy.

Women in the Confederacy

Middle-and planter-class white Southern women took a keen interest in European cultural trends throughout the antebellum era.[3] In the first half of the nineteenth century, these Southern women expressed a voracious appetite for European cultural exports: most often, food, fashion, and literature. This interest continued during the Civil War. For example, Clara Minor Lynn of Richmond described the Confederate interest in Victor Hugo's 1862 masterpiece, *Les Miserables*. When Lynn's friend was asked by a blockade runner what she would like, given the opportunity to have absolutely anything—especially considering the South's conditions of deprivation and austerity—she asked for *Les Miserables*: "A young friend was asked by a gentleman who was going to Nassau, a blockade runner, what he must bring her. She said 'Cosette,' though in her heart she longed to 'say shoes.'" Her friend did not expect to hear from the blockade runner again, but "a few weeks later a bundle was sent to her, with a polite note, expressing a hope that the 'article she ordered would fit'—behold a corset!! The poor man never having heard of the book did the best he knew."[4] Such an exchange illustrates the importance of French culture to some Southern planter women; presented with the rare opportunity to acquire more pragmatic goods for wartime, Lynn's friend instead requested a novel.

Through formal education, an affinity for Old World European culture was cultivated in privileged students of the South. Middle-and planter-class white women's education was designed to mold them into the highest quality wife for suitors, which required the amalgamation of academic and feminine accomplishments. According to Anya Jabour, women's academic curricula fell into three broad categories. First, basic education consisted of history, mathematics, and English. Second, advanced studies most often consisted of the sciences and philosophy but could also include the classics. Third, "the extras" (or electives) were classes designed specifically for the cultured and leisured lifestyle of elite Southern women and required additional fees. These classes most often included modern languages (French, Spanish, and German), art, music, sewing, and embroidery. If the student was to only study one language, planter-class daughters usually chose French.⁵ Parents encouraged their daughters to excel academically like their brothers, but they also desired their daughters to master "feminine accomplishments" such as music, drawing, letter writing, and European languages.⁶

While middle-and planter-class white Southern women's relationship to Europe was generally focused on cultural pursuits before the war, with the advent of war, women became more concerned with European politics. French and British recognition of the Confederacy was a crucial pressure point for the Confederate cause in the first half of the war. Broadly speaking, the Confederate ruling class believed that foreign recognition, and its accompanying economic and military assistance, would be a key to winning the war. Politically, Jefferson Davis sent diplomats James Mason and John Slidell to Europe to lobby the case for recognition through formal political channels in governments. Outside of formal government channels, Henry Hotze, a Swiss-born Confederate agent, went to Britain in 1861 to strengthen the Southern cause in Europe. There, Hotze published the *Index* between 1862 and 1865 as an unapologetic and brazen organ of Confederate propaganda to sway not only political elites but the population at large. He also led a concerted drive to publish Confederate propaganda pieces in mainstream British newspapers from early 1862. Militarily, Robert E. Lee believed that a Confederate victory on Union soil would prompt foreign recognition of the Confederacy, which at least partially motivated Lee's Gettysburg campaign. Economically, surrogates raised capital for the Confederacy abroad, such as Liverpool merchant James Spence. These issues did not have an immediate impact on the everyday lives of middle-and planter-class women, but these women still took a keen interest in their development over the course of the war.

Conservative middle-and planter-class white women's investment in these issues testifies to their commitment to political questions beyond the scope of their individual lived experiences. On July 1, 1862, Amanda Virginia Edmunds from Fauquier County wrote in her diary, much too optimistically, "France has positively recognized the Confederacy & England expects to follow her course in a few days."⁷ On September 25, 1863, from Norfolk County, Elizabeth Curtis Wallace inaccurately recorded, "We heard this evening that France had certainly recognized the Confederacy."⁸ Writing from just outside of Charlottesville, recalling how her Christmas of 1862 was overshadowed with news from abroad, Lucy Wood Butler lamented, "it fled all that made us bright and merry then, for we were buoyed up by false and extravagant hopes of peace from the interference of England in our behalf, and the friends who were gathered around us were all soon scattered."⁹ While they did not always possess accurate information, these women monitored news of the Confederacy's progress abroad. On February 12, 1863, after reading one of Davis's speeches—most likely his address to the First Confederate Congress in January 1863—Lucy Buck of Front Royal angrily pontificated: "If 'Neutral Europe' does not feel ashamed after the perusal of this document I do not know what is to prevent them."[10]

Some women commented on more specific terms, particularly on the Trent Affair. Traveling to Europe on the British vessel RMS *Trent* on November 8, 1861, Confederate commissioners James Mason and John Slidell were seized by the Union navy. According to Britain, this incident violated British neutrality and could have led to war between the Union and Britain. A diplomatic compromise was eventually brokered, and Mason and Slidell were released. Writing from Winchester, Cornelia McDonald Peake lambasted the Yankee occupation of the homes of Confederate commissioners Mason and Slidell.[11] In *Macaria*, Augusta Jane Evans delivered a stirring condemnation of the Trent Affair. Eric boarded the steamer *Trent* in Southampton, "which was destined subsequently to play a prominent part in the tangled role of Diplomacy, and to furnish the most utterly humiliating of many chapters of the pusillanimity, sycophancy, and degradation of the Federal government."[12]

Some women articulated a greater awareness of these issues given their proximity to Confederate political leaders negotiating these transatlantic relationships. Betty Herndon Maury Maury, who was married to her cousin, Confederate judge advocate general William A. Maury, was the daughter of Matthew Fontaine Maury. Serving in the U.S. Navy since 1825 and rising to superintendent of the U.S. Naval Observatory, Maury resigned his commission at the outbreak of war to serve as a commander in the Confederate navy. As discussed in chapter 2, he was a staunch supporter of the work of the Ladies' Defense Association in Richmond. At the end of 1862, he ran the blockade and traveled to England via Bermuda to advocate for the Confederacy in Europe. Maury was widely respected in the global community. In the first year of the war, Betty Maury revealed that her father received invitations from both Constantine the Grand Admiral of Russia and Napoleon to live in Russia and France, respectively. In the midst of the Trent Affair, Betty Maury meticulously chronicled the events as they unfolded, spliced with her own critiques. When news of the Trent Affair first broke, she boldly stated, "England will have lost much of her old pride and arrogance if she submits to such an insult!"[13] However, after the release of Mason and Slidell, Maury was far less incendiary and became resigned to the lack of Confederate recognition on the world stage, "The English Government expresses itself as satisfied with United States Secretary of State William

Seward's *apology* and the return of Mason and Slidell. There is no hope for foreign recognition now."[14]

While Betty Maury could offer little assistance to the diplomatic mission of Confederate recognition in Europe, she boldly inserted herself into her father's diplomatic mission in Cuba. In early October 1861, her father was ordered to Cuba to pay for arms that the Confederacy had purchased. Betty Maury objected to this assignment as any naval ensign could effectively carry out this duty; this was not within the remit of a commander. Earlier that year, in July 1861, Maury felt that her father was being unfairly treated by the Davis administration given his steadfast record of service to the cause: "They have old grudges against him, I think, and would be glad to put him out of their way. It is weak and wicked of them!"[15] Maury pleaded to accompany her father as "If the worst comes to the worse and we are captured, they certainly would not put a woman in Fort Lafayette."[16]

After her father's refusal to bring her on his mission to Cuba, Betty Maury wrote a letter to Charles M. Conrad, the chairman of the Committee of Naval Affairs, to petition for her father's orders to be recalled. She was concerned that the United States Consul in Cuba could take egregious and unlawful actions against her father. She also made it clear that her father had no knowledge of the letter, since a woman intervening on a man's behalf would undermine the Southern culture of masculinity and honor. Of her letter, she confided to her diary, "I signed it with my maiden name because I thought he might give it more attention if he thought I was a pretty young girl."[17] Given that her maiden and married names were both Maury, it is likely Maury signed this letter Betty Herndon Maury, and not Betty Herndon Maury Maury. Just over two weeks later, her father's orders were recalled without explanation. Significantly, Maury manipulated gender conventions twice to try to help her father. First, she asked him to take her with him, rationalizing that in case of capture even Union sympathizers would not imprison a woman. She planned to manipulate accepted conventions of female weakness to avert her father's potential captivity. Second, she signed her letter with her maiden name to appeal to the letter's male recipient with the prospect of romance and/or courtship. Maury was cognizant of the ways in which female weakness and desirability could be shaped to advance her own agenda. While it is unlikely that Maury possessed political intent in intervening on her father's behalf—she seems to have been far more driven by individual emotions—her actions still seem to have had a tangible political effect. This was not an effect in terms of political ideology or policy but of political bureaucratic assignments. Maury negotiated a new relationship with the wartime state; she advocated for her father's naval career and ensured that her concerns were registered by the government.

While not possessing Maury's close familial ties with Confederate political leaders, Charlotte Burckmyer lived in France throughout the war years. While her husband, Cornelius, returned to the United States to support the Confederacy, Charlotte remained in Europe. Her residency abroad gave her unfettered access to international debates and discourses surrounding Confederate recognition. She often commented on the changing political landscape between the Old and New World with fluency. Writing to her husband on March 21, 1863, from Tours, Burckmyer noted the importance of financial support over political recognition: "it was a financial recognition that will do us more good than any other. It does look like folks ere 'beginning to think we would be successful in achieving our independence,' their taking a 32 million loan when we only asked for 15 million. Hurra for dear old Dixie!"[18]

Three months later, in June 1863, Bruckmyer seems to have lost her optimism for the Confederate case with the British government, but not the British people: "Tomorrow night Mr. Roebuck is expected to make his motion respecting recognition of the Southern Confederacy. I don't hope much from this, but it may be that the people compel the Govt to move—nothing else will affect them I am sure." Bruckmyer went on to make it clear she found more solace within the domestic developments of the Confederacy than the foreign relations endeavors: "General Lee's movements have cheered my heart a great deal more, as I know we can depend upon him, and as yet our European cousins have been found wanting."[19] By the end of February 1864, Burckmyer had completely lost hope in the prospect of an effective program of European intervention in the war, "I do not hope for this [recognition] and I hope our people will never allow themselves to be buoyed up by any expectations of foreign intervention. It will never come until we no longer need or care for it."[20] Burckmyer's letters offer an individualistic and emotional trajectory of waning hope for Confederate recognition. In early 1863, the possibility of Confederate recognition was ripe with hope, but by early 1864 the possibility for recognition seemed to be ill-fated. This was not a sentiment restricted to Confederate political elites but also was expressed by individual women, such as Charlotte Burckmyer.

Granted, in their concerns over Confederate recognition in Europe, middle-and planter-class white women like Maury and Burckmyer did not construct a new political discourse; rather, these women were interpreting and further circulating a political issue already framed by the Confederate ruling elites. In his November 18, 1861, address to the Confederate Congress, President

Jefferson Davis outlined the importance of acknowledging the rights and powers of the Confederacy as a nation-state on the global stage: "In conducting this war we have sought no aid and proposed no alliances offensive and defensive abroad. We have asked for a recognized place in the great family of nations, but in doing so we have demanded nothing for which we did not offer a fair equivalent."[21] In his 1863 article, "The Revolutions of 1776 and 1861 Contrasted," in the *Southern Literary Messenger,* Confederate firebrand and proslavery ideologue George Fitzhugh drew familial linkages between England and the South to advocate British recognition of the Confederacy. He concluded his article describing English Conservatives as "American cousins" and urged the South that, "We should cherish and cultivate the friendship of the English Tory party; for that friendship is not accidental or affected, but proceeds from concurrence in political doctrine and blood relationship; for we are descended from Tory stock."[22] The issue of Confederate recognition was omnipresent in Southern newspapers, from the outbreak of war to mid-1863. Local publications, like the *Alexandria Gazette,* and key newspapers in the capital, like the *Richmond Enquirer* and *Daily Dispatch,* commented on the progress of the case for the Confederacy abroad. Reprinting coverage from Northern and British publications, as well as creating their own original editorial content, Southern newspapers were committed to presenting the progress of the Confederacy abroad to its readership until mid-1863.[23]

Middle-and planter-class white women, situating themselves within the networks of knowledge and language produced and circulated by Confederate elites, tracked and chronicled developments in the campaign for European recognition of the Confederacy. While women's interest in this issue and the ways in which it was discussed may not have been particularly unique, insightful, or even accurate, it does reveal an emerging conservative political consciousness in diplomacy and foreign relations, albeit through the lens of the Confederate war effort. Middle-and planter-class white women accommodated a wider-angle frame to contextualize the political issues that held meaning for the Confederacy, even if these issues did not hold an immediate tangible impact on their own daily lives. In so doing, these women engaged with political culture in new ways. Looking across the Atlantic, middle-and planter-class white women considered not only the cultural but also increasingly the political role of Europe in defining the parameters of the American Civil War and the Confederate republic. Such women forged a new relationship with the state in which they were cognizant of and commented on international political issues that affected the Confederacy but, crucially, they did not have or want the full rights as citizens in the

Confederate political sphere. Conservative women's investment in these political issues was aligned with Confederate nationalism; their work was national devotion that amplified core Confederate aims.

Confederate Women in Britain

Confederate sympathizers in Britain also looked across the Atlantic; they looked to the roles of Southern women in the Confederate war effort. The pro-Confederate movement in Britain identified suffering Confederate women on the home front (i.e., "the weaker sex in war") as an emotive representation of the unjust and inhumane Union war effort, and the subsequent need for British intervention to protect Southern women.[24] Confederate supporters in Europe did not differentiate Southern women by state, class, or race but identified them as one homogenous group; they were "Southern" or "Confederate" women. From the eve of 1862, in gendered discussions of aid, support, and recognition of the Confederacy in the wartime British press, traditional tropes and language of female weakness were used to champion the Confederate cause.

Proposing a mutually constituted support network based on both class and gender, on December 28, 1861, in a reprint from *Reynold's London Weekly*, the *Richmond Daily Dispatch* published the British paper's call for transatlantic working-class solidarity through gender: "We call upon our country; aye, and upon our country women, to take instant and energetic action in this matter. But, to the working classes in an especial and emphatic manner, we address our appeal—Why should they see their wives in rags, their children famishing, their cupboards empty, their grates fireless."[25] Drawing on ideas of women's weakness and the gendered expectations of men to protect women and families, this transatlantic appeal used accepted nineteenth-century gender conventions to try to forge working-class solidarity. Class consciousness, wedded to Victorian gender norms, was employed to widen the scope of and sympathy for the Confederate cause. In the rhetoric presented to the British public, this was not simply a foreign war; this was a class war with relevance to the daily lives of working-class men and women.

As the war progressed, Confederate sympathizers in Britain strengthened this rhetoric and repeatedly tried to forge transatlantic female solidary support networks; Confederate women needed British women to intervene to protect them against gender-specific humanitarian abuses. For example, a December 1862 address given by the Confederate Aid Society in London titled "To the British Public and all Sympathizers in Europe" portrayed the women of the

South as victimized and called on the women of Britain to help. First, the address presented the problem: The Union had "insulted, imprisoned, flogged, violated and outraged the women of the South in the most inhuman and savage manner." Then, the address presented the solution, calling on women of Britain to intervene on Southern women's behalf: "Fairest and best of Earth! For the sake of violated innocence and the honor of your sex, come in woman's majesty and omnipotence, and give strength to a cause that has for its object the highest aims—the amelioration and exaltation of humanity."[26] Implicitly referencing the need for a transatlantic women's solidarity network, the Confederate Aid Society in London called upon women in Britain to save the "violated" women of the Confederacy for the "exaltation of humanity." British women's aid was not just necessary to ameliorate the conditions of Southern women in the context of the Civil War but also to advance the cause of mankind on more universal terms.

In a similar vein, on October 7, 1864, the *Times* published an advertisement for an upcoming bazaar for the Southern Prisoners' Relief Fund to be held at St. George's Hall, Liverpool. The bazaar would not just benefit Confederate prisoners but also the wives and children of these prisoners: "the multitudes of widows to whom nothing remains, and of orphans unable to help themselves . . . this work, which is wholly one of humanity—of sympathy for the great sorrows and suffering that now afflict a people of our own race."[27] The wives of leading politicians, financiers, and aristocrats from across Britain hosted the event, which raised over £20,000. This was apolitical work suitable for wealthier women to undertake under the guise of charity. According to its organizers, this fundraiser did not support the political project of the Confederacy, it supported the relief of prisoners of war, and their wives and children, using the rhetoric of universalism and humanitarianism. However, while the bazaar organizers and surrogates framed the event as apolitical and humanitarian in its intent, it was not perceived to be apolitical in its effect. When the organizers tried to send the recently raised funds to Confederate prisoners in Union camps, U.S. secretary of state William Seward refused to let them send the money behind Union lines. The women organizers envisioned these funds as benefitting the Confederate people on humanitarian grounds; Seward envisioned these funds as benefitting the Confederate state on political grounds. Or to put it another way, Seward envisioned this transatlantic women's solidarity network as a political threat to the Union war effort.

Not only did some British newspapers but some British individuals championed the Confederate cause. James Spence, a Liverpool merchant and one of the most esteemed and powerful advocates for the Confederacy in Britain, repeatedly and meticulously justified Confederate recognition through political and economic rationale rather than moral impetus. While his *The American Union* (1861) was a bestseller and has received much scholarly attention, his *On Confederate Recognition* (1862), published one year later, has received less scrutiny. As in *The American Union*, Spence avoided discussing women in direct terms in *Confederate Recognition*. However, he fervently contested the use of abolitionist preacher Henry Ward Beecher's gendered metaphor of Mother Britain to elicit British support for the Union and reconfigured it to support his own pro-Confederate agenda. Spence quoted Beecher, "'If there was any nation under heaven that we looked to for sympathy and help it was the mother country, England. But how did she treat us? She sympathized with our enemies.'" Spence fired back with a gendered critique of this gendered metaphor: "Here is a minister of the gospel of the peace educating his people in this spirit—so ignorant of human nature as to expect that a 'Mother' would be pleased to see a big son trampling on a weaker one—[the Union is] so incapable of manly sentiment."[28]

Spence focused on the political and economic issues surrounding the conflict, but he recognized the potential of this familial rhetoric to resonate with the British masses; he responded by refuting the family metaphor and emasculating the Union cause as "unmanly." Spence concluded the pamphlet with a call for the betterment of not just nations but mankind: "Are we to evade from trouble or shrink to this responsibility before us? The existence of the famishing, the welfare of commerce, the claims of humanity, the laws of all nations, the interests of America, all demand our decision."[29] While not explicitly aligning the Southern cause with female vulnerability, Spence used a language of gender and power to portray the weak condition of the Confederacy and called for British intervention for the sake of humanity. In doing so, he reformatted Beecher's pro-Union gospel and created a British-Confederate transatlantic support system based on family and kinship structure: Britain had a familial duty to intervene to protect the Confederacy as the former mother country.[30]

Confederate sympathizers in Britain attempted to forge a common identity between the Confederacy and Britain to elicit support for the Southern cause along the lines of gender, class, and family. These messages were crafted to make a distant global conflict more tangible, relatable, and intimate. Constructed around the political symbolism of Southern women's victimization, these messages situated the American Civil War in a context that had the potential to resonate with the British public and strengthen emotional investment in its outcome. Weak and victimized Confederate women were salient and emotive touchstones of a political and military conflict on the other side of the Atlantic

Ocean. Significantly, this call for intervention did not include specific and directed measures to improve the rights and status of women as individual citizens. Rather, such rhetoric implied that giving material aid to the Confederacy as a collective would improve the conditions of its women. Such measures were not so much about supporting individual women as much as supporting the Confederacy.

Women Confederate agents in Britain, those born in the United States and sanctioned by Jefferson Davis to promote the cause of the Confederacy abroad, offered a physical embodiment of this humanitarian crisis: Southern women taking refuge in Britain from the brutal Union military. Rose Greenhow and Belle Boyd were not only Confederate agents in their personhood but also in their prose. Greenhow and Boyd acted as Confederate spies and, later in the war, as Confederate emissaries in Europe. Both women published narratives calling for British recognition of the Confederacy based on their specific individual experiences of suffering as Southern women as well as more general pleas to uphold accepted standards of humanity. Greenhow and Boyd called on *all* members of British society to aid the Confederacy. Their direct, detailed, and harrowing accounts of their personal wartime experiences gave their narratives an unparalleled visceral authenticity to British audiences that simply could not be found in third-person journalistic articles and sympathizers' speeches.[31]

Henry Hotze had tried to employ a version of this highly effective propaganda strategy; the *Index* often published first-person accounts of individual Southern women to convey the severe conditions of suffering and degradation faced by the collective Confederacy. Framing the case for Southern recognition through a more intimate, emotional, and gendered lens was a persuasive and compelling way to present the Confederate case to the British public. However, Greenhow and Boyd intensified the British readership's experience of first-person narratives, like those found in the *Index*, from simply an account on the printed page. With Greenhow's arrival to London in 1863 and Boyd's arrival the following year in 1864, these women brought the physical embodiment of victimized Southern women to the British public. These two conservative women did not have, or lobby for, political credentials at home, but they held significant influence in the British political sphere. Greenhow and Boyd shaped and projected their performance of national devotion to an international audience. They brought animation to the inanimate symbolism of Southern women's victimization. They also brought an explicit demand with them: British recognition of the Confederacy.

Rose Greenhow may not hold the same celebrity recognition as a daughter of Virginia as Confederate spy Belle Boyd, but if Greenhow was to be the daughter of any state of the Confederacy, it would be Virginia. Maria Rosetta O'Neale was born in Maryland and spent time in Washington, D.C., as a teenager. After marrying Robert Greenhow Jr., she followed her husband's work with the State Department moving to Mexico City and San Francisco. After her husband's death in 1854, she was based in Washington, D.C. Rose Greenhow lived an itinerant life and rejected her birth state's disloyalty to the Confederacy with the outbreak of war. Her husband had hailed from a prominent Virginia planter family.

Soon after the war began, Greenhow served as a Confederate spy passing intelligence to the South through her home in Washington, D.C. In August 1861, Allan Pinkerton, head of the Union Secret Service, arrested her and placed her under house arrest for espionage. While imprisoned, she wrote a letter to U.S. secretary of state Seward, which was then forwarded to the *Richmond Whig* for publication by a Confederate (or at least Greenhow) sympathizer in Seward's office. The letter is a forceful rebuke of Greenhow's imprisonment, the Union cause, and, in particular, Seward's leadership. She even used Seward's own condemnation of a *London Times* reporter to protest her wrongful imprisonment: "I must be permitted to quote from a letter of yours, in regard to [William Howard] Russell of the London Times, which you conclude with these admirable words: 'Individual errors of opinion may be tolerated, as long as good sense is left to combat them.'"[32] She was then imprisoned in the Old Capitol Prison in Washington, D.C., from January to June 1862. Of her devotion and sacrifice to the Confederacy, husband of wartime diarist Mary Chesnut, and Confederate brigadier general James Chesnut claimed that the "Confederacy owes her a debt it can never pay."[33] After her release from prison in 1862 she chose to move to Richmond, the last place she would ever live on American soil. Greenhow became an adopted daughter of Virginia, choosing Richmond, Virginia, as her adopted Civil War home.

Following her move to Richmond, Jefferson Davis sent her to Europe as a Confederate emissary to Britain and France. She playfully described her appointment by Davis, "I saw the President this morning and he affords me every facility [. . .] in carrying out my mischief."[34] In the summer of 1863, while still in the Confederacy and preparing for her assignment abroad, she was in contact with European diplomats and journalists. The Spanish Consul visited her, and she reported that "the new Spanish Minister at Paris had been sent there for the purpose of urging the recognition."[35] Greenhow then dutifully passed this intelligence on to Davis. Likewise, a journalist from the *London Illustrated News*, Frank Vizitelli, briefed her on the siege at Vicksburg and then told her he believed "the European world will never allow the reconstruction of the

American Union—that their sympathies are naturally with the Anglo-Saxon race who are represented in the South."[36] He went on to say that only if the South looked to be facing imminent military defeat would Europe intervene. Again, Greenhow passed this information to Davis; she was embedded in an intelligence network and communicated political and diplomatic information to Confederate leaders.

After arriving in Europe, in a February 1864 letter to her frequent correspondent Virginian politician Alexander Boteler, Greenhow relayed an account of her time in Paris: "I was treated with great distinction great kindness, and my audience in Court Circles was pronounced *une grande success*—and altho the Emperor was lavish of expressions of admiration of our President and cause there was nothing upon which to hang the least hope of aid unless *England acted simultaneously* [emphasis her own]."[37] Greenhow then offered her hopeful reading of the British public's response to the Confederate state: "My belief is that from England alone are we to expect material aid. The better classes here are universally in our favor and the debates now going on in both houses of Parliament show the strong opposition to the Gov."[38] Greenhow was cognizant of the significant role the British public played in determining the outcome of Confederate recognition, and, as a result, the outcome of the war.

An earlier 1863 letter to Boteler showcased her drive to ensure the British press reported positive news of the Confederacy and portrayed the new republic in an encouraging way. She described her frustration with the circulation of what she considered to be misinformation and distortion in British print culture: "All the accounts come through the Yankee press. Just now we have the news of Bragg's disastrous defeat and falling back from Lookout Mountain—with loss of 60 pieces of artillery small arms &c. and 8000 prisoners. [...] This news has brought down the Confederate loan from 60 to 31." In spite of this, she maintained her optimism for the Confederate cause in Britain: "My friend you know not the importance of sending correct information, which can be used so as to counteract the Yankee accounts I believe that all classes here except the Abolitionists sympathize with us and are only held back from recognizing us for fear of war with the United States."[39] Greenhow believed she had her finger on the pulse of British society and could accurately determine the British public's allegiance in the Civil War. Communicating this important information to male political leaders in Richmond made her a key contact in transatlantic networks to advocate for the Confederate cause in Europe.

Greenhow also found a confidante in Georgiana Freeman Gholson Walker during her time in Europe. Walker's husband was sent to Bermuda by the

Confederate War Office in November 1862. In the spring of 1863, she ran the blockade to join him in Bermuda, and Walker saw her old friend while Greenhow was passing through Bermuda on her way to Europe in 1863. Then Walker visited Greenhow in London in mid-1864, the last time she would see her before Greenhow's death later that year. Greenhow wrote to Walker to convey her triumphs in Paris and Britain. In December 1863, Walker received a letter from Greenhow about her visit to the French capital: "Mrs G is much delighted with her visit to Paris, and considers her mission to have been a successful one. She had an audience with the emperor, and was treated with marked attention. She says she advocated our cause warmly and earnestly; and left not one point uncovered." Walker went on to describe Napoleon's consideration for Greenhow: "the Emperor received her as one directly from the President and bade her tell the President that his sympathy was all with him; and that he should do all in his power to aid him."[40] Napoleon recognized that Greenhow had direct lines of communication and an unmediated relationship with the Confederate president. Napoleon accepted Greenhow as an emissary in the political sphere and communicated to Davis through Greenhow. In this instance, a leader abroad acknowledged the significance of Greenhow, as a Confederate woman, to represent and strengthen the Confederate cause in Europe.

Walker was also keen to learn of Greenhow's successes in Britain. "She has been wonderfully well received in England. . . . I do not wonder at that for she is a very clever woman, and has the ability to show those Yankees up in their true characters." Walker went on to praise Greenhow's manipulation of nineteenth-century gender conventions to serve the Confederate diplomatic mission: "She says a smart thing in her letter. She writes 'I consider the cultivation of my good looks a duty which I owe to my country.' . . . *She is one of the most beautiful women I ever saw. She knows this; and like a sensible woman, does not pretend to think the contrary* [emphasis her own]."[41] According to Walker, Greenhow used her feminine beauty as a tool of gendered manipulation and advancement in her diplomatic exchanges with men in Europe. In this way, Greenhow's diplomatic efforts can be seen as enhanced, rather than compromised, by her position as "the weaker sex in war."

Greenhow published her narrative, *My Imprisonment and the First Year of Abolition Rule in Washington*, in London in 1863.[42] In her narrative, Greenhow described her suffering and the dangers she faced as a Southern woman in the context of war. She recalled the omnipresent and pervading threat of her arrest by Union authorities: "The words of the heroine Corday are applicable here: '*C'est le crime qui fait la honte, et non pas l'échafaud.*' My sufferings will afford a significant lesson to the women of the South, that sex or condition is no bulwark against the surging billows of the 'irrepressible conflict.'"[43] Furthermore, once she was arrested and imprisoned, she included an extract from her journal dated March 25, 1862: "I have been now eight months a prisoner, subject during that period to every insult and outrage which capricious tyranny could invent; my property stolen and destroyed; shut up in close imprisonment, and actually suffering the torments of hunger." Greenhow was also distraught over the inclusion of her daughter in her punishment, "To this treatment has my child of eight years been also exposed."[44] While such instances of women's imprisonment for supporting the Confederacy were rare, these exceptional cases did offer an opportunity for the Union to deter other Southern women from engaging in similar pursuits. These exceptional cases also offered the Confederacy the opportunity to admonish the Union for its harsh and inhumane treatment of Confederate women, like Greenhow, as "the weaker sex in war."

While these commentaries implicitly indicted the Union as the cause of her individual suffering, she spliced her narrative with explicit condemnations of the Union's lack of humanity in its interactions with Southern women. In her narrative, Greenhow included the second letter she wrote to U.S. secretary of war Edwin Stanton dated December 27, 1861, begging him to cease hostilities on the grounds of humanity, "if there be one latent spark of philanthropy still dormant in your soul, to kindle it in the cause of suffering humanity. For this cruel war lies at your door, and not at that of my brethren of the South."[45] Moreover, her entry from March 19, 1862, conveyed her sense of hopelessness and powerlessness at the hands of the Union. Greenhow's daughter accompanied her to prison and fell ill. Greenhow pleaded for medical help and finally a doctor was consulted, but the prospect of their release, even under these dire circumstances, seemed unlikely, "it [the doctor's visit] was only intended to gloss over their tyranny and afford a pretext for still greater oppression. I knew the chiefs of the Abolition Government too well to believe that humanity would guide their counsels."[46] Greenhow castigated representatives of the "Abolition Government"—both Stanton and its "chiefs"—in their failure to treat the South and its people with humanity.

After delivering her own personal account of suffering as a Southern woman and identifying the source responsible for her suffering—the Union government—Greenhow concluded her narrative with a call to British abolitionists to take a role of nonintervention in the conflict. Their doing so in debates surrounding Confederate recognition would silence some of the most vocal critics of the Confederacy abroad and make the prospect of Confederate recognition more likely. Greenhow explained how the South would address philanthropic and humanitarian concerns surrounding slavery on its own terms: "I think, English philanthropists may safely leave to Southern statesmen the removal of such abuses as cling to this in common with all other human institutions."[47] Greenhow was aware of the powerful effect of the language of humanitarianism in this conflict. The final lines of her narrative recognized the leading critique of the Confederacy—the Confederacy violated standards of humanity in its perpetuation of the institution of slavery—and attempted to counter this critique within the same rhetorical lexicon. According to Greenhow, the South might not advocate immediate abolition, but its leaders were considering the wider and global philanthropic and humanistic debates surrounding the institution of slavery. The South, like the English philanthropists, was concerned with the betterment of mankind and common humanity. Greenhow used the position and power granted to her by Davis to try to mediate the interests of Britain and the Confederacy, in both her encounters with foreign leaders and the publication of her narrative abroad. Davis did not empower Greenhow or any other Confederate woman as an official ambassador, and her activities did not signal conservative women's entry into formal politics, but he did afford her a version of diplomatic status that allowed her to contribute to debates over Confederate support in Britain. Greenhow did not need to enjoy the rights of full citizenship to make a forceful conservative intervention into these political and diplomatic issues.

In August 1864, Greenhow attempted to return to the Confederacy on a British blockade runner. After an altercation with a Union ship off the coast of Wilmington, North Carolina, Greenhow drowned. Sewn into her clothes were $2,000 of royalties from the sale of her memoir in Europe. These proceeds from her narrative, embedded in her garments for travel, hindered her ability to swim to safety. A letter published in the *Wilmington Sentinel* described how Greenhow's funeral was planned to be as "public as possible" and her "corpse would lie in state" given her service to the Confederate state: "It was a solemn and imposing spectacle . . . the silent mourners, sable-robed, at the head and foot; the tide of visitors, women and children with streaming eyes, and soldiers, with bent heads and hushed stares, standing by, paying the last tribute of respect to the departed heroine."[48] This episode became a perfect snapshot of Southern women's victimization at the hands of the Union military; both her memoir and her death illustrated the vulnerability of Confederate women. According to Confederate advocates, Britain had saved and protected Greenhow; the Union had persecuted and killed her. In her life and death, Greenhow was a heroine for the Confederate cause.

Like Greenhow, Belle Boyd hailed from a wealthy family; she was born in Martinsburg, Virginia (later West Virginia), and her family held strong Confederate sympathies. After being acquitted of murder for shooting a Union soldier in 1861 who tried to enter her family home, Boyd carried intelligence to Confederate military lines in Virginia. The Northern press lambasted her as a prostitute for her activities to support the Confederacy.[49] The Southern press hailed her as a heroine of the cause. Myrta Lockett Avary recalled the kindness and generosity of Boyd after she had spent a night sheltering in her family's house early in the war: "Once, when riding out to review some troops near Winchester, she met a soldier, a mere boy, trudging along painfully on his bare feet. She took off her own shoes and made him put them on."[50] Boyd was arrested by Union authorities in July 1862 and imprisoned in the Old Capitol Prison, the same as Greenhow, and was released one month later. She was arrested again in 1863 but was quickly released. Soon after, she ran the blockade and traveled to Britain, when her vessel was intercepted by a Union ship. Boyd's vessel was eventually permitted to travel on to Britain and, in August 1864, she married an officer on the Union ship that allowed her to pass, Samuel Wylde Hardinge. Soon after the marriage, Hardinge was imprisoned by the Union under suspicion of aiding a Confederate spy. While historians do not agree on the fate of Hardinge, most believe he was released from prison in early 1865 and died soon after. Like Greenhow, once in Britain and pregnant with Hardinge's child, Boyd published a memoir of her trials in the Confederacy titled *Belle Boyd in Camp and Prison. In Two Volumes* (1865).[51] Boyd's narrative, particularly in commentaries dated from 1862, is a testament to the enduring vulnerability and insecurity Southern women faced in the war—even if they were considered to be the "Rebel Joan of Arc" or "Cleopatra of Secession." Boyd described the war's impact on her family in the summer of 1861 in a description that could be applied to many households across the South at this early point in the war: "the excitement caused by our exertions to equip our father for the field had ceased, and the reaction of feeling had set in.... Our nights were not passed in sleep, but in thinking painfully of the loved one who was exposed to the dangers and privations of war."[52] Later, she recalled a less generalized experience of suffering in the Old Capitol Prison: "Years may roll by, but my sufferings in that prison, both mental and physical, can never be obliterated from my memory; and to attempt to describe them would be utterly impossible."[53]

Boyd was meticulous in identifying the cause of her suffering: the Union's violations of standards of humanity. Boyd described one of her many scathing confrontations with the Union navy, "I calculated far too much upon the forbearance and humanity of Yankees; and these qualities were seldom exhibited when their enemies were defenseless and, consequently, at their mercy."[54] Furthermore, Boyd not only discussed her own suffering, but the suffering of others she encountered. She described "a piteous spectacle" at Fort Delaware: "Four [Confederate] men, old and decrepit, one of them tottering on the entrance to the valley of shadows, gray beards and venerable aspects ought to have commanded at least sympathy from the presiding powers at Washington, were brought in as prisoners [to the Union]."[55] She then provided the text of the petition written by the four prisoners to the commander at Fort Delaware asking him to support their petition for release and their oath of allegiance to the Union if he found it in accordance with his own "views of duty and humanity."[56] The Union not only transgressed the bonds of humanity in its relations with Southern women but also frail older Southern men; the Union preyed upon the South's weakest people. In her selection of this visceral and emotive anecdote to include in her narrative and complement her first-person account, Boyd widened the scope of sympathy to include not only victimized women but victimized men. Whereas Confederate sympathizers in Britain used the language of humanity to forge bonds of commonality between Britain and the Confederacy, Greenhow and Boyd used the language of humanity to demonize the Union. Still, both of these rhetorical strategies were deployed to strengthen British support of the Confederate war effort.

After building her case for Southern women's victimization as a result of Union abuses of humanity, the final words of Boyd's two-volume narrative advocate for European recognition of the Confederacy in memory:

> Englishmen! I appeal to your impartial judgment! I look to you for the discountenancing of the foul charge which Mr. Stanton has thrown upon the shoulders of our Southern leaders [that the South is responsible for Lincoln's assassination] that he might thereby induce the European Powers to withdraw their recognition of Southern belligerency.[57]

Boyd had submitted her narrative to the publisher before the assassination of Lincoln and was able to add a final chapter after his assassination. In fact, on January 25, 1865, she had written to Lincoln with a proposal. She would withdraw her memoir from publication if Lincoln released her husband. She described the politicization of her narrative: "My book was not originally intended to be more than a personal narrative, but since my husband's unjust arrest, I had intended making it political." She then went on to describe this politicized narrative's threat to Lincoln, "[I] had introduced many atrocious circumstances respecting your government with which I am so well acquainted which would open the eyes of Europe to many things which the world on this side of the water little dreams."[58] She gave him a deadline of March 25 to release her husband or else her memoir would be published. Given there is no record of a response from Lincoln to Boyd, and Boyd did publish her narrative in 1865, it is very unlikely her letter had an impact on Lincoln. She may have been unsuccessful in forging a relationship with Lincoln and lobbying for her husband, but her letter to Lincoln still reveals her claim to an expanded wartime role; she believed she had the right to petition Lincoln herself for her own interests. After the surrender at Appomattox and assassination of Lincoln, Boyd still perceived European recognition of the Confederacy to be crucial to the preservation of its legacy.[59] Boyd was acutely aware that the Southern war effort would not only be remembered in a national context but in a more global landscape. European recognition of the Confederacy was not just important to the Confederate war effort before 1865 but to the memory of the Confederacy after 1865.

After the war, still experiencing financial strain, Boyd became an actress. In 1866, she played Pauline in Manchester Theatre Royal's production of *The Lady of Lyons*. Soon after, she returned to the United States and gave her theatrical debut in St. Louis. She then toured the South and Southwest with a theater company. Before her March 1869 marriage to John Swainston Hammond, a former British officer, she gave up her acting career.[60] In her immediate postwar activities, Boyd maintained a public transnational presence and found a new venue to explore performance and the fluidity of identity. In some ways, she applied the same skill set she had developed during the war as a spy to her work after the war as an actress. Whereas during the war she performed the role of a Confederate spy and deceived the Union as to her true identity, after the war she performed many theatrical roles as an actress to entertain commercial audiences. Her wartime performance projected ideals of Confederate nationalism and the legitimacy and worthiness of the Confederate cause to audiences inside and outside of the Confederacy. Like Greenhow, Boyd controlled both her performative and written narrative of her devotion to the Confederate cause and offered Confederate supporters a sensational and charismatic emissary to circulate their ideas.

The Rhetoric of Confederate Womanhood in Britain

From 1862, espoused by both British-born Confederate sympathizers and American-born women Confederate agents, one way in which the appeal for Confederate recognition in Britain was framed was through a rhetoric of what today would be called "humanitarianism" justified through Southern women's vulnerability and victimization. Often in newspapers and political debates, economic and political treatises on taxation and the constitutional rights to secession became secondary to moralistic supplications for support of the Southern cause to protect the rights of humanity and promote the betterment of mankind. This was a more inclusive rhetorical frame with a wider appeal. This rhetoric was presented in simple and easily accessible language that was generally secular and void of complex political theory. Also, it was not just aimed at the political and economic elites but the masses. As such, it held the potential to incorporate more voices in the debate across a more diverse range of classes and backgrounds. This was not just about defining international relations from above but shaping popular opinion from below.

The rhetoric of Confederate recognition evolved from a more political and economic argument to one of moralism and common humanity from 1862. By the start of 1862, after several months of fighting, the sacrifices of war were no longer an abstract concept as they had been in the early months of 1861, but an actual lived reality for the Confederate home front. As such, this new rhetoric was a response to the new hardships and culture of self-sacrifice on the Southern home front born out of the conditions of war. Also, in more specific terms, this change in rhetoric was a response to the Union's alleged aggressions against Southern women in the early months of the conflict. As Confederate secretary of state Judah P. Benjamin wrote to James Mason, the Confederate emissary in Britain, in late 1864, "While engaged in defending our country on terms so unequal the foes whom we are resisting profess the intention of resorting to the starvation and extermination of our women and children as a means of securing conquest over us." Benjamin ended his letter with a plea for Mason to ascertain whether England would, in fact, recognize the Confederacy for the sake of humanity: "If, then, the purpose of France and Great Britain have been, or be now, to exact terms or conditions before conceding the rights we claim [independence and foreign recognition], a frank exposition of that purpose is due to humanity. It is due now, for it may enable us to save many lives most precious to our country."[61] Benjamin, a keen observer of events in Europe and the promotion of the Confederate case abroad, captured the shift in pro-Confederate rhetoric in Britain in a letter to his diplomat: Southern civilians were suffering and required foreign intervention on humanitarian grounds.

In incidents that would garner international attention, as discussed earlier, Confederate spy Rose Greenhow was imprisoned in 1861 and Belle Boyd was imprisoned in 1862 and 1863. Between August 20 and August 24, 1862, *Reynold's Newspaper*, *Preston Guardian*, *Leeds Mercury*, and *Liverpool Mercury* all printed an article from the *New York Herald* describing Boyd's arrest and imprisonment.[62] In an infamous episode, Union general Benjamin Butler, occupying New Orleans from May 1862, issued General Order 28, an order that gave Union soldiers the right to treat New Orleans women displaying "insult" or "contempt" to their authority as "common women" or prostitutes. Inside and outside of the Confederacy, these incidents were framed as abuses of Union power and as victimization of Southern women and became lightning rods to critique the Union war effort.[63]

General Butler's order, while targeting Southern women in the Confederacy, did have international diplomatic ramifications. Lord Palmerston in the British House of Commons pontificated, "An Englishman must blush to think that such an act has been committed by one belonging to the Anglo-Saxon race."[64] Such anxieties surrounding General Order 28 prompted a prolonged confrontation between Palmerston and the American minister to Great Britain, Charles Francis Adams. National and local British newspapers reported on Butler's exploits in New Orleans. Many publications reprinted General Order 28 verbatim and responses to the order from both Northerners and Southerners. Both the *Standard* and the *Leicester Chronicle* published the text of Butler's General Order 28 and Confederate general P. G. T. Beauregard's General Order 44, a response to Butler's edict, on June 10, 1862, and June 14, 1862, respectively. Beauregard's General Order 44 highlighted the significance of gender: "shall our mothers, our wives, our daughters and our sisters, be thus outraged by the ruffianly soldiers of the North, to whom is given the right to treat, at their pleasure, the ladies of the South as common harlots?"[65] Male Confederate leaders harnessed women not only as symbols to strengthen the Confederate cause but to denigrate the "ruffianly" Union cause, and this rhetoric was circulated both inside and outside of the Confederacy.

What is more, New Orleans resident Eugenia Phillips was arrested, prosecuted, and imprisoned under Butler's General Order 28 for laughing at the procession of a Union soldier's funeral. In addition to visceral outrage throughout the South, this episode was prominently featured in newspapers across Britain. Between July 28 and August 6, 1862, the *Daily News*, the *Times*, *Penny Illustrated Paper*, *Belfast News-Letter*, and *Derby Mercury* all printed Butler's conviction order of Phillips's and Phillips's response to his order.[66] Three months after her imprisonment, Butler released Phillips and she became a physical representation of the suffering women of the Confederacy under inhumane Union military occupation. While she did not physically journey to Europe as Greenhow and Boyd did, news of Phillips's ordeal did travel to Europe and helped frame debates surrounding the suffering of Southern women and the merits of Confederate recognition. Again, the emerging rhetoric of gender and humanitarianism was a response to changing conditions inside the Confederacy and the Union's mismanagement of "unruly" Southern women.

From 1862, the rhetoric surrounding Confederate recognition had to grapple with the effects of the Union's plans for emancipation. In May 1861, while in command of Fort Monroe in Hampton, Virginia, Union general Butler refused to return fugitive slaves who had entered his camp to their Southern owners in a policy that became known as "Butler's Fugitive Slave Law." In August 1861, the Union passed the First Confiscation Act and the Second Confiscation Act in July 1862. After the Battle of Antietam in September 1862, Lincoln issued his preliminary Emancipation Proclamation and the final Emancipation Proclamation on January 1, 1863.[67] Lincoln's final Emancipation Proclamation changed the Civil War from the war to save the union, to the war to end slavery. The Emancipation Proclamation gave the Union an international humanitarianism cause and grounded its war efforts in moralism. This was a powerful and evocative message to an international audience: to support the Union was to support abolition.

On the other side, the Confederacy was founded on the right to own slaves. The Confederacy could not appeal to an international audience on humanitarian grounds on the issue of slavery. Confederate advocates tried to challenge the humanity of Lincoln's Emancipation Proclamation, but this was an impotent and ineffective strategy. Still, some tried. In addition to lobbying the case for Confederate recognition in parliament, Liberal M.P. for Sunderland William Schaw Lindsay also lobbied the case for Confederate recognition to the British public. At the annual meeting of the Middlesex Annual Agricultural Association in October 1863, Lindsay lambasted Lincoln's plans for emancipation on humanitarian grounds,

> It [Emancipation Proclamation] could not be humane to the slaves, who were not yet prepared for freedom; and it certainly would not be humane to the five or six million of white people in the Southern States because the real object, aim and end of the proclamation was nothing more or less than this [. . .] massacre your masters, massacre your mistresses, massacre their children so you can obtain your freedom. Instead of being a humane proclamation, it was in fact a specimen of the most horrible barbarity.[68]

According to Lindsay, the Emancipation Proclamation, not the Confederate cause and slavery, promoted unjust violence and inhumanity. In a similar lexicon of barbarity and depravity, Greenhow described the Emancipation Proclamation to Boteler in early 1864, "The French people are brutal ignorant and depraved to a degree beyond description and have no appreciation of our struggle they believe it is to free the slaves and all their sympathies are really on the Yankee side." While Greenhow harbored high hopes for British recognition of the Confederacy until her death, her critique of the French people's views on "the war to end slavery" reveals a dominant discourse across Europe, even in Britain, that Confederate advocates abroad failed to effectively contest. After January 1, 1863, it was widely believed the Union held a monopoly on humanitarian interests given its recently stated commitment to abolish slavery. Despite its best efforts, the Confederacy struggled to challenge this narrative.

However, Confederate sympathizers tried to change this narrative of humanitarian concerns in the Civil War using the rhetoric of gender and the nationalist symbolism of victimized Southern women as "the weaker sex in war." In this narrative, the Union became the belligerent force as it violated standards of common humanity and moralism. While the Union might have made the Civil War the war to end slavery, it also fought a war against Southern women. This rhetorical frame offered the Confederacy the opportunity to assume the moral high ground and combat Union influence in the court of international public opinion. Simply put, the Confederacy's embrace of common humanity rhetoric, based on abuses against Southern women, can be read as a response to the Union's emancipation plans to a global audience.

These humanitarian moralistic appeals cannot be qualified as apolitical. They not only requested financial support for specific Confederate causes (like Southern prisoners and Southern women) but also political support to recognize the Confederacy for the betterment of the family of nations and mankind. The rhetoric of common humanity, as justified through the victimization of Southern women, wedded the moral and political justifications for Confederate recognition. Placing these debates in a lexicon of humanitarianism made the struggle for Confederate recognition about more than the individual self-interest of one state and its citizens, but rather the collective interests of all states and mankind. In doing so, seemingly apolitical humanitarian discourses became political because they all had one aim: securing Confederate recognition in Britain by way of gendered rhetoric.

Therefore, the idea of victimized Southern women, or "the weaker sex in war," played a key role in debates to recognize the Confederacy in Britain. Confederate advocates and Confederate women in Britain were cognizant of the emotive political power of female vulnerability and victimization, especially in the context of war. Mobilizing this rhetoric to an international audience placed suffering Southern women at the center of the campaign to convince the British populace to lobby for their government recognizing Southern independence. Conservative women became a source of political capital showcased by Confederate sympathizers in Britain to advance their agenda of recognition. As seen in their first-person narratives and letters, some middle-and planter-class white women in the Confederacy did display a conservative political consciousness on diplomatic issues and desired European recognition of the Confederacy on the world stage. These conservative women were invested in political issues outside of their daily lived experience, and they were eager to chronicle and contribute to the Confederate cause. However, most of these women, save Rose Greenhow and Belle Boyd, had little impact as political actors on these issues inside or outside of the Confederacy.

Greenhow and Boyd were exceptional figures in this global narrative, and they carved out new and influential diplomatic relationships with Confederate and British as well as French leaders on both sides of the Atlantic. Male political leaders, in both the Confederacy and Britain, recognized the potential power of Greenhow and Boyd to shape both public perceptions and political alliances in Britain. In contrast to women's reform networks in the mid-nineteenth-century North, Greenhow and Boyd did not secure for themselves or lobby for others for the full rights of citizenship on the basis of their expanded roles in the political sphere, but they still affected important political and diplomatic issues for the Confederacy in formative ways. However, unlike Greenhow and Boyd, most Confederate women had the greatest impact as inanimate symbols referenced in transnational print culture and political speeches, without a voice or distinction as to their race or class status. Confederate supporters abroad used the idea of Southern women as "the weaker sex in war" symbolically to admonish the Union and gain sympathy for the Southern cause.

White Southern women were not only powerful ideological symbols geographically outside of the Confederacy, but temporally outside of the Confederacy. The women discussed so far in this book—in chapters 1 through 4—reveal how the advent of war changed middle-and planter-class white women's relationship to the state and how these women negotiated relationships with male political and military leaders. Women advocated their own agendas often linked to national devotion and increasingly engaged with political culture in new ways. After 1865, some white Southern women played key roles in the construction of Lost Cause ideology and in shaping the relationship between the Old South and the New South. In doing so, they often used the memory of these wartime women to legitimize and valorize their own Lost Cause organizations and actions.

CHAPTER 5

The Home for Needy Confederate Women

THE STATE OF VIRGINIA chartered the Home for Needy Confederate Women in 1898. The charter allocated "for the establishment and conduct of a home for needy widows, wives, sisters and daughters of Confederate soldiers."[1] The organization occupied three homes in Richmond over the course of the twentieth century to accommodate its expanding operation. In 1900, the first home opened on 1726 Grove Avenue and housed eleven residents. In 1903, the organization moved to 3 East Grace Street, caring for an average of forty to fifty women per year. Then, the home moved to 301 N. Sheppard Street in 1932.[2] The new building on Sheppard Street could house up to 100 residents, but the organization struggled to recruit residents later in the twentieth century. In 1977, twelve years before its closure in 1989, the home cared for fifty residents.

The home received significant support from the state of Virginia. From 1915 to 1982, the Virginia General Assembly awarded the home annual funding, though these awards were often subject to debate in the legislature over the amount. In 1915, in its first award of state funding, the legislature gave the home $5,000. By way of comparison, in 1918, the General Assembly gave the Lee Home for Confederate Veterans $90,000.[3] In addition, fundraising drives as well as donations from private individuals and other Confederate memorial organizations (in particular, the United Daughters of the Confederacy and Sons of the Confederate Veterans) supported the home to a far lesser extent.

In the early 1980s, in its final years of funding, the home was given $125,000 per year. Without state financial support the home could not operate, and it was increasingly reliant on the state of Virginia for its survival as the twentieth century progressed.[4] In this way, the home fit national patterns. Historians of twentieth-century veterans' homes have established that the funding patterns of these institutions show an early reliance on private funding, transitioning to a combination of private and state funding, and finally a reliance on state funding.[5] Historians of twentieth-century Confederate women's homes agree with this trajectory, albeit with an emphasis on changing definitions of—and gendered forms of—charity from the nineteenth to the twentieth century and the lessening role of the individual in ensuring social welfare programs as time progressed.[6] In addition to funding its work through private donations and state support, the home required that residents transfer their remaining financial assets to the home upon admittance. This policy led to criticism and claims that the home prioritized prospective residents with greater resources for admittance.[7] In 1989, seven years after the General Assembly withdrew state funding for the home and facing an ever-dwindling population of Confederate "widows, wives, sisters, and daughters" the home shut its doors and the remaining residents were relocated to nursing homes.[8]

The United Daughters of the Confederacy supported the establishment of similar homes for indigent Confederate women across the South at the beginning of the twentieth century, but the Home for Needy Confederate Women in the former capital of the Confederacy was in many ways a template for these later establishments.[9] The significance of these homes rested not with the quantifiable number of residents but the symbolism of caring for the female descendants of Confederate soldiers. In other words, the organization not only served the medical needs of its residents, the residents served the ideological needs of the organization as embodiments of Confederate memory, becoming living, breathing symbols of the Lost Cause. Women leaders of the home were actively and eagerly involved in constructing and circulating this symbolism of Confederate memory. Just as the women discussed in this book were committed to and helped strengthen the Confederate cause during the war, the female leaders of the home were committed to and helped build Confederate memory and the Lost Cause after the war.

Both during and after the war, the groups of women discussed in this book had control over how they contributed first to nationalist and later to Lost Cause ideologies. During the war, even though women did not hold the full rights of citizenship and were not concerned with attaining these rights, they still negotiated new roles in society and a new relationship with the state. Over the course of the twentieth century, coinciding with the life span of the Home for Needy Confederate Women, women gained more rights as citizens as well as direct access to the electoral political sphere as both voters and officeholders.[10] Still, despite this expansion of women's political rights as citizens and the introduction of women's roles in the electoral political sphere, the women involved with the home engaged with twentieth-century conservative political culture to champion an antiquated agenda from the previous century.

It is important to note here that "conservative" is not used in this chapter as an adjective for the Republican Party or to describe the twentieth-century political party spectrum. Conservative is used in the same way as in previous chapters, to denote women who were not concerned with advancing their individual rights or advocating for marginalized groups but rather were focused on the collective mission of sustaining the Confederacy during the war and the Lost Cause after the war. As such, these conservative women used progressive advancements of gender equality and women's expanded rights as citizens to lobby the state of Virginia for the establishment, funding, and maintenance of a Lost Cause organization. These conservative women used the new set of rights and powers given to women through liberal reforms over the course of the twentieth century to lobby for the Home for Needy Confederate Women and the Lost Cause. The conservative women of the home benefited from liberal reforms and then used them to advance a Lost Cause agenda.

The life of its most famous resident, Sally Tompkins, encapsulates the mission of the organization. As discussed in the introduction, at the outbreak of the war, Tompkins dedicated her life to the Confederate cause. She ran the Robertson Hospital, a private hospital in Richmond, which served 1,300 patients over the course of the war. When Jefferson Davis ordered that all hospitals be placed under military command, he commissioned Tompkins in the Confederate army, as an unassigned captain in the Confederate cavalry. She was the only woman to be commissioned in the Confederate army and was known as the Florence Nightingale of the Confederacy. After the war, having never married or had children, she continued her charity efforts in the Richmond area until she was no longer able to support herself. She was admitted to the Home for Needy Confederate Women in 1905 and stayed until her death in 1916. She was given military honors at her burial. The trajectory of Tompkins's life, from being a caregiver to the Confederate cause in the 1860s to being a convalescent of the Confederate cause in the 1900s, is a powerful illustration of the home's romantic ambitions—an important facet of the broader trend to commemorate Tompkins, to which the epilogue returns. In a reciprocal exchange of service, the home strove to care for women who had cared for the Confederacy. Just as women like Tompkins safeguarded the Confederate cause during the war, the home would safeguard her welfare and medical care after the war, in both symbolic and practical ways.[11]

While there is an abundant body of scholarship exploring the significance of Ladies' Memorial Associations from the end of the war to the beginning of the twentieth century, as well as the emergence of the United Daughters of the

Confederacy at the end of the nineteenth century, there is little mention of the Home for Needy Confederate Women other than to briefly reference its links to these other Lost Cause organizations.[12] This chapter examines how the home rejected lifeless stone monuments to focus on caring for its residents and using them as living, breathing vessels of Confederate memory and the Lost Cause.[13] Its admittance requirements bore a similarity to the United Daughters of the Confederacy (UDC) membership policy that stated: "widows, wives, mothers, sisters, nieces and lineal descendants of such men as served honorably in the Confederate army, navy or civil service."[14] Indeed, the home was similar to the UDC in its reliance on the history of the Confederacy to select who would be included in its organization and its ideological mission, but it was markedly different in its works.[15] Its women leaders focused on maintaining life links to the Confederacy, to protect aging women, and to promote the home as a symbol of the Lost Cause into the next century. This was not just about valorizing the past but integrating living symbols of Confederate memory into the twentieth-century social landscape of the South.[16] Through the work of its women leaders, the Home for Needy Confederate Women became a symbol of Confederate memory, not as a stone memorial, but through the collective physicality of its female lineal descendants.[17] This chapter explores how the home was a collective symbol of Confederate memory, not only in terms of its residents but in its goals and interventions into Virginia state politics.

Not only its women residents, but the home itself as a domestic space can be seen as a symbol of wartime gender and race power relations and postwar trauma. As Thavolia Glymph argues, after the war "The white home was reinvented as a highly gendered and racialized sanctuary. There, white women would continue to be 'ladies' and managers of domestic spaces, both white and black."[18] The Home for Needy Confederate Women was comprised of women from several households and functioned somewhere between traditional definitions of the private and public spheres, but Glymph's ideas of domesticity and memory still apply to this collective household's embrace of the previous century's gender and race relations. The organization's women leaders sought to maintain the values of nineteenth-century Southern "civilization" through the maintenance of the twentieth-century home.[19] The home never housed a Black resident and references to race in the organization's archival record are rare and reflect the ways in which gendered notions of domesticity were inflected with a race and class hierarchy in both the nineteenth and twentieth centuries. The women leaders of the home recorded issues they found to be important, and such issues rarely included race, despite the organization's life span over segregation, Jim Crow, and the Civil Rights movement. The home did not consider Black women's voices, ideas, and experiences in its conceptualization of the Old South and Civil War; instead, the home's women leaders focused on promoting Confederate memory based on white superiority. These conservative women were actively engaged with strengthening Lost Cause ideology through white women's associations of domesticity and civilization from the previous century.

Yet toward the end of the twentieth century, this symbolism came into conflict with the legislative agenda and political ideology of the Virginia General Assembly, the oldest democratic legislative body in the United States. The General Assembly was willing to financially support the home temporarily, as long as it restricted its admittance policy to the next generation of Confederate survivors (i.e., daughters). However, when the home modified its admittance policy to include all female lineal descendants in perpetuity in 1977, the General Assembly withdrew its funding. State support of female Confederate descendants for generations to come, into the twenty-first century and beyond, held potentially perilous and unstable ramifications for individual politicians and the legislative body as a whole since the home's symbolism stood in stark contrast to ideals of modernization.

Debates surrounding continued state support of the home reveal multidimensional and deeply embedded conflicts over the state's role in supporting Confederate memorials and memory—an issue still relevant today. Furthermore, the home's near complete dependence on state funding from 1915 for its operation speaks to the contested notion of state support of medical care, another issue still relevant today. The symbolism of the Home for Needy Confederate Women held social capital for two dissonant interests. For Confederate sympathizers, the survival of the home was one means by which to strengthen the Lost Cause. For the state legislature, the withdrawal of state support for the home was one means by which to showcase a political agenda committed to social and economic liberalism in the second half of the twenty-first century, as argued by Susan Hamburger. The evocative and emotionally charged conflict between these two interpretations of the symbolism of the home reveals how understandings of gender and memory from the nineteenth century continued to shape the Virginia body politic into the twentieth century. As discussed in previous chapters, during the war conservative Virginia women brokered new relationships and exchanges to support the Confederate republic and perform national devotion. After the war, as seen in the establishment of the Home for Needy Confederate Women, some conservative Virginia women pivoted to new roles to support the Confederate republic in memory. In a similar vein as their wartime counterparts, they lobbied male political and civic society leaders to safeguard the ideological legacy of the Confederacy as well as the physical survival of Confederate women.

The Rejection of Stone Monuments

By the turn of the twentieth century, some in the Lost Cause called for Confederate memorialization to move beyond the erection of stone memorials and amplify its celebration of Confederate women. A year before the Home for Needy Confederate Women was chartered by the state of Virginia, the Ladies' Auxiliary of the George E. Pickett Camp published a circular addressing this shift in attitudes surrounding memorialization. The Ladies' camp outlined the necessity to memorialize the cause beyond lifeless monuments and indicted the uneven processes of commemoration between Confederate soldiers and Confederate women: "You have provided generously for the disabled survivors of our heroic Confederate soldiery in their declining years: you have built monuments to the deathless dead who died for us and decked their graves with flowers." The appeal continued with a sense of urgency: "under the shadow of those lofty pillars and pyramids you have erected to the dead, those dearer to the living and dead than life itself are shivering in cold and almost nakedness, starving for lack of proper food, dying for lack of proper care."[20] Such a rhetoric created a hierarchy of memorialization priorities where preserving life, as opposed to commemorating death, was paramount.

The circular went on to make the gendered inequity in postwar recognition explicit. "In plain words—in calm, clear statement—what we mean is this: Here in Richmond, and, as we are informed and believe, throughout the Commonwealth, widows and sisters and daughters of the dead and disabled Confederate soldiers are in dire distress."[21] Foreshadowing the Home's central mission, the Ladies' Auxiliary of the George E. Pickett Camp rejected the utility of stone monuments and advocated the care of aging Confederate women.

The home's first acting president, Elizabeth Lyne Hoskins Montague, mastered the rhetorical lexicon of women as living symbols of the Confederacy to both political and civic audiences. In a 1915 speech to the Virginia General Assembly, Montague emphasized Confederate women as deserving of government support and protection: "The poor and needy women of the Confederacy define and segregate a class that should ever touch our hearts and quicken our hands. Deserving charity is always blessed, but when in its exercise we can identify glorious traditions and preserve the fine and stirring things of history, we indeed ennoble ourselves." Montague went on to reject lifeless stone monuments. "We have [been] building monuments, literally many hundreds of them, throughout the South-land. But the cry now is not for stone, but for bread."[22] Likewise, addressing a UDC convention in the late 1920s to ask for increased financial support, Montague did not temper her rhetoric on the rejection of monuments: "It is not fully written in history, but sacrifice, suffering, endurance and courage are indelibly traced on the minds and hearts of the Southern people, and the objects of need can be better memorialized by bread than by stone."[23] Again, such a rhetoric prioritized the basic needs of living Confederate descendants over the creation of monuments. Given that the UDC worked tirelessly to erect monuments throughout the region, this was a particularly targeted critique.

Two decades later, in a speech to the Virginia General Assembly in the 1940s, Montague indicted the legislators to do more to support the home after they had not voted to raise its annual appropriations budget, despite the fact that the overall budget had been increased that year and such an increase for the home was recommended in the governor's budget. Her closing comments encapsulated the core of the home's work: "thousands of dollars have been spent upon monuments to our Confederate soldiers in this State. But this is the only monument in the world to the brave women of the South. Gentlemen, surely none of you desire the dissolution of this monument."[24] Interpreted through a conservative prism, Montague employed the issue of gender equality to strengthen her argument for the home's funding.

This rhetoric seems to have been embraced by not only the home's leaders but also by its residents. In 1910, Caroline Gouldin praised her care in the home and claimed former Confederate soldiers would have supported this effort above all other forms of memorialization: "Are those who died bravely for the 'Lost Cause' in any way more honored than in this way to make comfortable and happy the declining years of the women who were dearer to them than life itself? I think I can truly say that this is the monument our honored dead would have preferred to any other."[25] Gouldin inserted a moralistic imperative based on mid-nineteenth-century concepts of Southern masculinity and honor to showcase the significance of the work of the home in the early twentieth century. Not only was the home trying to ensure the survival of Confederate women, the home's advocates articulated a Confederate value system to justify its work.[26] From its president to its residents, the home emphasized its life links to the Confederacy.

As seen in Montague's documented speeches and its other printed materials, the home was cognizant of the power of print culture to strengthen the organization and attract private donations. The home meticulously molded its vision and drive around these aged women as life links to the Confederacy. This coalesced message is perhaps most visible in a 1929 twenty-four-page booklet published as part of a fundraising drive for the new home on Sheppard Street. The first half of the booklet detailed "The Need" of the organization as "the Home must be a refuge for the future, as well as the present, glorifying the memory of those who gave their all by ensuring that their descendants shall not be in danger of becoming public charges, or subject to the mercy of generations who may have forgotten."[27] The booklet went on to explain "Why YOU Should Help": "[the home] has been rendering definite service to aged women of the Confederacy for over 28 years.... [It] offers worthy aged women a safe haven in their hour of need that in no way reflects upon or injures their natural pride of womanhood."[28] This appeal made it clear that the home honored the memory of the Confederacy by maintaining the Confederacy through its living female descendants. Through the bodies of these aged women, the Confederacy could exist outside of stone monuments into the twentieth century. President of the Richmond UDC chapter (1896–1927) Janet Henderson Weaver Randolph concurred. She opposed the building of a stone monument to honor Confederate women and instead advocated donations to the Confederate Museum as a way to celebrate Confederate womanhood in the present.[29]

An abbreviated form of the booklet was published as a pamphlet aptly titled, "A Monument of Service: To the Undying Memory of the Women of the Southern Confederacy." Furthermore, the editor of the *Richmond Times-Dispatch* published an independent pamphlet to support the fundraising drive: "Virginia's call must not be Denied." The pamphlet succinctly positioned the organization's goals as straddling the past and the present: "The women of the Confederacy who survive will never forget the tragedy of the splendid days through which they lived.... And those who shall live in the South as long as America lasts, should never, must never, forget the women who saw their very civilization being destroyed."[30] For some in the twentieth century, the Confederate republic was the definition of civilization and tradition to be revered and preserved. In not only its speeches and oral culture, but in its printed materials and print culture, the home presented a documented and detailed argument that the protection and support of Confederate women in the twentieth century would serve as a living, breathing memorial to the cause, a far more purposeful and effective strategy than the construction of lifeless stone monuments.[31]

Through these fundraising ventures and its attempts to attract a greater network of support from private donors, the home was at times in competition with other Lost Cause organizations. This rupture between the ideological Lost

Cause and the financial Lost Cause was most apparent in an early dispute between the Home for Needy Confederate Women and the George E. Pickett Camp of Confederate Veterans. There were sixteen homes for Confederate veterans in all former states of the Confederacy as well as in Maryland, California, Kentucky, Oklahoma, and Missouri.[32] UDC members in every state of the former Confederacy worked to establish and fundraise for veterans' homes.[33] The Sons of Confederate Veterans, while also actively involved in supporting veterans' homes, largely did not reciprocate this commitment to the establishment and support of Confederate women's homes.

Despite this gendered unevenness in support, both Confederate veterans' homes and Confederate women's homes showcased their residents as "living monuments" to the Confederacy. Such symbolism transcended the focus on monuments and illustrated the ways in which life links to the Confederacy could be memorialized and vindicated into the next generation.[34] In 1904, the Pickett camp and the home resolved a dispute over both organizations' claims to a shared Metropolitan Bank account totaling $1,511. The home initially suggested taking two-thirds of the account and the Pickett camp one-third of the account. The Pickett camp rejected this offer and proposed to evenly split the account. The home accepted this offer in order to "have the cheerful and cordial co-operation of the members of the George E. Pickett Camp" and to avoid litigation.[35] The home recognized the value of an affable and productive working relationship with a prominent organization with significant influence in Richmond rather than a more lucrative stand-alone payment. Prioritizing future collaborations and interorganizational support allowed the home to present itself as a willing partner in the network of Confederate organizations in Richmond. The future of the home was intrinsically tied to the power of Confederate memory in the twentieth century. Working with other organizations with a shared ideological drive to strengthen the legacy of the Confederacy was an advantageous strategy. Still, the resolution of this dispute mirrors the gender inequity in commemoration practices. The Pickett camp dictated the terms of the negotiation and the home acquiesced.[36]

Furthermore, from 1910 to 1913, a joint committee comprised of representatives from the Home for Needy Confederate Women and the United Daughters of the Confederacy presented a series of proposals exploring the option for the Virginia Division of the UDC to assume control of the struggling home. Ultimately, the UDC did not approve these measures and the home advocated "co-operation over domination." The home offered the UDC a "fair share in official control" in the form of board membership.[37] These proposals and subsequent discussions testify to the ways in which this shared mission of preserving the memory of the Confederacy could become fractured over strategy and the allocation of resources between organizations.

That said, these discussions in 1910–13 appear to be more aberrational in their tension when examining the longer narrative of the relations between these two overlapping organizations. In the home's annual reports from 1900 to 1904, the UDC donated more to the home than any other organization, with forty-two chapters giving donations. Later, in 1954, the Richmond chapter of the UDC donated twenty-five burial plots to the home in Riverview Cemetery, and the Elliot Grays chapter of the UDC donated fifteen burial plots in Maury Cemetery as the spaces allotted to the home by the city council had been used.[38] Over the course of the twentieth century, the relationship between the home and the UDC was more "cooperation than domination" prioritizing the ideology of the Lost Cause.

While veterans' homes and the UDC shared a commitment to the Lost Cause as an ideology, at times these organizations came into conflict with the home over how to enact this ideology into a tangible lived reality. These issues of Confederate memory and womanhood did not exist in a vacuum and were still shaped by human actors with a wide range of concerns and motivations. Still, this evidence suggests that although the home encountered some tension with other Lost Cause organizations, particularly in its early years, the home and its conservative women leaders were able to maintain productive relationships with these organizations in the longer term and safeguard their joint ideological commitment to women as living memorials to the Confederacy.

The Rise and Decline of the Home

When the home did look to the past, it tended to do so through the prism of Robert E. Lee. In terms of reverence of the past, there was no greater symbol of Confederate fortitude than Lee; the organization meticulously manicured links to Lee to bolster its profile in Lost Cause Richmond. Lee's daughter, Mary Custis Lee, was the first president of the organization and bridged the nineteenth-and twentieth-century celebrations of the Lee family in Virginia. While Lee served in an honorary role with little contribution other than the symbolism of her involvement, she still gave the home increased legitimacy and access to the social capital of the Lee legacy. Furthermore, as acting president under Lee, Montague tenaciously lobbied the Robert E. Lee Camp No. 1, United Confederate Veterans for land on their site to construct a new and expanded Home for Needy Confederate Women. In 1924, the Lee camp finally acquiesced. The Robert E.

Lee Camp No. 1, United Confederate Veterans gave the Home for Needy Confederate Women 2.5 acres of land on the site of their veterans' home. From the opening of the third and final site of the Home for Needy Confederate Women in 1932, the veterans' home named in honor of Lee and the Home for Needy Confederate Women would sit beside one another. This transfer of land between the organizations was approved by the Virginia General Assembly in 1926.[39]

Significantly, and foreshadowing later debates addressing the survival of the home into the twenty-first century, Governor Elbert Lee Trinkle vetoed the original bill authorizing the land transfer as he supported the position that the home should only admit widows, wives, sisters, and daughters (i.e., not female lineal descendants in future generations as had been allowed in a 1916 amendment to the charter).[40] Trinkle advocated for the admission requirements to reflect the original 1898 charter, not the 1916 amendments that included all female lineal descendants. Only after the state legislature amended the bill to address Trinkle's issues did it pass.

In these fundraising efforts to build the new home on the land of the Lee camp, the women regularly employed the legacy of Lee. In the 1929 promotional pamphlet for the building of the new home, an image of Lee occupied the front inside cover and Lee's Farewell Address appeared in its text.[41] Furthermore, the organization published a history of the home from 1900 to 1904 that offered a statement of support from Fitzhugh Lee, as a Confederate veteran, member of the Lee family, and former postwar governor of Virginia (1886–90):

> Referring to our conversation in Richmond in which, as a survivor of the war, I expressed my great appreciation of the noble work you and the ladies associated with you are doing... I want to make it more emphatic by voicing, in writing, the gratitude of southern soldiers generally.... I know of no better service that can be rendered to our Confederate comrades than the exalted charity which seeks to shelter, protect and provide for needy Confederate women.[42]

Situating itself in the genealogical and geographical legacy of Lee was a shrewd strategy to raise the organization's profile with a sympathetic and captive audience in Richmond. With his daughter at the helm from its inception, and its building on the land of the Robert E. Lee Camp No. 1, United Confederate Veterans, the Home for Needy Confederate Women could not be divorced from the memory of Robert E. Lee.

The leadership of Mary Custis Lee reveals another defining feature of the organization beyond the legacy of Lee as an individual: its relationships and exchanges with politically powerful men to advance its agenda. While the home's charter was relatively standard for an organization at the end of the nineteenth century, it did stipulate that all officers and members of the board of directors must be women.[43] Not only would the organization care for women, its leadership would be comprised of women (at least on paper). Such a measure presented a gendered performance of the Lost Cause; women were both recipients of and workers for charity efforts aligned with Confederate memory. Of course, in practice, white male advisors from Richmond's ruling elite offered various levels of guidance and counsel to the nascent organization. While generally speaking 1898 Virginia certainly offered more freedoms and rights to middle-class white women than in Confederate Virginia, women still struggled for power and authority in this more liberal and progressive society. The public performance of surrogacy by prominent men in the community validated the women's work to skeptical audiences and gave their mission legitimacy.

While Lee was the honorary president, Montague was the acting president and was responsible for the early survival and successes of the home. In 1889, she had married Andrew Jackson Montague, a leading Southern progressive who would go on to become the forty-fourth governor of Virginia (1902–6) and member of the U.S. House of Representatives (1912–37).[44] Montague's political career at both the state and federal levels operated within the long shadow of Confederate memory and at the nexus of the Old and New South. He was the first Virginia governor since the Civil War not to have served in the Confederate military, though he was named after his uncle who died at the Battle of Gaines' Mill in 1862. Even though Montague privately said the Confederacy's loss in the war had been "providential," he was a strong supporter of the home throughout his wife's tenure as president.[45] On March 14, 1905, he gave the introductory address to Alexander McClure's fundraising lecture "Our Country." He also provided a statement of support in a published history of the early history of the home: "Help in life is better than pains after death; and to the former task you and the ladies have committed yourself with an energy and self-sacrifice deserving of the sympathy of all who have sympathy for those whose present misfortunes and sorrows are nowise their own making."[46] Montague's comments draw on the culture of self-sacrifice of Confederate women during the war; the women leaders of the home were devoted to Confederate memory in the same way their wartime counterparts were devoted to the Confederate republic.

As First Lady of Virginia (1902–6), whose work was often publicly supported by her husband, Montague was able to showcase the organization's work on a more visible platform to a wider audience.[47] Such support also lent the organization legitimacy, which was especially important in its early days. After Montague's death in 1951, one of her three children, her daughter, Janet Montague Nunnally, took over as president. Then, after Nunanlly's resignation in 1976 until its closing, Nunnally's daughter and Montague's granddaughter, Janet Roy Burhans served as president. This matrilineal line of inheritance shows the social and political power held by some former elite Confederate families a century after Appomattox; the Montague family and its conservative women held a monopoly on the physical and ideological construction of the home over nearly nine decades.

In one instance, the First Lady of the United States and the former First Lady of Virginia worked together to strengthen the cause of the home on a national, as opposed to regional, stage. On December 30, 1926, the *New York Times* reported that Montague had taught First Lady Grace Coolidge, an expert knitter, how to make a pattern found on the bed of one of the home's residents. Coolidge then sold the directions on how to knit the pattern to a "newspaper woman" to publish to her readers for $250, which Coolidge donated to the home's building fund.[48] The First Lady's support had significant influence in publicizing the mission of the organization to a national audience. Montague had access to Coolidge through the political work and networks of their husbands; Andrew Jackson Montague served as a congressman during the administration of Calvin Coolidge (1923–29). While Coolidge was notoriously apolitical in her work as First Lady, this stand-alone act of charity gave the home some sense of approval and acceptance to Northern observers. The former First Lady of Virginia and the current First Lady of the United States worked in concert to promote the work of the home in a nonpolitically partisan and nonprogressive way.

Again, in an episode of solidarity between First Ladies, the past and present First Ladies of Virginia worked together to minimize the impact of state budget cuts on the home's residents. In 1943, the Virginia General Assembly cut thirteen widows' pensions from $12 and $15 a month to $5 month. The assembly justified this cut by pointing out that Montague had spoken to the assembly and claimed all the women's needs were met in the home and did not require a greater amount of funding. When this appropriations bill was passed, the home's leaders were outraged and lobbied the state for a restoration of the previous year's funding. In response, on July 14, 1944, the governor of Virginia, Colgate Darden Jr., wrote a letter to Montague explaining that he would not override the will of the assembly and provide state funding for the home as such an act would compromise the balance of power in state government and compromise the legislative democratic process. Instead, he wrote: "I am sending you a check herewith for $500 from

Mrs. Darden in order to allow the payments to continue on the old basis. She will send you another check at the turn of the year. I feel certain that when the Assembly again convenes the situation will have its attention."[49] Significantly, First Lady of Virginia Darden did not write to Montague; Governor Darden used the apolitical associations with the role of First Lady to privately support the home when the state failed to do so. The governor could not personally support such a project as doing so would critique the appropriations decision of the General Assembly. However, the First Lady could do this.

Whether Governor Darden would have provided this level of support to the organization had Montague not been a former First Lady of Virginia is debatable. It is clear that Montague's political connections aided the organization and gave it greater clout in political circles. Furthermore, the letter from Darden to Montague was leaked to a local newspaper by State Auditor L. McCarthy Downs. Downs "believed it proper to make the letter public because the pension situation had caused considerable comment lately."[50] It is unlikely Downs would have leaked this letter to the press with his name attached to the story without explicit approval from his immediate superiors and implicit approval from the governor. This letter portrayed the First Couple of Virginia as compassionate and caring, even willing to close the gap between the resources of the state and the needs of the citizenry out of their own personal funds. Darden's letter cannot be read as simply an altruistic measure to aid the organization; this situation also provided the opportunity to bolster his popularity with the people of Virginia. Just as Montague used her proximity to powerful political men to advance the home's interests, Governor Darden used the home to advance his political popularity. This was a mutually beneficial exchange that placed the home and its conservative women leaders and supporters at the forefront of state politics, and this conflict between the executive and legislature, for a fleeting moment.

In the aftermath of this heated funding debate, in 1946 the Quesenbery Commission was set up to investigate whether the state should continue to support the home. The following year, the commission recommended that the home only be allowed to admit wives, widows, daughters, and sisters (i.e., not female lineal descendants in perpetuity as the 1916 amendment had offered for ten years until the 1926 bill restored the wording of the original 1898 charter to only include wives, widows, daughters, and sisters).[51] As explored by Susan Hamburger, the Quesenbery Commission also critiqued the home's admittance policies as prioritizing candidates with larger endowments to transfer to the home upon their admittance.[52] The commission's findings foreshadowed later debates surrounding the closure of the home in the 1970s and 1980s and implied the state's support of the home should be temporary (for the current generation of Confederate women) and not permanent (for future generations of Confederate women). In sum, the state just needed to run out the clock for the last Confederate daughter to expire in its care. For the General Assembly, this was the most politically expedient and least controversial course of action.[53]

While the home kept its doors open and continued to accept residents, its financial situation became increasingly dire over the next few decades. In March 1977, after the home's extended lobbying campaign, the Virginia General Assembly amended the home's original 1898 charter (revised in 1926 to accommodate the transfer to land from the Lee camp to the home), to include "female lineal descendants" as beneficiaries of the home in addition to widows, wives, sisters, and daughters. This amendment signified the changing landscape for the process of Confederate memory and the need to address the widening passage of time from Appomattox to the present. The last daughters of the Confederacy were dying and to keep the home in existence, it needed to be permitted to admit the granddaughters of the Confederacy.[54] According to local media reports, the sponsors of the legislative amendment said Black female descendants of Confederate soldiers would be entitled for residency in the home, but the home never housed a Black resident.[55] Unsurprisingly, the home was hardly at the forefront of racial equality in the New South. In fact, ten years later, the home would be sued by one of its former employees for racial discrimination in management practices.[56]

In the late 1970s, the home's superintendent, Ellise Lipscomb, became increasingly demoralized in her annual reports as the home's residents became older and required more care than the budget or staff could accommodate. In 1976, the state of Virginia gave the home $125,000, but the operating costs of the home were over $252,000. Private donations did not make up the difference between state funding and the operating costs of the home. Frustrated by unsuccessful attempts to solicit private donations from individuals and other organizations, President Janet Burhans told the *Washington Post* in 1980, "'When you get right down to it, I suppose charity is a 19th century concept.'"[57] In the end, the assembly would discontinue annual appropriations to the home in 1982. (The home would receive appropriations in the 1986 budget due to relentless lobbying, but this was a singular one-off payment.)

In an August 20, 1980 letter, a program analyst from the Virginia Department of Planning and Budget, Robert F. White, wrote to President Janet Burhans asking why the General Assembly inserted "female lineal descendants" in the charter in 1977 only to revoke funding from 1982. Burhans responded: "Presumably this was a statement that they [the General Assembly] did not feel an obligation to support lineal descendants. That their obligation would stop with the Daughters of Confederate Veterans.... Possibly those 1977 legislators believed that no Daughters would survive beyond that date."[58] In 1980, the UDC estimated that there were 3,000 living daughters of the Confederacy and less than fifty living Confederate widows.[59]

After the Virginia General Assembly withdrew the home's annual funding in 1982 and in the context of struggling to attract residents to the home, President Burhans applied for Landmark status in 1984. It seems likely that given the home had not applied for Landmark status in its previous eighty-four years (and fifty-two years in its third and final building), that the organization acknowledged that its future was in jeopardy and wanted to do everything it could to survive. This is expressed in a letter from Burhans to an architect to request his sponsorship of the application: "If we are to profit by Landmark status in seeking grants or other building maintenance funding then we must do so before we lost the last Confederate Daughter in our care. Our future, if any, depends upon qualifying as a Landmark: by September of 1985, our building could well be levelled and in use of parking for the museum."[60] Burhans recognized the symbolic power of the National Register of Historic Places to bolster support at this crucial moment. Furthermore, it seems that Burhans was aware that if the home did collapse, such a status would ensure its symbolism beyond the lifetime of the organizational mandate. Like other women discussed in this book, Burhans tried a new strategy to champion her agenda and petitioned an influential civic organization to advance her cause. Again, like other women discussed in this book, Burhans recognized the importance of developing communication networks and shared goals with leaders and organizations in political and civic society to secure women's aims.

The home was given Landmark status on November 11, 1985. Significantly, in its evaluation form of the home's application received in October 1985, the National Park Service crossed out "Needy" from the name on the application acceptance sheet. The National Park Service would only recognize "The Home for Confederate Women" not "The Home for Needy Confederate Women." The National Park Service seems to have recognized that the national government could not sanction the uneasy descriptor of "needy Confederate." Debates surrounding the determination of deserving recipients of state funding and what constituted "needy" ravaged the national and state political landscapes, especially after the publication of the Moynihan Report in 1965.[61] Enveloping the home's residents in these debates surrounding class and welfare (as well as race), the modifier of "needy" created more of a pressure point for censure and critique.⁶² Whereas a former state of the Confederacy endorsed such language, the national government was unwilling to do so. Regardless, Landmark status was not enough to save the home from financial ruin as it closed a mere four years later. Harnessing the architectural value of the house, which was built based on James Hoban's plans for the north façade of the White House, delivered an aesthetic symbolism of the building, if not the tangible works or the organization, beyond the lifetime of the Home for (Needy) Confederate Women. And, close to Burhans prediction, though not quite a parking lot, the former home is now the Center for Education and Outreach for the Virginia Museum of Fine Arts.

By the 1980s, the Virginia General Assembly had withdrawn financial support for the Home for Needy Confederate Women. In 1989, the home closed and its last seven residents were relocated to other care facilities at the state of Virginia's expense. One of the final residents, ninety-eight-year-old Lila Lee Riddell, filed a lawsuit against her relocation from the home. The Richmond Circuit Court denied her request and the case was taken to the Virginia Supreme Court where it was again rejected. She then filed a temporary injunction, but this was rejected by the Federal District Court.⁶³ While her mission was ultimately unsuccessful, Ridell shows the ways in which women at least attempted to forge new relationships and lobby their interests related to Confederate memory, with city, state, and federal governments long after the war.⁶⁴ This collective legacy of the Confederacy, intertwined with her individual medical care and welfare, drove Riddell to lobby the various levels of the judicial branch to ensure these symbiotic causes after the state legislative system failed the home and its residents.

Other Confederate women's homes closed around the same time due to a declining population of potential residents, such as the Confederate Women's Home in Fayetteville, North Carolina (1915–81). Likewise, Confederate veterans' homes closed due to a dwindling population of Confederate veterans around 1950. The Lee Camp Soldiers' Home, which neighbored the home in its third and final site, closed in 1941. The challenges facing the Home for Needy Confederate Women were not unique and reflected standard life cycle patterns. Living survivors of the Confederacy who had been born in the mid-nineteenth century were dying by the mid-twentieth century. However, the home was unique in its response to this demographic crisis: to expand admission eligibility to include all female lineal descendants into future generations. Such an accommodation raised issues related to the relationship between the government and Confederate memory. Did the inclusion of female lineal descendants provide a window for Confederate identity to be extended into the twenty-first century and beyond? And should the state support such a project led by conservative women a century after the Civil War?

The state's withdrawal of funding for the home after it amended its constitution to include female lineal descendants beyond daughters exposes changing understandings of Virginia's obligation to processes of memory surrounding Confederate womanhood. First, these issues of Confederate memory did not exist in a political vacuum; they were wedded to broader national issues of social and economic policy in the late twentieth century. Ronald Reagan's election in 1980 ushered in the era of neoliberalism with an emphasis on privatization and limited state support for social programs.[65]

In terms of the wider societal landscape, a commitment to Confederate memory did not hold the same political capital as it had with the electorate during Reconstruction, Jim Crow, and segregation.[66] While the Lost Cause held meaning for voters earlier in the twentieth century and provided a channel to try to resurrect antebellum racial hierarchies and glorify the Old South, by the last few decades of the century, the Lost Cause was losing support. While it is difficult to measure armchair supporters of the Lost Cause, the membership decline in the UDC over the twentieth century reveals a formative pattern. In 1918, the UDC reported its national membership as 100,000 women.[67] In 2001, the UDC estimated its membership to be 20,000 women.[68] For elected politicians, endorsing the Lost Cause did not hold the same appeal for attracting votes as it had a century earlier. Still, the General Assembly continued to support some Confederate groups and projects, and continues to support some today. From 2009–18, the state of Virginia awarded the UDC over $800,000 for the maintenance of Confederate graves and cemeteries. During the same time, the state of Virginia paid $174,000 for the maintenance of the Lee statue on Monument Avenue in Richmond.[69]

The General Assembly did not abandon all Confederate memory drives, but it did abandon the home after its decision to extend its admittance to female lineal descendants. As its cornerstone, from its establishment in 1898, the home offered a "living" and "breathing" monument to the Confederacy. The home, and Montague in particular, elevated living women over the lifeless stone monuments championed by other Lost Cause organizations. Confederate women, as descendants from the nineteenth century, were the breathing vessels to champion the Confederacy and keep the Confederacy "alive." The conservative women leaders of the home, and Montague in particular, played instrumental roles in molding it as a symbol of the Lost Cause. This focus on the maintenance of life, as opposed to memorialization of death, allowed the home to differentiate itself from other Lost Cause organizations. However, this also allowed the Virginia General Assembly to differentiate it from other organizations in terms of financial support. While the General Assembly supported the first generation of female Confederate descendants (i.e., daughters), it was unwilling to support all generations of female Confederate descendants as included in the organization's 1977 amendments. The assembly would not support Confederate women into the twenty-first century and beyond.[70] Confederate women needed to be restricted to the past tense, to memory; this was not a permissible present-tense identity label in the late twentieth century. The General Assembly was still willing to financially support some organizations and projects dedicated to the maintenance of Confederate memory, just not the maintenance of life links to the Confederacy.

Confederate memory needed to commemorate the past, not maintain life links to the Confederacy in the present. With the demise of the home, a century of a particular strain of conservative Southern women's engagement with public causes and political leadership had also come to an end. Until the 1980s, some conservative women had been active and forceful contributors to Lost Cause ideology, just as some conservative women in the previous century had been active contributors to Confederate nationalism. This gendered labor, first for Confederate national devotion and then Confederate memory, held emotive political capital for audiences inside and outside of the geographic borders of the Confederacy, and during and after the life span of the Confederate republic. The conservative women leaders of the home used their recently expanded rights as citizens, secured by progressive women's rights campaigners over the twentieth century, to lobby for this Lost Cause ideology. Yet their efforts in the end resulted in the dismantling of the Home for Needy Confederate Women as both an actual physical site for medical care as well as its projected imagery as a living, breathing symbol of Confederate womanhood.

Epilogue

WITH THE ADVENT OF the American Civil War, middle-and planter-class white women engaged with Confederate political culture and nationalism in new ways. Women undertook actions that had tangible effects on the strength and growth of Confederate nationalism. Confederate leaders in both government and civic society used and projected these women and their work as symbols of the Confederate republic. Women controlled the ways in which they participated in and performed such exercises of national devotion, and they were willing and eager to be used by Confederate leaders to advance the cause. These women not only held social and economic power in the plantation household before the war, they also held nationalistic power outside of the plantation household during the war. From the antebellum period through the war, women's power was underpinned by slavery. As slaveholders, they exercised social and economic power in the plantation household. As supporters of a republic established for the right to own enslaved persons, they held nationalistic power in their performance of national devotion as "the weaker sex in war." Working with male Confederate leaders, in action and rhetoric, Confederate women played important roles in the construction and circulation of Confederate nationalism to audiences inside and outside of the Confederacy, before and after the war.

The formative roles these women played in wartime nationalism shows the significance of gendered work in civic society, and the ways in which women's ideas and labor from civic society permeated the political sphere. Women may not have had full rights as citizens in the political sphere, but they were still able to influence male Confederate leaders and nationalistic ideas in the political sphere through their work in civic society. Emerging from the revolution, women of the antebellum South had indirect and limited relationships with the state mediated through their husbands and their civic obligation was to their husbands rather than to the state. As the daughters and granddaughters of Republican mothers, Confederate women brokered direct relationships with the wartime state as individuals. Despite this expansion in women's relationship with the state, these women did not lobby for the advancement of their rights as individual citizens. Instead, they used this new relationship with the state to advance the collective cause of Confederate nationalism.

Such an agenda was in stark contrast to their counterparts in the North. The Northern women's rights movement championed women's equality with men through the attainment of the full rights of citizenship across gender. In a liberal tradition, the Northern women's rights movement advocated rights in the political sphere, whereas Confederate women rejected this progressive campaign and instead embraced conservative political culture. In this way, Confederate women's engagement with conservative political culture stands as an oppositional counterpoint to the narrative of first-wave feminism; it reveals the ways in which women could make decisive interventions to the mid-nineteenth-century American political landscape beyond individual rights and social reform. Just because these women were not progressive does not mean they were not important to wider debates surrounding nationalism and citizenship. This rejection of this progressive mandate of women's equality and full rights of citizenship also supported Confederate nationalism. This representation of Confederate women as unequal with men, including in terms of the rights of citizenship, and more broadly as "the weaker sex in war" in need of protection, proved to be a compelling way to frame the cause.

This wedding of gender and nationalism created an arsenal of evocative rhetoric and images ready to be deployed to advance the ideological mission of the Confederate republic. The project of Confederate nationalism was dynamic and fluid, with women decisively shaping the narrative from below. This relationship between gender and nationalism became a key focus of Confederate political culture for both men in power and women on the home front—a relationship that would also become a key focus of Confederate memory from the second half of the nineteenth century to the present.

Virginia Women's Monument and Sally Tompkins

In 2010, approaching the concurrent 100th anniversary of the congressional passage of the Nineteenth Amendment and the 400th anniversary, in 2019, of both representative democracy in Virginia and the first arrival of enslaved persons to Virginia, the Virginia General Assembly established the Virginia Women's Monument Commission to recommend a monument to celebrate Virginia women. As the Virginia Civil Rights Memorial was unveiled in 2008 in Capitol Square, and "Mantle," a monument dedicated to Virginia's Native American tribes was unveiled in 2018, the commission recommended the erection of twelve life-sized bronze statues of Virginia women on a granite plaza to rectify this inequity and narrate the history of Virginia's women in Capitol Square (see figure 6). The commission, chaired by Governor Ralph Norcom and composed of Virginia political and civic leaders, sought to address that "From the Founding of the Commonwealth, the genius and creativity of women and their presence and contributions have been evident in every aspect of Virginia history . . . however, they have received very little appreciation, recognition, or official acknowledgment."[1] The twelve women were selected by the commission, in consultation with historians, to portray the history and regional distinctions of Virginia from the settlement of Jamestown to the late twentieth century. As a collective, the monument is called *Voices from the Garden* and over 200 names of women are shown on a glass Wall of Honor surrounding the twelve statues representing the contributions of other Virginia women, with space to add additional names in the future:

> Voices from the Garden draws visitors into an oval forum to interact with the twelve women who await them. At the center stands a bronze sundial on a granite pedestal. Tempered glass panels, a metaphor for the social filter that has long obscured women's accomplishments from public view, provide space for the names of additional important women of history, with room to add the names of women today and tomorrow.[2]

The monument lies west of the Virginia State Capitol in Capitol Square.

At the dedication ceremony on October 14, 2019, where Girl Scouts unveiled the first seven statues, Governor Norcom stated, "[This] is the first monument in [the] nation to celebrate both the individual and collective accomplishments of women over four centuries. . . . With the addition of the Women's Monument to Capitol Square, we're finally telling a more inclusive story, a more complete story, about Virginia."[3] Clerk of the Senate and commission member Susan Clarke Schaar claimed, "No pedestals, no weapons, no horses . . . [the commission] wanted it to be approachable. They wanted it to be warm and welcoming. And they wanted to convey a sense of consensus building."[4] Ivan Schwartz, the sculptor for the new monument as well as the Thomas Jefferson statue already in the State Capitol, reified the comments of Norcom and Clerk on a more national scale, "women have been excised from the marble pedestal of history. . . . [This] gentlemen's club, which has occupied our national living room, our nation's public spaces, has at last started to admit women, African Americans, and Native Americans."[5] In October 2019, seven of the planned twelve statues of these women were unveiled in Capitol

FIGURE 6. Virginia Women's Monument in October 2019, Capitol Square, Richmond, Virginia. Photograph by the author.

Square: Anne Burras Laydon, Cockacoeske, Mary Draper Ingles, Elizabeth Keckley, Laura Copenhaver, Virginia Randoph, and Adele Clark. The remaining five statues—Martha Washington, Clementina Rind, Maggie L. Walker, Sarah G. Jones, and Sally Tompkins—required further funding for their construction. An additional $200,000 needed to be raised per statue to fund its construction by StudioEIS, the sculpture and design firm contracted to build the monument. Donors, which include individuals, nonprofit organizations, and businesses around Virginia, could specify which monument they wanted to support with their giving. For instance, two women each donated $100,000 for the construction of the Cockacoeske statue ensuring its commission.[6] At the start of 2019, only half of the required $200,000 had been raised for the construction of the Tompkins statue.[7] In 2020, the Virginia Women's Monument Commission announced the successful completion of their $3.8 million fundraising effort.

The project has received criticism. In a less ideological vein, the sundial at the center of the monument depicting the regions of Virginia misspelt Loudoun as "Loudon." This was quickly noted after the October dedication ceremony by the *Richmond Times-Dispatch* and *Loudoun Times-Mirror*.[8] More significantly, some Virginians oppose the inclusion of slaveholders and/or Confederate women in the monument. Community activist Chelsea Wise Higgs lamented, "the Women's Monument includes indigenous women and multiple African American women, giving many Virginians permission to grant this monument tolerance." She went on to censure the selection of these twelve women: "Just as many women of color are forced to stand in rooms today where their voices aren't heard, their bodies are violated, and their narratives are twisted, so are our women heroes being forced to share their legacy with Clementina Rind, Martha Washington, and Sally Louisa Tompkins."[9] The printing pioneer and wife of the first president were both slaveholders, but only Tompkins was both a slaveholder and a Confederate.

The controversy over the inclusion of Tompkins in the monument highlights debates over Confederate memorialization that have intensified since the June 2015 mass shooting in the Charleston Emmanuel African Methodist Episcopal Church where Confederate sympathizer and white supremacist Dylann Roof murdered nine African Americans at a Bible study group. The August 11–12, 2017, Unite the Right Rally to protest the removal of the Robert E. Lee statue in Charlottesville, where one counter-protester was killed, further enflamed these issues. More recently, the reignited nationwide debate over the removal of statues of Confederates in the aftermath of the murder of George Floyd in May 2020 contributed to wider discussions of race, violence, and inequality in the present-day United States. Namely, is the valorization of the Confederacy acceptable in twenty-first-century America?[10]

The proposed location for the Tompkins statue, in the former Confederate capital city of Richmond, exacerbates these tensions. Confederate statues of J. E. B. Stuart, Matthew Fontaine Maury, and Stonewall Jackson lined Richmond's nearby Monument Avenue until the city of Richmond removed them in the summer of 2020 and have been a recurrent focus of the statue debate. Monument Avenue's statue of Jefferson Davis was pulled down by Black Lives Matter protestors in June 2020 and the Lee statue was removed following a Virginia Supreme Court ruling in September 2021.[11] Prior to the statue removals, critics called Monument Avenue a 1.5-mile shrine to the Confederacy. Its defenders called it a necessary part of Virginia's history and a means to celebrate individual men without celebrating the Confederacy and slaveholding. Artist Kehinde

Wiley created *Rumors of War* (2019), an equestrian statue of an African American man, as a critique of Richmond's grandiose Confederate statue culture. *Rumors of War* was unveiled outside of the Virginia Museum of Fine Arts in December 2019, blocks away from Monument Avenue and less than a mile from the Lee statue. In an earlier attempt to diversify Richmond's Confederate statue culture, as discussed in the introduction, Salvador Dalí proposed a design of a statue of Tompkins to be constructed on Monument Avenue in 1966.

Criticisms of the construction of the statue of Tompkins, as a Confederate, insert Tompkins into this debate over the memory of the Confederacy in twenty-first-century Virginia. The same rationale used to oppose statues of male Confederate political and military leaders (i.e., these men are symbols of Confederate nationalism and valorize the Confederacy) has been extended to include Tompkins (i.e., this woman is a symbol of Confederate nationalism and valorizes the Confederacy). Tompkins is not primarily recognized as a nurse or caretaker in these debates; she is recognized as a Confederate in a similar way to how Robert E. Lee, Stonewall Jackson, and others are. In processes of memorialization in the present day, at least for some, Tompkins holds a similar nationalistic power as male leaders of the Confederacy. In a similar vein to how Confederate women were used as symbols of Confederate nationalism during the war, such discourses acknowledge the ways in which Tompkins can be interpreted as a symbol of Confederate nationalism in memory. This salient relationship between Confederate nationalism and gender is not restricted to the historical landscape but continues to permeate the present-day sociopolitical terrain in divisive and decisive ways. Representations of Confederate women are an evocative and effective touchstone for controversies addressing Confederate memory and the Lost Cause in contemporary society. The idea of "the weaker sex in war" that proved to be so effective in the Confederate war effort still holds a place in Lost Cause ideology today, and in the case of Sally Tompkins, has intersected with the Virginia state executive and legislative agenda. Confederate women's performance of and contributions to nationalism in civic society shaped debates and issues in wartime political society, and the memory of these contributions continues to play a role in the nexus between Confederate memory and politics and governance today.

NOTES

Preface

1. The plantation household, and the relationship between planter women and enslaved women, has been a rich topic in the historiography since the 1980s. For early works, see Catherine Clinton, *The Plantation Mistress: Woman's World in the Old South* (New York: Pantheon Books, 1982), 6, 204–5; and Deborah Gray White, *Ar'n't I A Woman?: Females Slaves in the Plantation South* (New York: W.W. Norton, 1985; reprint 1999), 6, 162, 186. See also Elizabeth Fox-Genovese, *Within the Plantation Household: Black and White Women of the Old South* (Chapel Hill: University of North Carolina Press, 1988), 29, 372–73; Marli Weiner, *Mistresses and Slaves: Plantation Women in South Carolina, 1830–80* (Urbana: University of Illinois Press, 1998), 89–112; and Joan E. Cashin, *A Family Venture: Men and Women on the Southern Frontier* (New York: Oxford University Press, 1991), 99–118.

2. Literary theorists Suzanne Bunkers and Victoria Stewart have noted the importance of individual life writing in understanding the broader social and political context of the society in which the writer produces their narrative. See Suzanne Bunkers, "Reading and Interpreting Unpublished Diaries by Nineteenth-Century Women," *alb: Auto/Biography Studies* 2.2 (1986): 15; and Victoria Stewart, *Women's Autobiography: War and Trauma* (New York: Palgrave Macmillan, 2003), 22. For more information on the life and literary processes of diaries, see Ellen Gruber Garvey, "Anonymity, Authorship and Recirculation: A Civil War Episode," *Book History* 9 (2006): 159–78.

3. For an example of how women's first-person wartime experiences can be used to comment on the broader landscape of political history, see Stephanie McCurry, *Women's War: Fighting and Surviving the American Civil War* (Cambridge, MA: Harvard University Press, 2019), 124–202.

4. Jean Friedman argues that unlike their Northern sisters, elite Southern white women's kinship connections in their gender-integrated evangelical communities shaped their identities and preserved their traditional roles, thus limiting their individual autonomy. According to Friedman, this rural evangelical kinship system stunted Southern women's reforming zeal through the nineteenth century and these women only played significant roles in benevolent and charity associations after the Civil War. This book challenges this premise and shows the ways in which middle-and planter-class

white Southern women formed organizations during the war. See Jean E. Friedman, *The Enclosed Garden: Women and Community in the Evangelical South, 1830–1900* (Chapel Hill: University of North Carolina Press, 1985), xi–xiii. Other scholars assert that Southern women's organizations existed before 1865. See Elizabeth R. Varon, *We Mean to Be Counted: White Women and Politics in Antebellum Virginia* (Chapel Hill: University of North Carolina Press, 1998); Drew Gilpin Faust, *Mothers of Invention: Women of the Slaveholding South in the American Civil War* (Chapel Hill: University of North Carolina Press, 1996), 23–24; and Anne Firor Scott, *Natural Allies: Women's Associations in American History* (Urbana: University of Illinois Press, 1991), 19–20.

5. Clara Minor Lynn, "The Last Days of the Confederacy," Confederate Memorial Literary Society (CMLS), Virginia Museum of History and Culture (VMHC), Richmond, Virginia, 4.

6. Emily to Richard Noble: June 11, 1863, Richard G. Noble Correspondence, Special Collections, Virginia Polytechnic Institute and State University, Blacksburg, Virginia. Again, such written accounts require literacy from both their creators and recipients. In some episodes, like the Richmond bread riot, documentation composed and circulated by its participants is more limited as a result of these explicit education and implicit class constraints.

7. Suzanne Lebsock, *The Free Women of Petersburg: Status and Culture in a Southern Town, 1784–1860* (New York: W.W. Norton, 1984), 138–41.

8. Thavolia Glymph, *Out of the House of Bondage: The Transformation of the Plantation Household* (Cambridge: Cambridge University Press, 2008), 24–25; and Stephanie E. Jones-Rogers, *They Were Her Property: White Women as Slave Owners in the American South* (New Haven, CT: Yale University Press, 2019), xx.

9. Jones-Rogers, *They Were Her Property*, xx.

Introduction

1. For (edited) first-person accounts by Confederate nurses, see Phoebe Yates Pember, *A Southern Woman's Story: Life in Confederate Richmond*, ed. Bell Irvin Wiley, 2nd ed. (Atlanta, GA: Mockingbird Books, 1974); Ada Bacot, *A Confederate Nurse: The Diary of Ada W. Bacot, 1860–1863*, ed. Jean V. Berlin (Columbia: University of South Carolina Press, 1994); and Kate Cumming, *The Journal of Kate Cumming: A Confederate Nurse, 1862–1865*, ed. R. Harwell, 2nd ed. (Savannah, GA: Beehive Press, 1975).

2. Mary Chesnut, *A Diary from Dixie*, ed. Isabella D. Martin and Myrta Lockett Avary (New York: D. Appleton and Company, 1905), 111–12. The 1984 edition of Chesnut's diary, the publication of her original 1860s diary with minimal editorial revisions, provides a more austere commentary on the hospital visit: "[The patients] had all bright, pleasant faces"; Mary Chesnut, *The Private Mary Chesnut: The Unpublished Civil War Diaries*, ed. C. Vann Woodward and Elisabeth Muhlenfeld (New York: Oxford University Press, 1984), 140. From early 1862, Judith White McGuire also visited the

hospital on several occasions. See Judith White McGuire, *Diary of a Southern Refugee, During the War* (New York: E. J. Hale and Son, 1868).

3. "Robinson Hospital," *Richmond Whig*, December 3, 1862. The Robertson Hospital is often mistakenly referred to as the Robinson Hospital in the press. There is no record of a Robinson Hospital, and the newspapers list the Robinson Hospital's address as the same one as the Robertson Hospital. For more early wartime Richmond newspaper accounts of the Robertson Hospital, see "The Sick and Wounded," *Richmond Whig*, August 6, 1861; "Another Hospital," *Richmond Enquirer*, August 5, 1861; and Advertisement (Tompkins thanks St. Paul's Church), *Richmond Dispatch*, August 8, 1862.

4. Commission of Sally L. Tompkins, September 9, 1861, Sally Tompkins Papers, Confederate Memorial Literary Society (CMLS), Virginia Museum of History and Culture (VMHC), Richmond, Virginia.

5. For more on Confederate medical care and nursing generally, see Carol C. Green, *Chimborazo: The Confederacy's Largest Hospital* (Knoxville: University of Tennessee Press, 2004), 1–18, 41–64; H. H. Cunningham, *Doctors in Gray: The Confederate Medical Service* (Baton Rouge: Louisiana State University Press, 1958), 10–72; Jane E. Schultz, *Women at the Front: Hospital Workers in Civil War America* (Chapel Hill: University of North Carolina Press, 2004), 11–141; and Libra R. Hilde, *Worth a Dozen Men: Women and Nursing in the Civil War South* (Charlottesville: University of Virginia Press, 2012). For more on Tompkins specifically, see E. Susan Barber, "Sally Louisa Tompkins: Confederate Healer," in *Virginia Women: Their Lives and Times*, ed. Cynthia A. Kierner and Sandra Gioia Treadway (Athens: University of Georgia Press, 2015), 344–62; and Ron Maggiano, "Captain Sally Tompkins: Angel of the Confederacy," *Organization of American Historians Magazine of History* 16.2 (2002): 32–38.

6. Barbara Mann Wall, Kathleen Rogers, and Ann Kutney-Lee, "The North vs. the South: Conditions at Civil War Hospitals," *Southern Quarterly* 53 (2016): 37–55.

7. Commission of Sally L. Tompkins, September 9, 1861, VMHC.

8. Barber, "Sally Louisa Tompkins: Confederate Healer," 352.

9. "Mayor's Court," *Richmond Sentinel*, November 5, 1864.

10. The use of enslaved labor was standard in Confederate hospitals throughout the South.

11. For more on the Home for Needy Confederate Women, see chapter 5, this volume.

12. "Miss Sallie Tompkins: Portrait of the Southern Heroine Presented at the Confederate Museum," *Richmond Times*, June 1, 1889.

13. "Captain Sallie Tompkins Takes Part in Unique Ceremony," *Richmond Times-Dispatch*, December 14, 1910.

14. Barber, "Confederate Healer," 349–51.

15. Ed Grimsley, "Dali's Plan for Statue Given Cool Reception," *Richmond Times-Dispatch*, April 28, 1966.

16. Stephanie McCurry, *Confederate Reckoning: Power and Politics in the Civil War South* (Cambridge, MA: Harvard University Press, 2010); and Laura Edwards, *Scarlett Doesn't Live Here Anymore: Southern Women in the Civil War Era* (Urbana: University

of Illinois Press, 2000) have both made significant contributions in recentralizing the experiences of lower-class white women and enslaved women to Confederate history.

17. For an assessment of generational responses to the war, focusing on young planter women's perceptions and experiences, see Giselle Roberts, *The Confederate Belle* (Columbia: University of Missouri Press, 2003); Anya Jabour, *Scarlett's Sisters: Young Women in the Old South* (Chapel Hill: University of North Carolina Press, 2007); and Victoria Ott, *Confederate Daughters: Coming to Age during the Civil War* (Carbondale: Southern Illinois Press, 2008).

18. For studies of the centrality of marriage as an institution to the functionality of the plantation household in the mid-nineteenth-century South, see Carol Bleser, ed., *In Joy and Sorrow: Women, Family, and Marriage in the Victorian South* (New York: Oxford University Press, 2001). While the ideal white Confederate woman would sacrifice her son and husband to the war effort, some women were single and contributed to the culture of self-sacrifice. See Marie S. Molloy, *Single, White, Slaveholding Women in the Nineteenth-Century American South* (Columbia: University of South Carolina Press, 2018); and *An Evening When Alone: Four Journals of Single Women in the South, 1827–67*, ed. Michael O'Brien (Athens: University of Georgia Press, 1993). Also, for the politics of sexual and social control, inside and outside of marriage, see Martha Hodes, *White Women, Black Men: Illicit Sex in the Nineteenth-Century South* (New Haven, CT: Yale University Press, 1997); and Victoria Bynum, *Unruly Women: The Politics of Social and Sexual Control in the Old South* (Chapel Hill: University of North Carolina Press, 1992).

19. Jacqueline Glass Campbell argues that Southern women's daily interactions with Union soldiers affected their commitment to the Confederate cause; often after a period of war weariness, Southern women would rededicate themselves to the Southern cause. See Jacqueline Glass Campbell, *When Sherman Marched North from the Sea: Resistance on the Confederate Home Front* (Chapel Hill: University of North Carolina Press, 2005), 69. For more on "enemy women," see Stephanie McCurry, *Women's War: Fighting and Surviving the American Civil War* (Cambridge, MA: Harvard University Press, 2019), 25–45. For instance, women in New Orleans faced occupation beginning in May 1862.

20. Upper-class women's wartime diary writing can be read as an exercise in autonomy and/or resistance. See Steven M. Stowe, *Keep the Days: Reading the Civil War Diaries of Southern Women* (Chapel Hill: University of North Carolina Press, 2018); Kimberly Harrison, *The Rhetoric of Rebel Women: Civil War Diaries and Confederate Persuasion* (Carbondale: Southern Illinois Press, 2013); and Sarah Gardner, *Blood and Irony: Southern White Women's Narratives of the Civil War, 1861–1937* (Chapel Hill: University of North Carolina Press, 2004).

21. Drew Gilpin Faust asserts that elite women's commitment to Confederate nationalism waned after mid-1863 due to increasing battle losses and that the loss of Southern women's morale played a decisive role in the Confederate defeat. See Drew Gilpin Faust, *Mothers of Invention: Women of the Slaveholding South in the American Civil War* (Chapel Hill: University of North Carolina Press, 1996), 238–47. This thesis has been contested. Gary Gallagher states women's commitment to Confederate nationalism

remained strong throughout the war, to 1865. See Gary W. Gallagher, *The Confederate War: How Popular Will, Nationalism, and Military Strategy Could Not Stave Off Defeat* (Cambridge, MA: Harvard University Press, 1997), 3–5, 65–80. William A. Blair concurs; see *Virginia's Private War: Feeding Body and Soul in the Confederacy, 1861–1865* (New York: Oxford University Press, 1998).

22. Sewing Confederate soldiers' uniforms was work often given to enslaved women and men. This was not just elite white women's nationalistic labor. See Thavolia Glymph, *Out of the House of Bondage: The Transformation of the Plantation Household* (Cambridge: Cambridge University Press, 2008), 113. Also, according to Anne Firor Scott, for the plantation mistress, "The experience of years of providing food and clothing for slaves was now applied to feeding and clothing an army." See Anne Firor Scott, *The Southern Lady: From Pedestal to Politics, 1830–1930* (Chicago: University of Chicago Press, 1970), 82.

23. For a discussion of ideas of "women outside of war," see McCurry, *Women's War*, 13–14, 19, 24–25, 40–41, 61.

24. According to Thavolia Glymph and Stephanie E. Jones-Rogers, enslaved persons recognized this link between the Confederate war effort and the protection of elite white Southern women. See Thavolia Glymph, *Out of the House of Bondage*, 101; and Stephanie E. Jones-Rogers, *They Were Her Property: White Women as Slave Owners in the American South* (New Haven, CT: Yale University Press, 2019), 161. Glymph also argues that the protection of the elite white home was central to the Confederate project, and elite white women refugees represent failures in the Confederate project. See Thavolia Glymph, *The Women's Fight: The Civil War's Battles for Home, Freedom, and Nation* (Chapel Hill: University of North Carolina Press, 2020), 19–54, especially 21–22, 28.

25. Scott, *The Southern Lady*, 3, 6–7.

26. The Greek classic roles of women in war, Antigone and Cassandra, support this definition of the "weaker sex." Both Antigone and Cassandra engage with the wartime state in new critical ways, but they both still require the protection of men. See Linda Kerber, *No Constitutional Right: Women and the Obligations of Citizenship* (New York: Hill and Wang, 1998), 237–38. Also, in examining the early republic, Linda Kerber argues that "Women's weakness became a rhetorical foil for republican manliness." Kerber, *No Constitutional Right*, 11.

27. Glymph, *Out of the House of Bondage*; and Jones-Rogers, *They Were Her Property*.

28. McCurry, *Confederate Reckoning*, 87. While McCurry focuses on yeoman and poor white Southern women (i.e., soldiers' wives) who made up the vast majority of the white Confederate home front, she also considers planter women (see McCurry, *Confederate Reckoning*, 100–132) and enslaved women (see McCurry, *Confederate Reckoning*, 218–309, especially 237–46).

29. McCurry, *Confederate Reckoning*, 100–113.

30. McCurry, *Confederate Reckoning*, 121–30.

31. Drew Gilpin Faust, *The Creation of Confederate Nationalism: Ideology and Identity in the Civil War South* (Baton Rouge: Louisiana State University Press, 1989), 21. Faust also proposes the creation of culture is a "self-conscious" process of nationalism.

32. In addition to Faust and Gallagher (see note 21 above), several historians have grappled with the contradictory and conflict-ridden definition of Confederate nationalism, as well as the cultural and political dimensions of its short-and long-term successes and failures. See George C. Rable, *The Confederate Republic: A Revolution against Politics* (Chapel Hill: University of North Carolina Press, 1994), 74–75, 208, and *Civil Wars: Women and the Crisis of Southern Nationalism* (Urbana: University of Illinois Press, 1991); Anne Sarah Rubin, *A Shattered Nation: The Rise and Fall of the Confederacy, 1861–68* (Chapel Hill: University of North Carolina Press, 2005), 2–4, 134–38; Michael T. Bernath, *Confederate Minds: The Struggle for Intellectual Independence in the Civil War South* (Chapel Hill: University of North Carolina Press, 2010), 13–34; Robert E. Bonner, *Mastering America: Southern Slaveholders and the Crisis of American Nationhood* (Cambridge: Cambridge University Press, 2009), 217–322; and Ian Binnington, *Nationalism, Symbolism and the Imagined South in the Civil War* (Charlottesville: University of Virginia Press, 2013). Binnington focuses on the importance of symbols in constructing Confederate nationalism, but this study neglects a comprehensive consideration of gender.

33. For the ways in which Confederate nationalism looked to Europe and the wider world to contextualize its legitimacy, see Paul Quigley, *Shifting Grounds: Nationalism and the American South, 1848–1865* (Oxford: Oxford University Press, 2011), 128–213; and Don Doyle, *The Cause of All Nations: An International History of the American Civil War* (New York: Basic Books, 2015).

34. Gallagher, *Confederate War*, 72–111. In a similar approach as Gallagher, the following chapters also examine the connections between the home front and front lines in Confederate nationalism. In their diaries and letters, women carefully chronicled battle news and praised military leaders. As chapter 2's analysis of the Ladies' Defense Association (LDA) shows, some women actively supported the military through fundraising efforts and the formation of gunboat societies.

35. For more on the relationship between the establishment of political legitimacy to the strength of nationalism, see Ernest Gellner, *Nations and Nationalism* (Oxford: Basil Blackwell, 1983). On the importance of a shared culture to projects of nationalism, see Anthony D. Smith, *Theories of Nationalism* (London: Duckworth, 1971).

36. Faust, *Confederate Nationalism*, 21.

37. See Paul D. Escott, *After Secession: Jefferson Davis and the Failure of Confederate Nationalism* (Baton Rouge: Louisiana State University Press, 1978); and Richard E. Beringer et al., *Why the South Lost the Civil War* (Athens: University of Georgia Press, 1986).

38. On the importance of print capitalism to nationalism, see Benedict Anderson, *Imagined Communities: Reflections on the Origins and Spread of Nationalism* (London: Verso, 1983).

39. Glymph, *Out of the House of Bondage*, 133–36 (quote 136).

40. Kerber, *No Constitutional Right*, 305. Likewise, according to McCurry, "[Antebellum] women had a particular kind of citizenship and a secondhand relationship to the state." McCurry, *Women's War*, 20–24, (quote 24).

41. However, the legal doctrine of coverture was not always applied evenly in practice; some women continued to own property after they were married. Some women even continued to own enslaved persons after marriage. See Jones-Rogers, *They Were Her Property*, 29–31, 55.

42. Kerber, *No Constitutional Right*, xxiii. For a discussion of the relationship between the "patriarchal home" and its impediments to women's claims to citizenship, see Glymph, *Women's Fight*, 3.

43. Kerber, *No Constitutional Right*, 243. Of course, some women served in disguise in Confederate armies and some women served as Confederate spies, as discussed in chapter 4, this volume.

44. For a discussion of the Union's gendered struggle to define civilians and combatants in the Confederacy, see McCurry, *Women's War*, 53–54.

45. In the context of the American Revolutionary War, Kerber examines the uneasy relationship between women and treason (i.e., can a woman be convicted of treason?). See Kerber, *No Constitutional Right*, 3–46, *Women of the Republic: Intellect and Ideology in Revolutionary America* (Chapel Hill: University of North Carolina Press, 1980), 115–36, and *Toward an Intellectual History of Women* (Chapel Hill: University of North Carolina Press, 1997), 261–302. As McCurry notes, the historiography on gender and treason in the Civil War is not as developed. McCurry, *Confederate Reckoning*, 102, and *Women's War*, 31–32. While my book does not engage with the relationship between gender and treason, the relationship between gender and loyalty is central to understanding Confederate women's relationship to the state, as the following chapters will demonstrate.

46. Conservative is used in this introduction not to denote nineteenth-century European conservative movements, or later twentieth-century American conservativism, but as one of many ways to articulate the temporal (antebellum vs. wartime) and geographic (North vs. South) differences in women's relationship to the state. Such a lexicon does not suggest a distinct conservative movement at this time but rather a relational consideration of women's societal roles and power. This is consistent with how Michael O'Brien conceptualizes the conservative intellectual history of Southern women and gender, especially Louisa McCord, Augusta Jane Evans, and Mary Chesnut, in *Conjectures of Order: Intellectual Life and the American South*, vols. 1 and 2 (Chapel Hill: University of North Carolina Press, 2004). In this context, conservative is useful as a term as it highlights O'Brien's importance of change and modernity to the South, and the ways in which Southern society moved beyond traditionalism. For more on the limitations of traditionalism (and the difficulties in defining conservativism in the antebellum North), see Adam I. P. Smith, *The Stormy Present: Conservativism and the Problem of Slavery in Northern Politics, 1846–1865* (Chapel Hill: University of North Carolina Press, 2016), 5–13. Also, for a classic study of the relationship of the Old South and conservative intellectual history, see Eugene Genovese, *The Slaveholders' Dilemma: Freedom and Progress in Southern Conservative Thought, 1820–1860* (Columbia: University of South Carolina Press, 1992), 10–40, especially 35–38. My definition of conservative

women is also consistent with Elizabeth Varon's usage in *We Mean to Be Counted: White Women and Politics in Antebellum Virginia* (Chapel Hill: University of North Carolina Press, 1998), 9.

47. Linda Kerber, "The Republican Mother: Women and the Enlightenment—An American Perspective," *American Quarterly* 28.2 (1976): 202–5, and *Women of the Republic: Intellect and Ideology in Revolutionary America* (Chapel Hill: University of North Carolina Press, 1980), 11–12, 228–31, 269–88. See also Rosemarie Zagarri, "The Rights of Man and Woman in Post-Revolutionary America," *William and Mary Quarterly* 55 (1998): 203–30.

48. This conceptualization of political culture as including women's actions outside of the electoral sphere was developed by Elizabeth R. Varon in her analysis of women's conservative politicization in antebellum Virginia: Varon, *We Mean to Be Counted*, 2–4. More recently, Caroline Janney and Stephanie McCurry have applied a similar definition of political culture to include the work of postwar Ladies' Memorial Associations and wartime lower-class women, respectively. See Caroline E. Janney, *Burying the Dead but Not the Past: Ladies' Memorial Associations and the Lost Cause* (Chapel Hill: University of North Carolina Press, 2008), 5–6; and McCurry, *Confederate Reckoning*, 3–7. Thavolia Glymph considers the home and plantation household as a "political space," as well as the home as a site of "warring intimacies" and an "embattled workplace." Glymph, *Out of the House of Bondage*, quotes 3, 37, 41. See also Glymph, *Women's Fight*, 4, 9, 14. Jacqueline Glass Campbell also argues that during the war, elite white women saw themselves as "viable political actors with interests that extended beyond the immediate concerns of friends and family." See Campbell, *When Sherman Marched*, 69. Linda Kerber sees women as part of national political culture from the revolution through the twentieth century. See Kerber, *No Constitutional Right*, especially 308. For another earlier engagement with women's relationship to politics in the public sphere, see Mary P. Ryan, *Women in Public: Between Banners and Ballots* (Baltimore, MD: Johns Hopkins University Press, 1990), 5–15.

49. For a theoretical discussion of the doctrine of separate spheres outside the nineteenth-century United States, see Amanda Vickery, "Golden Age to Separate Spheres? A Review of the Categories and Chronology of English Women's History," *Historical Journal* 36.2 (1993): 383–414; and Leonore Davidoff and Catherine Hall, *Family Fortunes: Men and Women of the English Middle Class, 1780–1850* (Chicago: University of Chicago Press, 1991). For a discussion of the interplay of separate spheres in antebellum and Civil War America, see Nancy Cott, *The Bonds of Womanhood: "Woman's Sphere" in New England, 1780–1835* (New Haven, CT: Yale University Press, 1977); Elizabeth Fox-Genovese, *Within the Plantation Household: Black and White Women of the Old South* (Chapel Hill: University of North Carolina Press, 1988), 63–64; Linda Kerber, "Separate Spheres, Female Worlds, Women's Place: The Rhetoric of Women's History," *Journal of American History* 75.1 (1988): 9–39; Barbara Welter, "The Cult of True Womanhood 1820–1860," *American Quarterly* 18 (1966): 151–74; and Catherine Clinton, *The Plantation Mistress: Woman's World in the Old South* (New York: Pantheon Books, 1982), 10–12. For a discussion of the complication of non-family members

performing labor (enslaved and paid) in the domestic private sphere, see Glymph, *Out of the House of Bondage*, 43. Most recently, Glymph moved away from the separate spheres approach to focus on "the contexts of previous wars, gender and class struggles, and slave resistance" in her groundbreaking study *Women's Fight*, especially 11.

50. See Varon, *We Mean to Be Counted*; and Janney, *Burying the Dead*.

51. For arguments that Southern women had far greater social and economic opportunities after the war and this ushered in an area of "new womanhood," see Anne Firor Scott, *Natural Allies: Women's Associations in American History* (Urbana: University of Illinois Press, 1991), 79–80, 83, and *The Southern Lady*, especially 110–15, 118–24; and Jane Turner Censer, *The Reconstruction of White Southern Womanhood, 1865–1895* (Baton Rouge: Louisiana State University Press, 2003), 276–80. Other historians argue that for Southern women, the Civil War was "change without change"; Southern women's postbellum societal roles and opportunities mirrored their antebellum societal roles and opportunities. See Rable, *Civil Wars*, 265–88; and Faust, *Mothers of Invention*, 247–54. For more arguments of how Confederate women's politicization extended into Reconstruction, see Janney, *Burying the Dead*, 39–103; and Hilde, *Worth a Dozen Men*, 204–21.

52. Glymph, *Out of the House of Bondage*, 3–4, 11, 17, 26–29, 31, 62, 92.

53. Stephanie E. Jones-Rogers, *They Were Her Property*, xii–xvi, 151, 156–57, 180.

54. Emory M. Thomas, *The Confederate State of Richmond: A Biography of the Capital* (Baton Rouge: Louisiana State University Press, 1971), 113–14.

55. Stephen V. Ash, *Rebel Richmond: Life and Death in the Confederate Capital* (Chapel Hill: University of North Carolina Press, 2019), 139.

56. The First Battle of Bull Run was the first major battle to be fought in Virginia. Minor battles occurred in the state before the action in Manassas, such as the Battle of Big Bethel in June 1861.

57. United States National Park Service: The Civil War, https://www.nps.gov/civilwar/search-battles.htm, last accessed September 10, 2019.

58. University of Virginia, Historical Census Browser, 1860 Census, http://mapserver.lib.virginia.edu/ php/state.php, last accessed February 1, 2013.

59. Samuella Hart Curd, Diary: February 19, 1861, VMHC.

60. Daniel W. Crofts, *Reluctant Confederates: Upper South Unionists in the Secession Crisis* (Chapel Hill: University of North Carolina Press, 1989), 308–33; and William A. Link, *Roots of Secession: Slavery and Politics in Antebellum Virginia* (Chapel Hill: University of North Carolina Press, 2003), 213–44.

61. David R. Zimring, "'Secession in Favor of the Constitution': How West Virginia Justified Separate Statehood during the Civil War," *West Virginia History: A Journal of Regional Studies* 3.2 (2009): 23–51; and William A. Link, "'This Bastard New Virginia': Slavery, West Virginia Exceptionalism and the Sectional Crisis," *West Virginia History: A Journal of Regional Studies* 3.1 (2009): 37–56.

62. For more on Unionism in Virginia, see Barton A. Myers, *Rebels Against the Confederacy: North Carolina's Unionists* (Cambridge: Cambridge University Press 2014), 1–15; Margaret M. Storey, *Loyalty and Loss: Alabama's Unionists in the Civil War and Reconstruction*

(Baton Rouge: Louisiana State University Press, 2004), 18–36; Victoria E. Bynum, *The Long Shadow of the Civil War: Southern Dissent and Its Legacies* (Chapel Hill: University of North Carolina Press, 2010), 15–54; Richard Nelson Current, *Lincoln's Loyalists: Union Soldiers from the Confederacy* (Boston, MA: Northeastern University Press, 1992); Ash, *Rebel Richmond*,123–38; Charles F. Irons, "Reluctant Protestant Confederates: The Religious Roots of Conditional Unionism," in *Virginia's Civil War*, ed. Peter Wallenstein and Bertram Wyatt-Brown (Charlottesville: University of Virginia Press, 2005), 72–86; and Wayne Wei-Siang Hsieh, "'I Owe Virginia Little, My Country Much': Robert E. Lee, the United States Regular Army, and Unconditional Unionism," in *Crucible of the Civil War: Virginia from Secession from Commemoration*, ed. Edward L. Ayers, Gary W. Gallagher, and Andrew J. Torget (Charlottesville: University of Virginia Press, 2006), 35–57.

63. Elizabeth R. Varon, *Southern Lady, Yankee Spy: Elizabeth Van Lew, a Union Agent in the Heart of the Confederacy* (New York: Oxford University Press, 1995).

64. Joan E. Cashin, *First Lady of the Confederacy: Varina Howell Davis's Civil War* (Cambridge, MA: Harvard University Press, 2008).

65. Glymph, *Out of the House of Bondage*, 100–124, and *Women's Fight*, 6, 89, 96–106; and Jones-Rogers, *They Were Her Property*, 158–59. The war changed planter women's conception of home and household slave management, particularly for elite white refugees. See Glymph, *Women's Fight*, 34–42, 51–52.

66. For other works with a focus on wartime Virginia, see Aaron Sheehan-Dean, *Why Confederates Fought: Family and Nation in Civil War Virginia* (Chapel Hill: University of North Carolina Press, 2007); Peter S. Carmichael, *The Last Generation: Young Virginians in Peace, War, and Reunion* (Chapel Hill: University of North Carolina Press, 2005); Ayers, Gallagher, and Torget, eds., *Crucible of the Civil War*; and Blair, *Virginia's Private War*. For a gendered focus on one community in Virginia on the eve of the Civil War, see Suzanne Lebsock, *The Free Women of Petersburg: Status and Culture in a Southern Town, 1784–1860* (New York: W.W. Norton, 1984); and for a gendered focus on the state of Virginia, see Varon, *We Mean to Be Counted*.

Chapter 1

1. George Washington to Lafayette: February 1, 1784, National Archives: Founders Online, https://founders.archives.gov/documents/Washington/04-01-02-0064, last accessed October 1, 2018.

2. Jefferson Davis, "Second Inaugural Address," February 22, 1862.

3. Positioning itself within the legitimate legacy of the American Revolution was not the only rhetorical device used by the Confederacy to define, disseminate, and strengthen its nationalist message. Among the most frequently used strategies were the Confederacy's claim that its republic was providentially sanctioned within a Christian tradition of covenant theology as well as its preferable benevolent paternalist model of

labor relations (through the institution of slavery) compared to the free labor industrialized North. See introduction, notes 21 and 32 for a discussion of the definition of Confederate nationalism.

4. Thavolia Glymph, *Out of the House of Bondage: The Transformation of the Plantation Household* (Cambridge: Cambridge University Press, 2018), 65.

5. Glymph, *Out of the House of Bondage*, 74–76 (quote 75).

6. For a discussion of the breakdown of elite white women's conception of "home" during the war, see Thavolia Glymph, *The Women's Fight: The Civil War Battles for Home, Freedom, and Nation* (Chapel Hill: University of North Carolina Press, 2019), 19–53.

7. Elizabeth R. Varon, *We Mean to Be Counted: White Women and Politics in Antebellum Virginia* (Chapel Hill: University of North Carolina Press, 1998), 124–36. More recently, Edward Everett's efforts to save Mount Vernon (including his relationship with the MVLA) has been examined in Matthew Mason, *Apostle of Union: A Political Biography of Edward Everett* (Chapel Hill: University of North Carolina Press, 2016), 211–83. Furthermore, the architectural history of the estate and the MVLA's role in its preservation and refurbishment is chronicled in Lydia Mattie Brandt, *First in the Homes of His Countrymen: George Washington's Mount Vernon in the American Imagination* (Charlottesville: University of Virginia Press, 2016), 54–57, for information on the Civil War. Several works financed by the Mount Vernon Ladies' Association chronicle the history of the organization through the war, but these works tend to omit references. For instance, see Gerald Johnson, *Mount Vernon: The Story of a Shrine* (New York: Random House, 1953); Elswyth Thane, *Mount Vernon Is Ours: The Story of Its Preservation* (New York: Duell, Sloane and Pearce, 1966); Dorothy Troth Muir, *Mount Vernon: The Civil War Years* (Mount Vernon, VA: Mount Vernon Ladies' Association, 1993); and Stephen A. McLeod, *The Mount Vernon Ladies' Association: 150 Years of Restoring George Washington's Home* (Mount Vernon, VA: Mount Vernon Ladies' Association, 2010).

8. Tracy to Cunningham: August 13, 1861, Mount Vernon Ladies' Association Early Records (MVLA), Fred W. Smith National Library for the Study of George Washington, Mount Vernon, VA.

9. "To the Ladies of the South," *Charleston Mercury*, December 2, 1853.

10. Sarah Agnes Rice Pryor, "The Mount Vernon Association," *The American Historical Register and Monthly Gazette of the Historic, Military, and Patriotic-Hereditary Societies of the United States of America* (January 1895), in *Museum Origins: Readings in Early Museum History and Philosophy*, ed. Hugh H. Genoways and Mary Ann Andrei (New York: Routledge, 2008), 30.

11. In a similar vein, LeeAnn Whites asserts women's postwar Lost Cause contributions needed to position themselves as working to strengthen masculinity. See Whites, *The Civil War as a Crisis of Gender, Augusta, Georgia, 1860–1890* (Athens: University of Georgia Press, 1995), 149–50. This wartime and postwar thematic connection in women's work is even clearer in the discussion of the LDA in chapter 2, this volume.

12. Sarah Agnes Rice Pryor, "The Mount Vernon Association," *The American Historical Register and Monthly Gazette of the Historic, Military, and Patriotic-Hereditary Societies of the United States of America* (January 1895), in *Museum Origins: Readings in Early Museum History and Philosophy*, ed. Hugh H. Genoways and Mary Ann Andrei (New York: Routledge, 2008), 32.

13. Judith Anne Mitchell, "Ann Pamela Cunningham: 'A Southern Matron's' Legacy" (MA thesis, Middle Tennessee State University, 1993), 17.

14. Mitchell, "Ann Pamela Cunningham," 24.

15. Tracy to Cunningham: April 30, 1861, MVLA.

16. Brandt, *First in the Homes of His Countrymen*, 55.

17. Scott E. Casper, *Sarah Johnson's Mount Vernon: The Forgotten History of an American Shrine* (New York: Hill and Wang, 2008), 83.

18. Tracy to Cunningham: May 2, 1861, MVLA.

19. Casper, *Sarah Johnson's Mount Vernon*, 77.

20. Casper, *Sarah Johnson's Mount Vernon*, 73–74.

21. List of property taken by Federal Forces from the Mount Vernon Farm of John Augustine Washington III, June 8, 1861, John Augustine Washington Manuscripts, Fred W. Smith Library for the Study of George Washington, Mount Vernon, VA.

22. See chapter 2, this volume.

23. "Purchase of Mount Vernon," *The Liberator*, December 31, 1858.

24. "Purchase of Mount Vernon," *The Liberator*, December 31, 1858.

25. "In Memoriam," *The News and Observer*, Raleigh, North Carolina, January 5, 1908.

26. See Stephen A. McLeod, *The Mount Vernon Ladies' Association: 150 Years of Restoring George Washington's Home* (Mount Vernon, VA: Mount Vernon Ladies' Association, 2010), for listings of vice regents.

27. Mary Chesnut to Ann Pamela Cunningham: April 3, 1860, Anna Pamela Cunningham Papers, South Caroliniana Library, University of South Carolina, Columbia, South Carolina.

28. Tracy to Cunningham: May 2, 1861, MVLA.

29. James A. Minish, The Civil War Diary and Letters of Private James A. Minish, Co. "F," 105th Regiment, Pennsylvania Volunteers, ed. M. L. Brown, Special Collections, Fred W. Smith Library for the Study of George Washington, Mount Vernon, VA.

30. Tracy to Comegys: July 15, 1861, MVLA.

31. Tracy to Cunningham: Jan 29, 1861, MVLA.

32. "Affairs North and South," *Alexandria Gazette*, January 25, 1861.

33. "The Remains of Washington," *New York Herald*, May 18, 1861.

34. Comegys to *Philadelphia Evening News*: May 16, 1861, MVLA.

35. Tracy to *National Intelligencer*: May 20, 1861, MVLA.

36. "A Visit to Mount Vernon. The Tomb of Washington Unmolested," *New York Times*, May 26, 1861.

37. Drew Gilpin Faust, *The Creation of Confederate Nationalism: Ideology and Identity in the Civil War South* (Baton Rouge: Louisiana State University Press, 1988), 21. See also

Anthony D. Smith, *Theories of Nationalism* (London: Duckworth, 1971); and Benedict Anderson, *Imagined Communities: Reflections on the Origins and Spread of Nationalism* (London: Verso, 1983). See the introduction for more on the application of Anderson's theory of nationalism to the Confederate context.

38. The MVLA had a strong relationship with the *Richmond Enquirer* in the 1850s; Anna Cora Mowatt Ritchie, the first vice regent of Virginia, was married to its editor, William Ritchie. In this context it is particularly striking the newspaper did not publish a letter or statement refuting these rumors. However, Ritchie stepped down as editor in 1860. (The same year, Ritchie left her husband and moved to Europe.)

39. Everett to Cunningham: May 30, 1861, MVLA.

40. Orlando B. Wilcox, "A Staff for the Holy Land," in *Experiencing Mount Vernon: Eyewitness Accounts, 1784–1865*, ed. Jean B. Lee (Charlottesville: University of Virginia Press, 2006), 190.

41. Everett to Scott: May 24, 1861, MVLA.

42. In 1883, following the Supreme Court decision in *U.S. v. Lee* (1882) the U.S. paid George Washington Custis Lee $150,000 for the seizure without due process of Arlington House in the Civil War.

43. Winfield Scott, General Order 13 (handwritten copy), MVLA.

44. Tracy to *National Intelligencer*: August 1, 1861, MVLA.

45. Scott's order did not completely eradicate dissent. Occasionally, the Northern press published articles critiquing Cunningham's leadership of the MVLA after July 31, 1861. For instance, see "Mount Vernon to Be Confiscated," *New York Times*, September 28, 1861. Still, after July 31, 1861, such articles were published with far less frequency and were the exception rather than the norm.

46. Mount Vernon Ladies' Association, Annual Meeting Minutes, 1900, 17. I am indebted to Mary Thompson for pointing me to this memorial.

47. Clopton, 1864: Account Book, 8–12, Clopton Papers, CMLS, VHMC.

Chapter 2

1. Drew Gilpin Faust, *Mothers of Invention: Women of the Slaveholding South in the American Civil War* (Chapel Hill: University of North Carolina Press, 1996), 28; and Judith E. Harper, *Women during the Civil War: An Encyclopedia* (New York: Routledge, 2004), 180.

2. Caroline Janney sees women's membership and involvement in gunboat associations as a testament to the strength of women's Confederate nationalism while Faust sees gunboat associations as symptomatic of the erosion of women's commitment to Confederate nationalism. Caroline Janney, *Burying the Dead but Not the Past: Ladies' Memorial Association and the Lost Cause* (Chapel Hill: University of North Carolina Press, 2008), 21–26; and Faust, *Mothers of Invention*, 28–29. Janney also claims the formation of gunboat associations foreshadowed the structure of Ladies' Memorial Associations

after the war. Janney, *Burying the Dead*, 22. See also LeeAnn Whites, *The Civil War as a Crisis in Gender Augusta, Georgia, 1860–1890* (Athens: University of Georgia Press, 1995), 59–60; Marie Tyler-McGraw, *At the Falls: Richmond, Virginia, and Its People* (Chapel Hill: University of North Carolina Press, 1994), 154; Anne Firor Scott, *Natural Allies: Women's Associations in American History* (Urbana: University of Illinois Press, 1991), 71; Judith E. Harper, *Women during the Civil War: An Encyclopedia* (New York: Routledge, 2004), 180–81; John Coski, *Capital Navy: The Men, Ships and Operations of the James River Squadron* (El Dorado Hills, CA: Savas Beatie, 1996), 82, 85; Cara Vandergriff, "'Petticoat Gunboats': The Wartime Expansion of Confederate Women's Discursive Opportunities Through Ladies' Gunboat Societies" (MA thesis, University of Tennessee, 2013), especially chapter 1; and Edna Susan Barber, "'Sisters of the Capital': White Women in Richmond, Virginia, 1860–1880" (PhD diss., University of Maryland, 1997), 199–206.

3. Barbara Mann Wall, Kathleen Rogers, and Ann Kutney-Lee, "The North vs the South: Conditions at Civil War Hospitals," *Southern Quarterly* 53 (2016): 37–55.

4. Adelaide Clopton to Namie Clopton Nichols: July 12, 1862, Maria Gaistkell Foster Clopton of Richmond, VA Papers, 1862–1872, Confederate Memorial Literary Society Collection (CMLS), Virginia Museum of History and Culture (VMHC), Richmond, VA.

5. Rebecca Barbour Calcutt, *Richmond's Wartime Hospitals* (Gretna, LA: Pelican, 2005), 156–58.

6. This kind of work is consistent with the restriction of elite Southern women's activities and interests to their kinship groups and oriented around benevolent charities put forth in Jean Friedman, *The Enclosed Garden: Women and Community in the Evangelical South, 1830–1900* (Chapel Hill: University of North Carolina Press, 1985).

7. Minute Book, Ladies' Defense Association Papers (LDA), VMHC, 2, 4.

8. "Ladies' Defense Association: Progress and Prospects," *Richmond Dispatch*, April 21, 1862.

9. Minute Book, LDA, 12.

10. LeeAnn Whites explores the ways in which women's postwar Lost Cause contributions could be seen as supporting and strengthening masculinity. Like women's work with the wartime LDA, women's postwar work could complement and augment, but never compromise, the work of men and constructions of masculinity. See Whites, *Crisis of Gender*, 149–50.

11. Anne Firor Scott, *The Southern Lady: From Pedestal to Politics, 1830–1930* (Chicago: University of Chicago Press, 1970), 6–7, 16–17.

12. Thavolia Glymph, *Out of the House of Bondage: The Transformation of the Plantation Household* (Cambridge: Cambridge University Press, 2008), 31.

13. Stephanie E. Jones-Rogers, *They Were Her Property: White Women as Slave Owners in the American South* (New Haven, CT: Yale University Press, 2019), 151.

14. Glymph, *Out of the House of Bondage*, 26–29; and Jones-Rogers, *They Were Her Property*, 10.

15. Jacqueline Glass Campbell, *When Sherman Marched North from the Sea: Resistance on the Confederate Home Front* (Chapel Hill: University of North Carolina Press, 2003), 69–74.

16. Campbell, *When Sherman Marched*, 71.

17. Campbell, *When Sherman Marched*, 69.

18 As discussed in the introduction and Linda Kerber, *No Constitutional Right to Be Ladies: Women and the Obligations of Citizenship* (New York: Hill and Wang, 1998), 243. Also, as Robert Bonner argues, some nationalist symbols, like flags, can wed the home front and front lines, civilian and military cultures, more closely. See Robert E. Bonner, "Flag Culture and the Consolidation of Confederate Nationalism," *Journal of Southern History* 68 (2002): 322–24.

19. "Ladies' Defense Association: Progress and Prospects," *Richmond Dispatch*, April 21, 1862.

20. Minute Book, LDA, 14.

21. Duncan to Clopton: April 21, 1862, LDA.

22. "Ladies' Defense Association: Progress and Prospects," *Richmond Dispatch*, April 21, 1862.

23. According to Linda Kerber, women in societies across time and place shamed their male counterparts to serve in the army and further the interests of the state. See Linda Kerber, "'History Can Do It No Justice': Women and the Reinterpretation of the American Revolution," in *Toward an Intellectual History of Women*, ed. Linda Kerber (Chapel Hill: University of North Carolina Press, 1997), 79. Also see Kerber, *No Constitutional Right*, 241.

24. Bertram Wyatt-Brown identifies fighting, horse racing, gambling, swearing, drinking, and wenching as critical competitions among school boys to prove their honor. Later, in Southern men's colleges, honor was an unofficial yet omnipresent element in the curriculum. See Bertram Wyatt-Brown, *Southern Honor: Ethics and Behavior in the Old South* (New York: Oxford University Press, 1982), 164–65. For a wider reflection on Wyatt-Brown's work and Southern cultures of masculinity, see Lisa Tendrich Frank and Daniel Kilbride, eds., *Southern Character: Essays in Honor of Bertram Wyatt-Brown* (Gainesville: University of Florida Press, 2011). Kenneth Greenberg offers dueling as a key socialization mechanism in antebellum manhood, with fathers encouraging such behavior as a sign of maturation in their sons. See Kenneth S. Greenberg, *Honor and Slavery: Lies, Duels, Noses, Masks, Dressing as a Woman, Gifts, Strangers, Death, Humanitarianism, Slave Rebellions, the Proslavery Argument, Baseball, Hunting, and Gambling in the Old South* (Princeton, NJ: Princeton University Press, 1996), 58–64. For a critique of Southern dueling culture, and the call to vote such Southern politicians out of political office, see Lyman Beecher, *The Remedy for Dueling. A Sermon, delivered before the Presbytery of Long-Island, at the Opening of their Session, at Aquebogue, April 16, 1806* (New York: J. Seymour, 1809). Also see Edward L. Ayers, "Honor's Southern Journey," in *The Field of Honor: Essays on Southern Character and American Identity*, ed. John Mayfield and Todd Hagstette (Columbia: University of South Carolina Press, 2017), ix–xviii.

25. For a wide-ranging thematic examination of the centrality of masculinity to Old South society, see Craig Thompson Friend and Lorri Glover, eds., *Southern Manhood: Perspectives on Masculinity in the Old South* (Athens: University of Georgia Press, 2004).

26. Wyatt-Brown demonstrates how the observation of violence against enslaved persons was an educational device for elite white men to train their sons in plantation management. See Wyatt-Brown, *Southern Honor*, 149–74. Likewise, Stephanie E. Jones-Rogers shows how some slaveholding women taught their daughters the importance of violence against enslaved persons. See Jones-Rogers, *They Were Her Property*, 4–6, 10, 15. Jones-Rogers's work suggests a more gender-integrated education in Southern values in childhood (leading to more gender-integrated models of power in the plantation regime in adulthood).

27. Nina Silber, *Gender and the Sectional Conflict* (Chapel Hill: University of North Carolina Press, 2008), 23–24; Scott, *Southern Lady*, 96–97, 99–101; and Stephen W. Berry, *All That Makes a Man: Love and Ambition in the Civil War South* (Oxford: Oxford University Press, 2003), 13. For a broad analysis of the significance of masculinity to the conflict, see Nina Silber and Catherine Clinton, eds., *Divided Houses: Gender and the Civil War* (New York: Oxford University Press, 1992), 43–91; and James J. Broomall, *Private Confederacies: The Emotional Worlds of Southern Men as Citizens and Soldiers* (Chapel Hill: University of North Carolina Press, 2019), 108–30.

28. Nina Silber, "Intemperate Men, Spiteful Women and Jefferson Davis," in *Divided Houses: Gender and the Civil War*, ed. Catherine Clinton and Nina Silber (New York: Oxford University Press, 1992), 295–305, and *The Romance of the Union: Northerners and the South, 1865–1900* (Chapel Hill: University of North Carolina Press, 1993), 29–37. Kenneth S. Greenberg describes Davis's capture dressed as a woman as an act of "unmasking," stripping a man of his honor. See Greenberg, *Honor and Slavery*, 25–31.

29. For an extended discussion of the fall of Richmond and the capture of Jefferson Davis, see Michael B. Ballard, *A Long Shadow: Jefferson Davis and the Final Days of the Confederacy* (Athens: University of Georgia Press, 1986), 93–177. In terms of image culture, see Mark E. Neely Jr., Gabor S. Boritt, and Harold Holzer, *The Confederate Image: Prints of the Lost Cause* (Chapel Hill: University of North Carolina Press, 1987), 80–96. According to Campbell, elite white Southern women struggled to accept the Confederate loss and reunion as it challenged Wyatt-Brown's constructions of honor and shame: "Southern culture, based on concepts of honor and shame, demanded outside recognition of the region's noble effort and a sense of dignity, even in defeat." See Campbell, *When Sherman Marched North*, 95.

30. Vernon is only referred to as "Mrs. Vernon" or "Mrs. V.E.W. Vernon" in the archival record without any reference to her first name. She seems to have embraced conservative couverture culture in naming practices, while advocating for women's expanded roles in civic society to support the Confederate cause. Women could support some conservative issues and some progressive issues at the same time.

31. Minute Book, LDA, 5.

32. Diary of Eliza Oswald Hill, Papers of Eliza Oswald Hill: March 5 1862 to June 31, 1863, Albert and Shirley Smalls Special Collection Library, University of Virginia, Charlottesville, VA, entry dated April 18, 1862.

33. Minute Book, LDA, 16–17. Some estimates claim the LDA raised $30,000. See Coski, *Capital Navy*, 85.

34. As discussed in Betty Herndon Maury Maury's diary entry on April 20, 1862. For more on Maury and her diary, see chapter 4, this volume.

35. Minute Book, LDA, 8.

36. Minute Book, LDA, 6.

37. Minute Book, LDA, 7.

38. "The Ladies' Gunboat Association," *Richmond Dispatch*, April 5, 1862.

39. See E. Susan Barber, "Cartridge Makers and Myrmidon Viragos: White Working-Class Women in Confederate Richmond," in *Negotiating Boundaries of Southern Womanhood: Dealing with the Powers That Be*, ed. Janet L. Coryell, Thomas H. Appleton Jr., Anastasia Sims, and Sandra Gioia Treadway (Columbia: University of Missouri Press, 2000), 199–214.

40. "Launching of the Ladies' Gunboat," *Richmond Enquirer*, June 30, 1863. This article also appears in the *Richmond Whig* (July 1, 1863), *Staunton Spectator* (July 7, 1863), and *Alexandria Gazette* (July 7, 1863).

41. Logan to Clopton: May 27, 1862, LDA.

42. "A Member" to Clopton: Undated, LDA.

43. Speed to Clopton: December 22, 1862, LDA.

44. Minute Book, LDA, 2–12.

45. "No. 8: Joint resolution of thanks to the patriotic women of our country for voluntary contributions furnished by them to the Army," First Session of the Confederate Congress, approved April 11, 1862.

46. Catesby Jones to Clopton: April 27, 1862, LDA.

47. Logan to Clopton: May 27, 1862, LDA.

48. Berkeley to Clopton: Undated, LDA.

49. "Meeting of the Ladies of Richmond," *Richmond Enquirer*, March 28, 1862.

50. "Meeting of the Ladies of Richmond," *Richmond Enquirer*, March 28, 1862.

51. "Obituary: Mrs. V.E.W. (McCord) Vernon," *Richmond Whig*, May 19, 1862.

52. Letter: Augusta Jane Evans to P. G. T. Beauregard, August 4, 1862, in *Augusta Jane Evans: A Southern Woman of Letters*, ed. Rebecca Sexton (Columbia: University of South Carolina Press, 2002), 42.

53. Letter: Augusta Jane Evans to P. G. T. Beauregard, August 4, 1862, 42.

54. Augusta Jane Evans, *Macaria; or, Altars of Sacrifice* (Richmond: West and Johnston, 1864), 137.

55. Evans, *Macaria*, 163.

56. For information on how the rhetoric surrounding Spartan motherhood challenged Confederate masculinity in its rejection of male desire, see Bella Zweig, "The Only Women Who Gave Birth to Men: A Gynocentric, Cross-Cultural View of Women in Ancient Sparta," in *Woman's Power, Man's Game: Essays on Classical Antiquity in Honor of Joy K. King*, ed. Mary DeForest (Wauconda, IL: Bolchazy-Carducci, 1993), 47. Also, see Sarah Pomeroy on Simone de Beauvoir's analysis of the "almost" equal gender relations of Spartan society due to the rejection of Victorian, Christian standards of womanhood:

Sarah Pomeroy, *Spartan Women* (Oxford: Oxford University Press, 2002), 71; Simone de Beauvoir, *The Second Sex*, trans. H. M. Parshley (New York: Knopf, 1952), 82.

57. Pomeroy, *Spartan Women*, 62; Faust, *Mothers of Invention*, 14–17. Sarah Pomeroy argues that Spartan women were the only women of ancient Greece whose thoughts, ideas, and concerns were considered worthy of citation; this is exemplified in Plutarch's *Sayings of Spartan Women*. Pomeroy rejects the premise that Plutarch's work is propaganda written by men, but insists that he recorded women's actual words as they offer an intimate portrayal of familial attitudes markedly different from other societies.

58. For example, speaking to the United Daughters of the Confederacy in 1902, Lelia Claudia Pullen Morris of La Grange, Georgia, concluded her recollections of the war with a valorization of her Southern sisters. First, she praised the women of Sparta, "Ancient history awarded the Spartan women the honor of being the bravest and most patriotic in the world, urging on their husbands, fathers and sons to battle, and sacrificing them upon the altar of their country rather than suffer defeat." Then, she positioned the women of the South in this revered legacy, "But my friends, modern history has awarded to Southern women, not only the honor of sacrificing their brave men, sires, and young boys, but given them the proud distinction of having the courage of defending their homes and firesides." Lelia Claudia Pullen Morris, "Recollection, 1902 February 13," CMLS, VMHC, 9.

59. As studies of Ladies' Memorial Associations have shown, Southern women's devotion to the cause encapsulated a romantic narrative of the Confederacy's struggle for independence. Janney, *Burying the Dead*, 69–103, 133–65; LeeAnn Whites, *Gender Matters: Civil War, Reconstruction and the Making of the New South* (New York: Palgrave, 2005), 85–94, and *Crisis in Gender*, 181–93.

60. Jefferson Davis, "Speech at Macon, Georgia," September 23, 1864.

61. Caroline Winterer, *The Mirror of Antiquity: American Women and the Classical Tradition, 1750–1900* (Ithaca, NY: Cornell University Press, 2007), 41.

62. This is not to preclude references to Roman culture in Civil War narratives. For instance, one of the most famous passages in Mary Chesnut's diary is Louisa McCord's retrieval of her son's body from the Second Bull Run battlefield by chartering a special train. Chesnut referenced *Caius Gracchus* in her description of the event, "'Mother of the Gracchi,' we cried." Mary Chesnut, *Mary Chesnut's Civil War*, ed. C. Vann Woodward (New Haven, CT: Yale University Press, 1981), 428. The analysis here focuses on references to Spartan women in order to complement and extend Winterer's examination of feminine classicism in eighteenth-and nineteenth-century America.

63. For more on the related concept of Republican Motherhood, see the introduction, this volume.

Chapter 3

1. J. B. Jones, *A Rebel War Clerk's Diary at the Confederate States Capital* (Philadelphia: Lippincott, 1866), 284–85.

2. See Stephanie McCurry, *Confederate Reckoning: Power and Politics in the Civil War South* (Cambridge, MA: Harvard University Press, 2010), 178–217 (especially 192–93). In a wider frame encompassing issues outside of the bread riots, McCurry considers soldiers' wives as formative local political actors who made demands on the Confederate state (even though they were still political dependents on their husbands). McCurry, *Confederate Reckoning*, 133–77 (especially 133–37).

3. Mary A. DeCredico, *Confederate Citadel: Richmond and Its People at War* (Lexington: University of Kentucky Press, 2020).

4. While most works on the Confederacy include some reference to the Richmond bread riot, it is usually limited to a brief discussion on the internal weaknesses of the Confederacy and its failure to unite disparate groups across the class spectrum. For example, see E. Merton Coulter, *The Confederate States of America, 1861–1865* (Baton Rouge: Louisiana State University Press, 1950), 422–23; and James McPherson, *Battle Cry of Freedom: The Civil War Era* (New York: Oxford University Press, 1988), 617–19. In particular, Drew Gilpin Faust sees the Southern bread riots as a barometer for the erosion of Confederate nationalism on the home front from mid-1863. Drew Gilpin Faust, *Mothers of Invention: Women of the Slaveholding South in the American Civil War* (Chapel Hill: University of North Carolina Press, 1996), 245.

5. Davis would issue nine days of fasting over the course of the war.

6. Emory M. Thomas, *The Confederate State of Richmond: A Biography of the Capital* (Baton Rouge: Louisiana State University Press, 1971), 113–14. See also Emory M. Thomas, *The Confederate Nation: 1861–1865* (New York: Harper and Row, 1979), 197–205.

7. For analyses of the Southern bread riots across the Confederacy (and not only in Richmond), see Drew Gilpin Faust, *The Creation of Confederate Nationalism: Ideology and Identity in the Civil War South* (Baton Rouge: Louisiana State University Press, 1988), 52–56; Drew Gilpin Faust, "Altars of Sacrifice: Confederate Women and Narratives of War," *Journal of American History* 76 (March 1990): 1200–28; Thavolia Glymph, *The Women's Fight: The Civil War's Battles for Home, Freedom, and Nation* (Chapel Hill: University of North Carolina Press, 2020), 70–73; George Rable, *Civil Wars: Women and the Crisis of Southern Nationalism* (Urbana: University of Illinois Press, 1989), 108–11; Harriet E. Amos, "All Absorbing Topics: Food and Clothing in Confederate Mobile," *Atlanta Historical Journal* 22 (Fall/Winter 1978): 17–28; Paul Escott, "The Moral Economy of the Crowd in Confederate North Carolina," *Maryland Historian* 13 (Spring/Summer 1982): 1–18, and *Many Excellent People: Power and Privilege in North Carolina, 1850–1900* (Chapel Hill: University of North Carolina Press, 1988), 65–67.

8. For detailed accounts of the Richmond bread riot, see McCurry, *Confederate Reckoning*, 178–217; William J. Kimball, "The Bread Riot in Richmond, 1863," *Civil War History* 7 (June 1961): 149–54; Michael B. Chesson, "Harlots or Heroines? A New Look at the Richmond Bread Riot," *Virginia Magazine of History and Biography* 92 (April 1984): 131–75; Douglas O. Tice, 'Bread or Blood!: The Richmond Bread Riot," *Civil War Times Illustrated* 12 (February 1974): 12–19; and E. Susan Barber, "Cartridge Makers and Myrmidon Viragos: White Working-Class Women in Confederate Richmond," in *Negotiating Boundaries of Southern Womanhood: Dealing with the Powers That Be*, ed.

Janet L. Coryell, Thomas H. Appleton Jr., Anastasia Sims, and Sandra Gioia Treadway (Columbia: University of Missouri Press, 2000), 199–214.

9. Hal Tutwiler to Netta Tutwiler: April 3, 1863, Netta L. Tutwiler Letters, Southern Historical Collection, University of North Carolina, Chapel Hill, North Carolina.

10. John Lancaster Waring to Warner Waring: April 2, 1863, Waring Family Papers, Virginia Museum of History and Culture (VMHC), Richmond, Virginia.

11. Barber, "Cartridge Makers and Myrmidon Viragos," 211; and Glymph, *Women's Fight*, 70.

12. Glymph, *Women's Fight*, 70.

13. Instead, service of Northern women was often presented in the Northern pictorial press. For instance, a drawing in the *Harper's Weekly* September 6, 1862, edition, "Our Women and the War," succinctly demonstrates Northern women's service in both the public and private spheres. In this image, women are captured in a variety of activities: sewing, nursing, providing spiritual support, and laboring on menial tasks for soldiers. In these depictions, Northern women are presented as industrious, self-sacrificing servants of the Union home front. See Brown, *Beyond the Lines: Pictorial Reporting, Everyday Life, and the Crisis of Gilded Age America* (Berkeley: University of California Press, 2002), 49. For more on the wider culture of pictorial journalism in the Civil War, especially in the North, see Joshua Brown, *Beyond the Lines*; W. Fletcher Thompson Jr., *The Image of War: The Pictorial Reporting of the American Civil War* (New York: Thomas Yoseloff, 1959); and William P. Campbell, *The Civil War: The Centennial Exhibition of Eyewitness Drawings* (Washington, DC: National Gallery of Art, 1961).

14. "Sowing and Reaping," *Frank Leslie's Illustrated Newspaper*, May 23, 1863. For these exceptional wartime images of Southern women, see *Harper's Weekly's* July 12, 1862, portrayal of New Orleans women's response to General Benjamin Butler's General Order 28. In the image, before the order, elite women spit in the face of a Union soldier. This first image conveys the idea that Southern women lack the decorum and subservience required of elite Southern women in the Old South. These women were engaging in crass behavior and challenging men in the public sphere. They were subverting the expectations of their gender and their class to express their support for the Confederacy. Their actions conflate deviant womanhood and Confederate womanhood. After the order, in the second image, the women acknowledge the Union soldier in a courteous manner. A November 15, 1862, image in *Frank Leslie's* serves a similar function. The image, "The Chivalrous Behavior of a Sesch Lady," shows a Southern woman lifting up her skirt, as a sign of disrespect, to a Union soldier. Furthermore, the Richmond bread riot is also depicted in the Northern press. The April 18, 1863, edition of *Harper's Weekly* contains a brief article about the Richmond bread riot, but it is not accompanied by a sketch. Also, the September 7, 1861, cover image of *Harper's Weekly*, "A Female Rebel in Baltimore—An Everyday Scene—," shows an extravagantly dressed Southern woman brazenly walking through the street attracting the whispers and sneers of Union soldiers. The woman is oblivious to the volatile political context and the realities of war. She is carefree and cavalier, unlike hardworking and sensible Northern women.

15. It is also important to note that the Northern pictorial press omitted Southern women from representations of some events where they were intrinsic to the narrative. This is particularly clear in depictions of Sherman's March to the Sea. *Harper's Weekly* presented drawings of Sherman's Atlanta Campaign and subsequent March to the Sea over a one-month period in the editions dated August 6, August 13, and September 3, 1864. Likewise, the August 6, 1864, edition of *Frank Leslie's* includes a drawing of Sherman's Georgia campaign. This process of selective memory implicitly recognized the potential of circulating images of vulnerable and victimized Southern women to a Northern audience; again, such images could humanize and illicit sympathy for the Southern cause. For more on the centrality of Southern women to Sherman's campaign, see Lisa Tendrich Frank, *The Civilian War: Confederate Women and Union Soldiers During Sherman's March* (Baton Rouge: Louisiana State University Press, 2015), and "Bedrooms as Battlefields: The Role of Gender Politics in Sherman's March," in *Occupied Women: Gender, Military Occupation and the American Civil War*, ed. LeeAnn Whites and Alecia P. Long (Baton Rouge: Louisiana State University Press, 2009), 33–48; Jaqueline Glass Campbell, *When Sherman Marched North from the Sea: Resistance on the Confederate Home Front* (Chapel Hill: University of North Carolina Press, 2005), 58–92; and Anne Sarah Rubin, *Through the Heart of Dixie: Sherman's March and American Memory* (Chapel Hill: University of North Carolina Press, 2017), 45–68.

16. The Confederate bread riots share some striking similarities to the women's march on Versailles in the French Revolution on October 5, 1789, from the route (first descending on the Hotel de Ville), the concern (acquisition of affordably priced bread), the target (the domestic government), and the "dress rehearsals" throughout the summer of 1789 to women's leadership. Furthermore, in the aftermath of both riots, the participants were falsely declared to be prostitutes by journalistic and governmental accounts. To characterize these events as simply spontaneity driven by women's emotional response to an inflationary economy would be to obscure the shrewd political insight of the women organizers and participants in both riots. For more on women in the march on Versailles, see Joan B. Landes, *Women and the Public Sphere in the Age of the French Revolution* (Ithaca, NY: Cornell University Press, 1988); David Garrioch, "The Everyday Lives of Parisian Women and the October Days of 1789," *Social History* 24 (1999): 231–49, and *Women in Revolutionary Paris, 1789–1795*, ed. Darline Gay Levy, Harriet Branson Applewhite, and Mary Durham Johnson (Urbana: University of Illinois Press, 1979). For more on the Richmond riot and prostitution, see Barber, "Cartridge Makers and Myrmidon Viragos."

17. Louis H. Manarin, ed., *Richmond at War: The Minutes of the City Council, 1861–65* (Chapel Hill: University of North Carolina Press, 1966), 311.

18. Manarin, ed., *Richmond at War*, 311–12.

19. Manarin, ed., *Richmond at War*, 311–12.

20. Manarin, ed., *Richmond at War*, 314.

21. Manarin, ed., *Richmond at War*, 317.

22. Manarin, ed., *Richmond at War*, 320.

23. Randolph's biographer, George Shackleford, claims his economic and political ideology can best be described as "pre-Marxist socialism." See George Green Shackleford,

George Wythe Randolph and the Confederate Elite (Athens: University of Georgia Press, 1988), 53.

24. Mary Chesnut, *A Diary from Dixie*, ed. Isabella D. Martin and Myrta Lockett Avary (New York: D. Appleton and Company, 1905), 105. Chesnut also accompanied Randolph on some of her hospital visits. In the 1905, 1949, and 1981 editions of her diary, the entry dated August 23, 1861, detailed the infamous anecdote of Chesnut fainting at Sally Tompkins's Robertson Hospital while on a charity visit with Mary Randolph. See the introduction, note 2, p. 125.

25. Chesnut, *Diary*, 107–8.

26. McCurry, *Confederate Reckoning*, 192. McCurry further asserts that lower-class white women's participation in the Richmond bread riot must be understood as a planned political action with political intent not a spontaneous event void of political meaning. For an excellent theoretical framework on the sociopolitical consciousness of "the mob," see E. P. Thompson, "The Moral Economy of the Crowd in the Eighteenth Century," *Past and Present* 50 (1971): 76–136.

27. "Richmond's Bread Riot: Jefferson Davis Describes a Wartime Event: Beauvoir Letter to the *Richmond Dispatch*," *New York Times*, April 30, 1889; and Varina Howell Davis, *Jefferson Davis, Ex-President of the Confederate States of America: A Memoir*, vol. 2 (New York: Belford, 1890), 374.

28. J. B. Jones, *A Rebel War Clerk's Diary*, 285.

29. Josiah Gorgas, *The Civil War Diary of Josiah Gorgas*, ed. Frank E. Vandiver (Tuscaloosa: University of Alabama Press, 1947), 28–29.

30. Gorgas, *The Civil War Diary of Josiah Gorgas*, 29.

31. McCurry links Confederate conscription policies that removed lower-class white laborers from smaller farms (while exempting plantation owners holding twenty or more slaves), as a motivating factor in the soldier wives' bread riots. See McCurry, *Confederate Reckoning*, 203–4.

32. "Bread Riot in Richmond: Three Thousand Hungry Women in the Streets. Government and Private Stores Broke Open," *New York Times*, April 7, 1863.

33. Sarah Agnes Rice Pryor, *My Day: Reminiscences of a Long Life* (New York: Macmillan, 1909), 237.

34. Margaret Wight, *A Refugee of Hanover Tavern: The Civil War Diary of Margaret Wight*, ed. Shirley A. Haas and Dale Paige Talley (Charleston, SC: History Press, 2013), 139.

35. Judith White McGuire, *Diary of a Southern Refugee, During the War* (New York: E. J. Hale and Son, 1868), 203. Also see Jones, *A Rebel War Clerk's Diary*, for further sympathy with the rioters.

36. White McGuire, *Diary of a Southern Refugee*, 204.

37. Chesson, "Harlots or Heroines?," 169.

38. William Alan Blair, *Virginia's Private Civil War: Feeding Body and Soul in the Confederacy, 1861–1865* (New York: Oxford University Press, 1998), 58–64, 81–84; Peter S. Carmichael, *The Last Generation: Young Virginians in Peace, War, and Reunion* (Chapel Hill: University of North Carolina Press, 2005), 174–76; Paul D. Escott, *After*

Secession: Jefferson Davis and the Failure of Confederate Nationalism (Baton Rouge: Louisiana State University Press, 1978), 80–88, 117–19, and *Military Necessity: Civil-Military Relations in the Confederacy* (Westport, CT: Praeger, 2006), 33–37, 168–69.

39. Drew Gilpin Faust, *Mothers of Invention: Women of the Slaveholding South in the American Civil War* (Chapel Hill: University of North Carolina Press, 1996), 240–42.

40. Stephanie E. Jones-Rogers, *They Were Her Property: White Women as Slave Owners in the American South* (New Haven, CT: Yale University Press, 2019), 161–62.

41. Thavolia Glymph, *Out of the House of Bondage: The Transformation of the Plantation Household* (Cambridge: Cambridge University Press, 2008), 100–124, and *Women's Fight*, 34–42, 51–52; and Jones-Rogers, *They Were Her Property*, 158–59.

42. Glymph, *Out of the House of Bondage*, 38.

43. Jones-Rogers, *They Were Her Property*, 172–74. Jones-Rogers also notes that Confederate soldiers impressed enslaved persons from slaveholding women, and women petitioned for payment for the loss of their property. Again, this shows slaveholding women's concerns with slavery as a means to ensure their own economic survival. See Jones-Rogers, *They Were Her Property*, 167–68.

44. Jones-Rogers, *They Were Her Property*, 175.

45. *The Statutes at Large of the Confederate States of America Passed at the Second Session of the First Congress; 1862*, ed. James M. Matthews (Richmond, VA: R. M. Smith, 1862), 77, http://docsouth.unc.edu/imls/csstat62/csstat62.html, last accessed October 1, 2021.

46. For an example of the usage of "rich man's war, poor man's fight" to describe the Confederate war effort, see Sam R. Watkins, *Co. Aytch: A Confederate Memoir of the Civil War*, 2nd ed. (Wilmington, NC: Broadfoot Publishing Co., 1987), 69.

47. *The Statutes at Large of the Confederate States of America Passed at the Third Session of the First Congress; 1862*, 158, https://babel.hathitrust.org/cgi/pt?id=osu.32435001714492&view=1up&seq=155, last accessed October 1, 2021. The exemption became even more restrictive in February 1864.

48. In February 1864, the Twenty Slave Law would be amended again to apply only to plantations with fifteen or more, instead of twenty or more, enslaved persons. Also, planters would be required to give the government 100 pounds of bacon, or a comparable substitute, for each enslaved person on his plantation as recompense. Again, the Confederate government revised expectations of both military and financial service from the Confederate elite.

49. M. E. Caperton to G. H. Caperton: May 9, 1861, Caperton Family Papers, Virginia Polytechnic Institute and State University, Blacksburg, Virginia.

50. Chesnut, *Diary*, 33.

51. Mary Norcott Bryan, *A Grandmother's Recollection of Dixie* (New Bern, NC: Owen G. Dunn, 1912), Documenting the American South, University Library, University of North Carolina at Chapel Hill, Chapel Hill, North Carolina, Letter IX, https://docsouth.unc.edu/fpn/bryan/bryan.html, last accessed December 5, 2018.

52. Faust, *Mothers of Invention*, 56–62.

53. Sarah Morgan, *The Civil War Diary of Sarah Morgan*, ed. Charles East (Athens: University of Georgia Press, 1991), 228.

54. Margaret Muse Pennybacker, "Reminiscences: War Memorial," Margaret Muse Pennybacker Personal Papers, Library of Virginia, Richmond, Virginia, 8.

55. Glymph, *Women's Fight*, 60–69, 73–76. Glymph also examines interactions between wealthy lowcountry refugees in poor white mountain communities to show how poor whites also expressed class-based resentment. Wealthy refugees often endangered these communities with their demands on already scarce resources.

56. Eugenia Phillips, "A Southern Woman's Story of Imprisonment in 1861 & 1862," CMLS, VMHC, 10.

57. Louise B. Clack, "My Experiences of the Civil War of 1861–65 by a New Orleans Woman," CMLS, VMHC, 4.

58. In such descriptions of their fears over the Union and lower-class whites, Southern women often referenced the French Revolution as a western touchstone for violent class warfare. For instance, in June 1862, two months before the Battle of Baton Rouge, Sarah Morgan reflected, "Here we two culprits [Miriam, her sister, and herself] stand alone before the tribunal of patriotism. Madame Roland, I take the liberty of altering your words and cry 'O Patriotism! How many base deeds are sanctioned by your name!' Don't I wish I was a heathen! In twenty four hours the whole country will be down on us." In aligning her subjectivity with that of one of the most famous women martyrs of the French Revolution, Morgan magnified the sense of imminent danger and class conflict on the home front. Morgan, *Diary*, 130.

59. Manarin, ed., *Richmond at War*, 312.

60. Manarin, ed., *Richmond at War*, 323.

61. Anne Firor Scott, *Natural Allies: Women's Organizations in America* (Urbana: University of Illinois Press, 1991), 68–72.

62. Clara Minor Lynn, "What the Confederates Wore," CMLS, VMHC, 6–7.

63. Public and private charity associations and efforts were prevalent in the antebellum South. See Timothy James Lockley, *Welfare and Charity in the Antebellum South* (Gainesville: University of Florida, 2007). For a study focused on charity in Richmond, Virginia, see Elna C. Green, *This Business of Relief: Confronting Poverty in a Southern City, 1740–1940* (Athens: University of Georgia Press, 2003), 40–84.

64. Elizabeth R. M. Callender, Unpublished Diary, Bird Family Papers, VMHC, 2.

65. McCurry identifies soldiers' wives as perceived worthy beneficiaries of state aid. McCurry, *Confederate Reckoning*, 133–37, especially 135–37.

66. Missouri did not grant pensions to widows; it only granted pensions to veterans. (Missouri was a border state in the war and never formally joined the Confederacy.)

67. Lockley, *Welfare and Charity in the Antebellum South*, 213, 217.

Chapter 4

1. The ways in which this case for Confederate recognition, as well as the concurrent opposing case for maintaining neutrality and abstaining from intervention, was circulated and received within domestic British society has been widely examined in

the current historiography. Richard Blackett explores which segments of British society supported the Union and Confederacy and their motivations for doing so. Blackett is particularly mindful of class and regional differences in shaping these affiliations; see Richard Blackett, *Divided Hearts: Britain and the American Civil War* (Baton Rouge: Louisiana State University Press, 2001), 89–212. In an earlier work, Mary Ellison refutes the premise that Lancashire cotton workers supported the North and argues that Lancashire opinion mainly supported the Confederacy; see Mary Ellison, *Support for Secession: Lancashire and the American Civil War* (Chicago: University of Chicago Press, 1972), 109–72. Both Blackett and Ellison show the importance of British public opinion in shaping British-Confederate relations. Through the lens of "Anglo-American criticism," Martin Crawford examines the impact of the *Times* on the Anglo-American relationship in the late antebellum and first two years of the Civil War acknowledging the significance of public opinion and newspaper culture; see Martin Crawford, *The Anglo-American Crisis in the Mid-Nineteenth Century: The Times and America, 1850–1862* (Athens: University of Georgia Press, 1987), 106–33, especially 126–33. For a more traditional top-down approach to international relations in the Civil War, see Howard Jones, *Blue and Gray Diplomacy: A History of Union and Confederate Foreign Relations, 1861–1865* (Chapel Hill: University of North Carolina Press, 2010), 47–82, and *Union in Peril: The Crisis over British Intervention in the Civil War* (Chapel Hill: University of North Carolina Press, 1992), 80–137; Frank Lawrence Owsley, *King Cotton Diplomacy: Foreign Relations of the Confederate States of America* (Chicago: University of Chicago Press, 1931), 294–494; and Robert May, ed., *The Union, the Confederacy and the Atlantic Rim* (West Lafayette, IN: Purdue University Press, 1995), 29–67. Don Doyle adroitly interrogates the role of state actors as well as global public opinion, international relations from above and below, in *The Cause of All Nations: An International History of the American Civil War* (New York: Basic Books, 2014).

2. The ways in which this rhetoric for Confederate recognition was constructed to the British public, specifically how it changed over time, has received less attention. Duncan Andrew Campbell, *English Public Opinion and the American Civil War* (Rochester, NY: Boydell, with the Royal Historical Society, 2003), 163–93; Charles P. Cullop, *Confederate Propaganda in Europe, 1861–1865* (Miami: University of Miami Press, 1969); and Tom Sebrell, *Persuading John Bull: Union and Confederate Propaganda in Britain, 1860–65* (New York: Lexington Books, 2014), 121–50, 173–90, offer rich studies of the construction of pro-Confederate rhetoric in Britain, but there are still important research questions to be explored in this area, particularly in terms of identity politics and gender.

3. Looking at the post–Civil War period, Kristin L. Hoganson examines middle-class white American women's consumption of European cultural imports as a way to consider the United States in a more global, as opposed to national, history in this period. Hoganson's concept of domestic gendered consumerism (or "contact zones") "looks at quintessentially domestic places ... to find evidence of international connections." This chapter utilizes a similar frame of analysis, interrogating white middle-class and planter Southern women's transnational interests, writings, and travels, for broader connections between the Confederacy and Europe in the diplomatic and political spheres. See

Kristin L. Hoganson, *Consumers' Imperium: The Global Production of American Domesticity, 1865–1920* (Chapel Hill: University of North Carolina Press, 2005), 8.

4. Clara Minor Lynn, "Last Days in a Confederate Home," Confederate Memorial Literary Society (CMLS), Virginia Museum of History and Culture (VMHC), Richmond, Virginia, 7.

5. Christie Farnham notes that the catalogue for the Greensboro Female College of the 1858–59 academic year was typical of the standard proportion of students enrolled in French language studies; of its 351 students, only fifty-seven studied French. This relatively low proportion of French students can be chiefly attributed to the additional fees required to enroll in the course, segregating enrollment in French studies along class lines. See Anya Jabour, *Scarlett's Sisters: Young Women in the Old South* (Chapel Hill: University of North Carolina Press, 2007), 47–82; Giselle Roberts, *The Confederate Belle* (Columbia: University of Missouri Press, 2003), 15–34; and Christie Farnham, *The Education of the Southern Belle: Higher Education and Student Socialization in the Antebellum South* (New York: New York University Press, 1994).

6. After the Southern defeat, some white planter Southern women took extended visits or settled in Europe, including former Confederate First Lady Varina Howell Davis and Georgiana Freeman Gholson Walker.

7. Amanda Virginia Edmonds Papers, 1857–1886, Section 2 1857, June 8–1862, September 12, VMHC, 216. Baird's edition of Edmonds's diary provides the following entry for July 1, 1862: "France has positively recognized the Confederacy and England is expected to do likewise in a few days." Amanda Virginia Edmonds, *Journals of Amanda Virginia Edmonds: Lass of the Mosby Confederacy, 1859–1867*, ed. Nancy Chappelear Baird (Stephens City, VA: Commercial Press, 1984), 102.

8. Elizabeth Curtis Wallace, *Glencoe Diary: The War-Time Journal of Elizabeth Curtis Wallace*, ed. Eleanor P. Cross and Charles B. Cross Jr. (Chesapeake, VA: Norfolk Historical Society, 1968), 61.

9. Lucy Wood Butler, Diary of a Civil War Bride, Lomax Family Papers, VMHC, 106; and Lucy Wood Butler, *The Diary of a Civil War Bride: Lucy Wood Butler of Virginia*, ed. Kristen Brill (Baton Rouge: Louisiana State University Press, 2017), 78.

10. Lucy Buck, *Shadows on My Heart: The Civil War Diary of Lucy Rebecca*, ed. Elizabeth R. Baer (Athens: University of Georgia Press, 1997), 186.

11. Cornelia Peake McDonald, *A Diary With Reminiscences of the War and Refugee Life in the Shenandoah Valley, 1860–1865* (Nashville, TN: Cullom and Ghertner, 1934), 73.

12. Augusta Jane Evans, *Macaria; or, Altars of Sacrifice* (Richmond: West and Johnston, 1864), 154.

13. Betty Herndon Maury, *The Civil War Diary of Betty Herndon Maury: Daughter of Lieut. Commander M. F. Maury 1861–63*, ed. Alice Maury Parmelee (Washington: Privately Printed, 1938), 51 (November 18, 1861).

14. Maury, *Diary*, 60 (February 23, 1862).

15. Maury, *Diary*, 19 (July 13, 1861).

16. Maury, *Diary*, 39 (October 6, 1861).

17. Maury, *Diary*, 41 (October 9, 1861).

18. Charlotte Burckmyer returned to South Carolina after the war, but her European base during the war make her comments invaluable in this transatlantic framework of analysis. *The Burckmyer Letters: March 1863–June 1865*, ed. Charlotte Rebecca Homes (Columbia, SC: The State Company, 1926), 12.

19. *Burckmyer Letters*, 66–67.

20. *Burckmyer Letters*, 252.

21. Jefferson Davis, "Address to the Congress of the Confederate States," November 18, 1861.

22. George Fitzhugh, "The Revolutions of 1776 and 1861 Contrasted," *Southern Literary Messenger* 37 (December 1863): 725.

23. For instance, see *Richmond Enquirer*: October 28, 1861, August 1, 1862, and October 14, 1862. See *Daily Dispatch*: June 4, 1861, September 17, 1861, and February 20, 1863. See *Alexandria Gazette*: August 25, 1862, and November 21, 1862.

24. For more on the Union's efforts to categorize Confederate civilians and combatants according to Lieber's code, see Stephanie McCurry, *Women's War: Fighting and Surviving the American Civil War* (Cambridge, MA: Harvard University Press, 2019), 15–62, especially 15–19.

25. "England Must Break the Blockade," *Richmond Daily Dispatch*, December 28, 1861. This article appears in the final days of 1861.

26. "The Rebel Address," *New York Times*, December 27, 1862. The address was provided by George Thompson, M.P. to the *New York Times* to reprint for American audiences.

27. "Bazaar in Aid of the Southern Prisoners' Relief Fund," *The Times,* October 7, 1864.

28. James Spence, *On the Recognition of the Southern Confederation* (London: Richard Bentley, 1862), 12–13. Also see James Spence, *The American Union; Its Effect on National Character and Policy* (London: Richard Bentley, 1861). Note that Richard Bentley published the pro-Confederate works of both Greenhow and Spence.

29. Spence, *On the Recognition of the Southern Confederation*, 47–48.

30. Confederate emissary to Britain James Mason at times adopted the same rhetoric in his private correspondence. Writing to Lord Bath on September 12, 1862, Mason thanked him for his "expressions of good will toward our infant country." In addition to using familial language (with respect to infancy), Mason used the first-person plural (our) as opposed to the first-person singular (my) to describe the Confederacy. Mason to Lord Bath: September 12, 1862, James Murray Mason Papers, Mason Family Manuscript Collection, Gunston Hall Library and Archives, Lorton, VA.

31. While not a member of the British press before 1862, the *Index* still published in Britain for a British audience from 1862 to 1865. See Robert E. Bonner, "Slavery, Confederate Diplomacy, and the Racialist Mission of Henry Hotze," *Civil War History* 51 (2005): 288–316; Stephen B. Oates, "Henry Hotze: Confederate Agent Abroad," *Historian* 27 (1965): 131–54; and Lonnie A. Burnett, *Henry Hotze, Confederate Propagandist*.

Selected Writings on Revolution, Recognition, and Race (Tuscaloosa: University of Alabama Press, 2008).

32. Letter to William Seward: November 17, 1861, Rose O'Neal Greenhow Papers: An On-Line Archival Collection, Special Collections Library, Duke University, https://library.duke.edu/rubenstein/scriptorium/greenhow/1861-11-17/1861-11-17.html, last accessed June 8, 2020.

33. Mary Chesnut, *A Diary from Dixie*, ed. Isabella D. Martin and Myrta Lockett Avary (New York: D. Appleton and Company, 1905), 176.

34. Letter to Alexander Boteler: June 13, 1863, Rose O'Neal Greenhow Papers: An On-Line Archival Collection, Special Collections Library, Duke University, https://library.duke.edu/rubenstein/scriptorium/greenhow/1863-06-19/1863-06-19.html, last accessed June 8, 2020.

35. Letter to Jefferson Davis: July 16, 1863, Rose O'Neal Greenhow Papers: An On-Line Archival Collection, Special Collections Library, Duke University, https://library.duke.edu/rubenstein/scriptorium/greenhow/1863-07-16/1863-07-16.html, last accessed June 8, 2020.

36. Letter to Jefferson Davis: July 16, 1863.

37. Letter to Alexander Boteler: February 17, 1864, Rose O'Neal Greenhow Papers: An On-Line Archival Collection, Special Collections Library, Duke University, https://library.duke.edu/rubenstein/scriptorium/greenhow/1864-02-17/1864-02-17.html, last accessed December 12, 2018.

38. Letter to Alexander Boteler: February 17, 1864.

39. Letter to Boteler: December 10, 1863, Rose O'Neal Greenhow Papers: An On-Line Archival Collection, Special Collections Library, Duke University, https://library.duke.edu/rubenstein/scriptorium/ greenhow/1863-12-10/1863-12-10.html, last accessed June 8, 2020.

40. Georgiana Freeman Gholson Walker, Private Journal of Georgiana F. Walker, Albert and Shirley Smalls Special Collections Library, University of Virginia, Charlottesville, VA, January 8, 1864.

41. Walker, Private Journal, December 17, 1863.

42. Rose O'Neal Greenhow, *My Imprisonment and the First Year of Abolitionist Rule at Washington* (London: Richard Bentley, 1863).

43. Greenhow, *My Imprisonment*, 123.

44. Greenhow, *My Imprisonment*, 275.

45. Greenhow, *My Imprisonment*, 180. Greenhow stated that Stanton never received the letter.

46. Greenhow, *My Imprisonment*, 263.

47. Greenhow, *My Imprisonment*, 352.

48. "The Late Mrs. Rose A. Greenhow," presumably from the *Wilmington Sentinel*, October 1, 1864, Rose O'Neal Greenhow Papers: An On-Line Archival Collection, Special Collections Library, Duke University, https://library.duke.edu/rubenstein/scriptorium/greenhow/1864-10-01-a/1864-10-01-a.html, last accessed December 12, 2018.

49. For instance, see "A Rebel Joan D'Arc at Front Royal," *Evening Star* (Washington, D.C.), May 31, 1862.

50. Myrta Lockett Avary, *A Virginia Girl in the Civil War, 1861–1865* (New York: D. Appleton and Company), 58.

51. Belle Boyd, *Belle Boyd in Camp and Prison. In Two Volumes. Vol. I* (London: Saunders, Otley and Co., 1865), 4.

52. Boyd, *Camp and Prison. Vol. I*, 5.

53. Boyd, *Camp and Prison. Vol. I*, 278.

54. Belle Boyd, *Belle Boyd in Camp and Prison. In Two Volumes. Vol. II* (London: Saunders, Otley and Co., 1865), 50.

55. Boyd, *Camp and Prison. Vol. II*, 219–20.

56. Boyd, *Camp and Prison. Vol. II*, 222.

57. Belle Boyd, *Camp and Prison. Vol. II*, 277, 279.

58. Belle Boyd Hardinge to Abraham Lincoln: January 24, 1865, Abraham Lincoln Papers: Series 1. General Correspondence. 1833–1916, Library of Congress, https://www.loc.gov/resource/mal.4022200/?st=gallery, last accessed September 12, 2019.

59. For more on women spies in the Civil War, see Karen Abbott, *Liar, Temptress, Soldier, Spy: Four Women Undercover in the Civil War* (New York: Harper Collins, 2014); Elizabeth Varon, *Southern Lady, Yankee Spy: The True Story of Elizabeth Van Lew, a Union Agent in the Heart of the Confederacy* (Oxford: Oxford University Press, 2005); Elizabeth D. Leonard, *All the Daring of a Soldier: Women of Civil War Armies* (New York: W.W. Norton, 1999); and Catherine Clinton, *Stepdaughters of History: Southern Women and the American Civil War* (Baton Rouge: Louisiana State University Press, 2016).

60. Ruth Scarborough, *Belle Boyd: Siren of the South* (Macon, GA: Mercer University Press, 1997), 180.

61. James M. Mason, *The Public Life and Diplomatic Correspondence of James M. Mason, with Some Personal History*, ed. Virginia Mason (Roanoke, VA: Stone Printing and Manufacturing Co., 1903), 545.

62. "A Rebel Spy," *Leeds Mercury*, August 20, 1862; *Preston Guardian*, August 20, 1862; "A Rebel Spy," *Liverpool Mercury*, August 21, 1862; "A Rebel Female Spy," *Reynold's Newspaper*, August 24, 1862.

63. For an extended discussion of Butler's General Order 28, see Chester G. Hearn, *When the Devil Came Down to Dixie: Ben Butler in New Orleans* (Baton Rouge: Louisiana State University Press, 1990). See also Alecia P. Long, "(Mis)Remembering General Order No. 28: Benjamin Butler, the Woman Order and Historical Memory," in *Occupied Women: Gender, Military Occupation and the American Civil War*, ed. LeeAnn Whites and Alecia P. Long (Baton Rouge: Louisiana State University Press, 2009), 20–32; Catherine Clinton, *Public Women and the Confederacy* (Milwaukee, WI: Marquette University Press, 1999), 33–37; Kristen Brill, "'I Had the Men from the Start': General Benjamin Butler's Occupation of New Orleans," *Women's History Review* 26.3 (2017): 319–28; and Drew Gilpin Faust, *Mothers of Invention: Women of the Slaveholding South in the American Civil War* (Chapel Hill: University of North Carolina Press, 1996), 207–13.

64. Hearn, *When the Devil Came Down to Dixie*, 105.

65. As detailed in the *Standard*, June 10, 1862, and *Leicester Chronicle*, June 14, 1862.

66. "America," *Daily News*, July 28, 1862; "The Civil War in America," *Belfast News-Letter*, July 30, 1862; "Foreign News," *Penny Illustrated Paper*, August 2, 1862; "The Civil War in America," *Derby Mercury*, August 6, 1862; and "The Federals in New Orleans," *The Times*, July 29, 1862.

67. For more on Lincoln's plans for emancipation, see Eric Foner, *The Fiery Trial: Abraham Lincoln and American Slavery* (New York: W.W. Norton, 2010), 206–47; Michael Vorenberg, *Final Freedom: The Civil War, Abolition of Slavery and the Thirteenth Amendment* (Cambridge: Cambridge University Press, 2004), especially 23–46; "Forum: The Emancipation Proclamation," *Civil War History* 59.1 (2013): 7–31; and John Hope Franklin, *The Emancipation Proclamation* (New York: Wiley-Blackwell, 1994).

68. "Mr. Lindsay, M.P. on the War in America," *Telegraph*, October 3, 1863.

Chapter 5

1. "Charter: Chapter 851, An Act to Incorporate the Home for Needy Confederate Women," Item 2, Charters, Bylaws, Rules and Regulations Governing the Home for Needy Confederate Women (Richmond: Whippet and Shepperson, 1910), 3, Home for Needy Confederate Women Records, 1862–1997 (HNCW), Library of Virginia, Richmond, Virginia.

2. *In Memory of the Heroes in Gray*, 1929, foreword, HNCW.

3. Jeffrey W. McClurken, *Taking Care of the Living: Reconstructing Confederate Veteran Families in Virginia* (Charlottesville: University of Virginia Press, 2009), 155.

4. For a discussion of the justifications for and administration of the federal pension system, from which the South and former Confederates were excluded, see Theda Skocpol, *Protecting Soldiers and Mothers: The Political Origins of Social Policy in the United States* (Cambridge, MA: Harvard University Press), 102–52.

5. Robin Bates, "'The Ideal Home of the South': The Robert E. Lee Camp Confederate Soldiers' Home and the Institutionalization of Confederate Veterans in Virginia," *American Nineteenth Century History* 17.1 (2016): 26, 28; McClurken, *Taking Care of the Living*, 143–72, especially 156–58; and R. B. Rosenburg, *Living Monuments: Confederate Soldiers' Homes in the New South* (Chapel Hill: University of North Carolina Press, 1993), preface.

6. Karen Cox, *Dixie's Daughters: The United Daughters of the Confederacy and the Preservation of Confederate Culture* (Gainesville: University of Florida Press, 2003), 74; Susan Hamburger, "'We Take Care of Our Womenfolk': The Home for Needy Confederate Women in Richmond, 1898–1990," in *Before the New Deal: Social Welfare in the South, 1830–1930*, ed. Elna C. Green (Athens: University of Georgia Press, 1999), 61–62; and Caroline E. Janney, *Burying the Dead but Not the Past: Ladies' Memorial Associations and the Lost Cause* (Chapel Hill: University of North Carolina Press, 2008), 1–14.

7. This critique reflected a broader discussion of class status and admittance into Confederate women's homes. At the 1910 UDC General Convention, Caroline Helene Plane proposed the establishment of a home exclusively for the elite modeled after the Louise Home in Washington, D.C. The UDC's response to this proposal was mostly critical and the home never came to fruition. See Cox, *Dixie's Daughters*, 80–81.

8. For more on the code of conduct in the Home for Needy Confederate Women, see Cox, *Dixie's Daughters*, 77.

9. Hamburger proposes the UDC was central to the Home for Needy Confederate Women in terms of raising their public profile and circulating their message to print media and political circles. See Hamburger, "We Take Care of Our Womenfolk," 66–67.

10. See Linda Kerber, *No Constitutional Right to Be Ladies: Women and the Obligations of Citizenship* (New York: Hill and Wang, 1988), 124–302.

11. For a broad overview of the changing definitions of women's organizations, benevolence, and charity immediately after the war, see Lori Ginzberg, *Women and the Work of Benevolence: Morality, Politics, and Class in the Nineteenth-Century United States* (New Haven, CT: Yale University Press, 1990), 174–213; Karen J. Blair, *The Clubwoman as Feminist: True Womanhood Redefined, 1868–1914* (New York: Holmes and Meier, 1980); Ruth Bordin, *Woman and Temperance: The Quest for Power and Liberty, 1873–1900* (Philadelphia: Temple University Press, 1980); and Anne Firor Scott, *Natural Allies: Women's Associations in American History* (Urbana: University of Illinois Press, 1991), 111–74. For more specific descriptions of Southern women's postwar organizations, see Anne Firor Scott, *Southern Lady: From Pedestal to Politics, 1830–1900* (Chicago: University of Chicago Press, 1970), 151–61; Jane Turner Censer, *The Reconstruction of White Southern Womanhood, 1865–95* (Baton Rouge: Louisiana State University Press, 2003), 203–4, 206; and Jean E. Friedman, *The Enclosed Garden: Women and Community in the Evangelical South, 1830–1900* (Chapel Hill: University of North Carolina Press, 1985), 5–7. For women's roles in Virginia organizations, see Antoinette G. Van Zelm, "Virginia Women as Public Citizens: Emancipation Day Celebrations and Lost Cause Commemorations, 1863–1890," in *Negotiating Boundaries of Southern Womanhood: Dealing with the Powers That Be*, ed. Janet L. Coryell et al. (Columbia: University of Missouri Press, 2000), 71–88; and Angie Parrott, "'Love Makes Memory Eternal': The United Daughters of the Confederacy in Richmond, Virginia, 1897–1920," in *The Edge of the South: Life in Nineteenth-Century Virginia*, ed. Edward Ayers and John C. Willis (Charlottesville: University of Virginia Press, 2000), 219–38; and E. Susan Barber, "Anxious Care and Constant Struggle: The Female Humane Association and Richmond's White Civil War Orphans," in *Before the New Deal: Social Welfare in the South, 1830–1930*, ed. Elna C. Green (Athens: University of Georgia Press, 1999), 120–37.

12. The only developed study of the home is Susan Hamburger, "'We Take Care of Our Womenfolk,'" 61–77. Hamburger provides a concise summary of the home's history from its establishment in 1898 to its closure in 1989 and notes the women's successes in an era of tightening state provisions for social programs. In her study of the United Daughters of the Confederacy, Karen Cox briefly mentions the home's relationship

to the Virginia chapters of the UDC. Cox, *Dixie's Daughters*, 76–78. Likewise, in his study of Virginia Confederate veterans' homes, Jeffrey McCluken touches on the home's links to the Lee camp for Confederate soldiers. See McClurken, *Taking Care of the Living*, 155–56.

13. For more on the memory of the Confederacy and Civil War in the New South, see Edward L. Ayers, *Southern Crossing: A History of the American South, 1877–1906* (New York: Oxford University Press, 1995), 261–63; Catherine Bashir, "Landmarks of Power: Building a Southern Past in Raleigh and Wilmington, North Carolina, 1885–1915," in *Where These Memories Grow: History, Memory, and Southern Identity*, ed. W. Fitzhugh Brundage (Chapel Hill: University of North Carolina Press, 2000), 139–68; W. Fitzhugh Brundage, *The Southern Past: A Clash of Race and Memory* (Cambridge, MA: Harvard University Press, 2005), 105–37; Gaines M. Foster, *Ghosts of the Confederacy: Defeat, the Lost Cause, and the Emergence of the New South, 1865–1913* (Oxford: Oxford University Press, 1989), 88–144, 163–79; William Blair, *Cities of the Dead: Contesting the Memory of the Civil War in the South, 1865–1914* (Chapel Hill: University of North Carolina Press, 2005), especially 106–70; David Blight, *Race and Reunion: The Civil War in American Memory* (Cambridge, MA: Harvard University Press, 2005), 255–99; Paul M. Gaston, *The New South Creed: A Study in Southern Mythmaking* (New York: Alfred A. Knopf, 1970), 159–77; and Marjorie Spruill Wheeler, *New Women of the New South: The Leaders of the Woman Suffrage Movement in the United States* (New York: Oxford University Press, 1993), 3–37.

14. "Constitution and By-Laws of the United Daughters of the Confederacy," United Daughters of the Confederacy Harvey Black Chapter records, 1862–2010, Virginia Polytechnic Institute and State University, Blacksburg, Virginia.

15. Ladies' Memorial Associations predated the UDC and Confederate women's homes. The LMAs focused on mourning, burying, and then commemorating the dead. For more on LMAs, see Jane Turner Censer, *The Reconstruction of White Southern Womanhood, 1865–95* (Baton Rouge: Louisiana State University Press, 2003), 191–203; Elizabeth R. Varon, *We Mean to Be Counted: White Women and Politics in Antebellum Virginia* (Chapel Hill: University of North Carolina Press, 1998), 172; and Drew Gilpin Faust, *This Republic of Suffering: Death and the American Civil War* (New York: Alfred A. Knopf, 2008), 239–48. Faust argues that the work of LMAs were "explicitly sectional" and women became symbols and "instruments of the dead's immortality" (247–48). See also Drew Gilpin Faust, *Mothers of Invention: Women of the Slaveholding South in the American Civil War* (Chapel Hill: University of North Carolina Press, 1996), 252–53. In addition to highlighting the reconstruction of white manhood and masculinity through this work, Whites asserts that members of the LMA united to establish a Widows' Home in Augusta, Georgia, in 1868; the Widows' Home reinforced the work and mission of the LMA. See LeeAnn Whites, *The Civil War as a Crisis in Gender: Augusta, Georgia, 1860–1890* (Athens: University of Georgia Press, 1995), 160–68, 182–95; as well as LeeAnne Whites, *Gender Matters: Civil War, Reconstruction and the Making of the New South* (New York: Palgrave, 2005), 86–94. Anne Sarah Rubin argues women's

work in LMAs adhered to socially acceptable gender roles and women's associations with the emotions over intellect. See Rubin, *Shattered Nation: The Rise and Fall of the Confederacy, 1861–68* (Chapel Hill: University of North Carolina Press, 2005), 233–39.

16. For more on Confederate widows as a prominent feature of postbellum political and social memorialization (as well as its attendant economic issues), see Robert Kenzer, "The Uncertainty of Life: A Profile of Virginia's Civil War Widows," in *The War Was You and Me: Civilians in the American Civil War*, ed. Joan E. Cashin (Princeton, NJ: Princeton University Press, 2002), 112–35; Jennifer Lynn Gross, "'And for the Widow and the Orphan': Confederate Widows, Poverty, and Public Assistance," in *Inside the Confederate Nation: Essays in Honor of Emory M. Thomas*, ed. Lesley J. Gordon and John C. Inscoe (Baton Rouge: Louisiana State University Press, 2005), 209–29, and "Good Angels: Confederate Widowhood in Virginia," in *Southern Families at War: Loyalty and Conflict in the Civil War South*, ed. Catherine Clinton (Oxford: Oxford University Press, 2000), 133–54; and Angela Esco Elder, "Married to the Confederacy: The Emotional Politics of Confederate Widowhood" (PhD diss., University of Georgia, 2016).

17. For an analysis of the work of the UDC compared to the Daughters of the American Revolution, as well as its impact on early twentieth-century white masculinity, see Brundage, *The Southern Past*, 12–54 and for a broader overview, see Foster, *Ghosts of the Confederacy*, 38–45, 127–29. Caroline Janney has written extensively on LMAs in the postwar South. See Janney, "Written in Stone: Gender, Race and the Heywood Shepherd Memorial," *Civil War History* 52.2 (2006): 117–41; and the definitive study, Caroline E. Janney, *Burying the Dead*, 167–94. Janney shows how the United Daughters of the Confederacy emerged out of the work of the LMA, offering a younger membership body and a more diverse agenda beyond the scope of cemeteries and monuments. From 1894, the LMAs tried to compete with the growing membership and political and social influence of the UDC (and there was significant overlap in membership between the two groups), but by 1915 it was clear the UDC would be the dominant force in women's roles in the Lost Cause.

18. Thavolia Glymph, *Out of the House of Bondage: The Transformation of the Plantation Household* (Cambridge: Cambridge University Press, 2005), 19–20.

19. Glymph, *Out of the House of Bondage*, 89. For more on the relationship between home, domesticity, and civilization in nineteenth-century America, see Amy G. Richter, *Home on the Rails: Women, the Railroad, and the Rise of Public Domesticity* (Chapel Hill: University of North Carolina Press, 2005), and *At Home in Nineteenth-Century America* (New York: New York University Press, 2015), especially 97–131. Also see chapter 1 for a discussion of the MVLA's efforts to promote "civilization" in George Washington's home of Mount Vernon. For more on the theory of separate spheres, see the Introduction, note 49, this volume.

20. "Will Build a Home," March 29, 1897, HNCW.

21. "Will Build a Home," March 29, 1897, HNCW.

22. Mrs. A. J. Montague, Notes for Speech to Virginia General Assembly, 1915, HNCW.

23. Mrs. A. J. Montague, undated speech to UDC convention, HNCW.

24. Mrs. A. J. Montague, Notes for Speech to Virginia General Assembly, 1940s, HNCW.

25. Caroline Gouldin Letter: March 1, 1909, HNCW.

26. For more on the ways in which the home sought to uphold Confederate standards of masculinity, see Cox, *Dixie's Daughters*, 78.

27. *In Memory of the Heroes in Gray*, 1929, "The Need," HNCW.

28. *In Memory of the Heroes in Gray*, 1929, "Why YOU Should Help," HNCW.

29. Janney, *Burying the Dead*, 175–76.

30. "Virginia's Call Must Not Be Denied," undated pamphlet, HNCW.

31. This ideological commitment to a celebration of the Confederacy beyond monuments reinforces Cox's findings on the UDC. The UDC was committed to not only memorialization, but *vindication* through various channels, perhaps most significantly to the education of children of the Confederacy. For Cox, this also underlines the importance of women in creating Lost Cause culture in the early twentieth century; men did not hold a monopoly on the formation and circulation of Lost Cause culture. See Cox, *Dixie's Daughters*, 1–5. In making this argument, Cox argues against scholars in the previous decade who posited women's roles in Lost Cause organizations supported a patriarchal social system with restricted, as opposed to expanded, liberties for women. See Whites, *The Civil War as a Crisis of Gender*, 160–208; and Faust, *Mothers of Invention*, 247–57. Supporting Cox, Janney showcases the ways in which Ladies' Memorial Associations deterred veterans from controlling their commemoration projects, including Memorial Day celebrations, in the second half of the twentieth century. In this context and overcoming conflict, particularly in the final decades of the twentieth century, the LMAs worked together and cooperated with veterans. See Janney, *Burying the Dead*, 133–65.

32. Bates, "Ideal Home of the South," 37, note 4.

33. Cox, *Dixie's Daughters*, 76.

34. As argued in Rosenberg, *Living Monuments*.

35. Dispute with George E. Pickett Camp of Confederate Veterans, 1904, HNCW.

36. Hamburger contends that Confederate veterans' camps took a more active, interventionist role in the daily operation of the home. See Hamburger, "We Take Care of our Womenfolk," 66–67. Indeed, in December 1910, "A Friend of the Camp" wrote a letter to the Pickett Camp detailing concerns over the management of the Home for Needy Confederate Women. This "friend" clearly identified Pickett's camp as holding some level of power and authority over the affairs of the home. See Concerns over Management of the Home, 1910, HNCW.

37. "To the United Daughters of the Confederacy of the Chapters of the Virginia Division," proposed takeover by the UDC: 1910–13, HNCW.

38. UDC Donation of Cemetery Plots, 1954, HNCW.

39. "To the Members of the General Assembly," February 11, 1932, HNCW.

40. Home for Needy Confederate Women; *Report of the Commission to the Governor and General Assembly of Virginia, House Document No. 11* (Richmond: Virginia Division of Purchasing and Printing, 1947), 4–5.

41. *In Memory of the Heroes in Gray*, 1929, HNCW.

42. *History of the Home for Needy Confederate Women, 1900–1904*, 47, HNCW.

43. "Charter: Chapter 851, An Act to Incorporate the Home for Needy Confederate Women," Item 2, Charters, Bylaws, Rules and Regulations Governing the Home for Needy Confederate Women (Richmond: Whippet and Shepperson, 1910), 4, HNCW.

44. William Larsen, *Montague of Virginia: The Making of a Southern Progressive* (Baton Rouge: Louisiana State University Press, 1965), 31.

45. Larsen, *Montague of Virginia*, 286.

46. *History of the Home for Needy Confederate Women, 1900–1904*, 49, HNCW.

47. Montague was particularly invested in the development of education and roadways, though he secured little legislative victories. Larsen, *Montague of Virginia*, 284–90.

48. "Mrs. Coolidge Earns $250 and Gives It Away," *New York Times*, December 30, 1926.

49. "Virginia's First Lady Revealed Helping Confederate Women," undated newspaper clipping, HNCW.

50. "Virginia's First Lady Revealed Helping Confederate Women."

51. Home for Needy Confederate Women; *Report of the Commission to the Governor*, 4–5.

52. Hamburger, "'We Take Care of our Womenfolk,'" 70–2.

53. This is consistent with the UDC's requirement to establish female lineal descent to join the organization from the end of the nineteenth century. Such a hereditary, bloodline provision was not required for LMA membership (with the exception of Fredericksburg), which only required the payment of a subscription fee. Such a measure can be seen to "thwart the fluidity of social boundaries at the turn of the century by relying on an objective standard, some groups could dismiss charges of exclusivity while maintaining their middle-and upper-class bias." See Janney, *Burying the Dead*, 174.

54. The home lobbied the assembly for this alteration to the charter to address dwindling residency numbers and to ensure the legality of a bequest from a donor's will.

55. Brian Kelly, "4 Words Could Save Confederate Home," *Washington Star*, January 29, 1977.

56. Mabel A. Taylor v. Home for Needy Confederate Women, 1987, HNCW.

57. "Confederate Spirit Lives in Richmond," *Washington Post*, July 26, 1980.

58. Burhans to White: August 29, 1980, HNCW.

59. "Confederacy Lives in Home for Aged Women," *Richmond News-Leader*, April 24, 1980.

60. Janet R. Burhans to Frederick H. Cox, Jr.: July 18, 1984, HNCW.

61. For the impact of the Moynihan Report, see Daniel Geary, *Beyond Civil Rights: The Moynihan Report and Its Legacy* (Philadelphia: University of Pennsylvania Press,

2016); and Susan Greenbaum, *Blaming the Poor: The Long Shadow of the Moynihan Report on Cruel Images about Poverty* (New Brunswick, NJ: Rutgers University Press, 2015). For more on Medicare and Medicaid after 1965, see Daniel Béland and Alex Waddan, *The Politics of Policy Change: Welfare, Medicare and Social Security Reform in the United States* (Washington, DC: Georgetown University Press, 2015); Jonathan Engel, *Poor People's Medicine: Medicaid and American Charity since 1965* (Durham, NC: Duke University Press, 2006); and Rosemary Stevens, Charles E. Rosenberg, and Lawton R. Burns, eds., *History and Health Policy in the United States: Putting the Past Back In* (New Brunswick, NJ: Rutgers University Press, 2006).

62. As an earlier nineteenth-century point of comparison, these debates surrounding "deserving" and "worthy" recipients of state support and welfare in Virginia can be found in the discussion of the Richmond bread riot in chapter 3, this volume.

63. "For Richmond's Confederate Home for Women, It's Finally Appomattox," *New York Times*, August 25, 1989.

64. This reinforces Caroline Janney's claim that the processes of burying the Confederate dead offered former Confederate women new ways to participate in government through their vested interests in the promulgation of Confederate memory. While Janney refers to the immediate postwar period, her argument still holds relevance here. Janney, *Burying the Dead*.

65. In particular, the Omnibus Reconciliation Act of 1981 was meant to give states more power to determine spend levels (including health care spend) in the award of block grants, but in fact states saw cuts in the amount of dedicated health care funding in real terms.

66. Susan Hamburger argues that the climate of limited social spending, executed by a white male ruling elite in Virginia, played a crucial role in the closure of the home in 1989. See Hamburger, "We Take Care of our Womenfolk," 72.

67. Cox, *Dixie's Daughters*, 28.

68. Caroline E. Janney, "United Daughters of the Confederacy," Encyclopedia of Virginia, https://www.encyclopediavirginia.org/United_Daughters_of_the_Confederacy, last accessed September 3, 2019.

69. Brian Palmer and Seth Freed Wessler, "The Cost of the Confederacy," *Smithsonian Magazine* (December 2018).

70. This relationship between sentimental identity and legislation is explored in Susan Mary-Grant, "The Lost Boys: Citizen-Soldiers, Disabled Veterans, and Confederate Nationalism in the Age of People's War," *Journal of the Civil War Era* 2.2 (2012): 233–59.

Epilogue

1. "Establishing a commemorative commission to honor the contributions of the women of Virginia with a monument on the grounds of Capitol Square," Senate Joint Resolution No. 11, Virginia General Assembly, January 13, 2010.

2. "About Us," Virginia Women's Monument Commission, http://womensmonumentcom.virginia.gov/about.html, last accessed November 3, 2019.

3. Cameron Thompson, "Virginia Women's Monument Unveiled after almost Decade of Work," WTVR, October 14, 2019.

4. "Women's Monument Unveiled on Capitol Square: 'No Pedestals, No Weapons, No Horses,'" Capital News Service, WTVR, October 15, 2019.

5. "Women's Monument Unveiled on Capitol Square."

6. "First Four Statues Commissioned for Va. Women's Monument at Capitol Square," WRIC Newsroom, July 18, 2018.

7. Sherry Hamilton, "Funding Sought for Sally Tompkins Statue in Richmond," *Gloucester-Matthews Gazette Journal*, January 30, 2019.

8. Staff Report, "Loudoun Misspelled on New Virginia Women's Monument in Richmond," *Loudoun Times-Mirror*, October 15, 2019.

9. Chelsea Wise Higgs, "Virginia Plans to Honor Slaveholders and Confederate on New Women's Monument," *RVA Magazine*, October 14, 2019; and Colleen Curan, "'A Monumental Day': Seven Statues Unveiled at Virginia Women's Monument on Capitol Square," *Richmond Times-Dispatch*, October 14, 2019.

10. Several articles and monographs, for both academic and popular audiences, exploring the post-2015 Confederate statue debate have been published. For a good example of this topical body of literature, see Catherine Clinton, W. Fitzhugh Brundage, Karen L. Cox, Gary W. Gallagher, and Nell Irvin Painter, *Confederate Statues and Memorialization* (Athens: University of Georgia Press, 2019).

11. Richmond's statue of Christopher Columbus was also pulled down, set on fire, and thrown into a lake by protestors in June 2020.

BIBLIOGRAPHY

Manuscripts

Albert and Shirley Smalls Special Collection Library, University of Virginia, Charlottesville, Virginia
    Eliza Oswald Hill Papers
    Georgiana Freeman Gholson Walker Private Journal
Fred W. Smith National Library for the Study of George Washington, Mount Vernon, Virginia
    Diary and Letters of Private James A. Minish
    John Augustine Washington Manuscripts
    Mount Vernon Ladies' Association Early Records
Gunston Hall Library and Archives, Lorton, Virginia
    James Murray Mason Papers
Library of Virginia, Richmond, Virginia
    Home for Needy Confederate Women Records, 1862–1997
    Margaret Muse Pennybacker Papers
South Caroliniana Library, University of South Carolina, Columbia, South Carolina
    Anna Pamela Cunningham Papers
Southern Historical Collection, University of North Carolina, Chapel Hill, North Carolina
    Netta L. Tutwiler Letters
Virginia Museum of History and Culture, Richmond, Virginia
    Ladies' Defense Association Papers
    Maria Gaistkell Foster Clopton of Richmond, Virginia Papers, 1862–72
    Robert E. Lee Headquarters Papers, 1850–76
    Bird Family Papers
    Waring Family Papers
    Samuella Hart Curd Diary
    Sally Tompkins Papers, Confederate Memorial Literary Society collection, formerly the Southern Women's Collection at the Museum of the Confederacy in Richmond, Virginia (CMLS)
    Lomax Family Papers

Amanda Virginia Edmonds Papers
Clara Minor Lynn Papers (CMLS)
Lelia C. Pullen Morris Papers (CMLS)
Louise B. Clack Papers (CMLS)
Virginia Polytechnic Institute and State University Special Collections, Blacksburg, Virginia
Caperton Family Papers
Richard G. Noble Papers
United Daughters of the Confederacy Harvey Black Chapter Records, 1862–2010

Online Archival Collections

Abraham Lincoln Papers, Library of Congress
Documenting the American South
Founders Online
Rose O'Neal Greenhow Online Papers, Special Collections Library, Duke University, Durham, North Carolina

Periodicals

Alexandra Gazette
Belfast News-Letter
Charleston Mercury
Daily News
Derby Mercury
Evening Star
Frank Leslie's Illustrated Newspaper
Gloucester-Matthews Gazette Journal
Harper's Weekly
Leeds Mercury
Liberator
Liverpool Mercury
Loudoun Times-Mirror
National Intelligencer
New York Herald
New York Times
Philadelphia Evening News
Preston Guardian
Reynold's Newspaper
Richmond Enquirer
Richmond Dispatch/Richmond Times-Dispatch

Richmond News-Leader
Richmond Sentinel
Richmond Whig
Southern Literary Messenger
Staunton Spectator
Times
Washington Post
Washington Star

Printed Sources

Abbott, Karen. *Liar, Temptress, Soldier, Spy: Four Women Undercover in the Civil War*. New York: Harper Collins, 2014.

Amos, Harriet E. "All Absorbing Topics: Food and Clothing in Confederate Mobile." *Atlanta Historical Journal* 22 (Fall/Winter 1978): 17–28.

Anderson, Benedict. *Imagined Communities: Reflections on the Origins and Spread of Nationalism*. London: Verso, 1983.

Ash, Stephen V. *Rebel Richmond: Life and Death in the Confederate Capital*. Chapel Hill: University of North Carolina Press, 2019.

Avary, Myrta Lockett. *A Virginia Girl in the Civil War, 1861–1865*. New York: D. Appleton and Company, 1903.

Ayers, Edward L. *Southern Crossing: A History of the American South, 1877–1906*. New York: Oxford University Press, 1995.

Ayers, Edward L., Gary W. Gallagher, and Andrew J. Torget, eds. *Crucible of the Civil War: Virginia from Secession to Commemoration*. Charlottesville: University of Virginia Press, 2006.

Bacot, Ada. *A Confederate Nurse: The Diary of Ada W. Bacot, 1860–1863*. Edited by Jean V. Berlin. Columbia: University of South Carolina Press, 1994.

Ballard, Michael B. *A Long Shadow: Jefferson Davis and the Final Days of the Confederacy*. Athens: University of Georgia Press, 1986.

Barber, E. Susan. "Anxious Care and Constant Struggle: The Female Humane Association and Richmond's White Civil War Orphans." In *Before the New Deal: Social Welfare in the South, 1830–1930*, ed. Elna C. Green, 120–37. Athens: University of Georgia Press, 1999.

Barber, E. Susan. "Cartridge Makers and Myrmidon Viragos: White Working-Class Women in Confederate Richmond." In *Negotiating Boundaries of Southern Womanhood: Dealing with the Powers That Be*, ed. Janet L. Coryell, Thomas H. Appleton Jr., Anastasia Sims, and Sandra Gioia Treadway, 199–214. Columbia: University of Missouri Press, 2000.

Barber, E. Susan. "Sally Louisa Tompkins: Confederate Healer." In *Virginia Women: Their Lives and Times*, ed. Cynthia A. Kierner and Sandra Gioia Treadway, 344–62. Athens: University of Georgia Press, 2015.

Barber, E. Susan. "'Sisters of the Capital': White Women in Richmond, Virginia, 1860–1880." PhD diss., University of Maryland, 1997.

Bashir, Catherine. "Landmarks of Power: Building a Southern Past in Raleigh and Wilmington, North Carolina, 1885–1915." In *Where These Memories Grow: History, Memory, and Southern Identity*, ed. W. Fitzhugh Brundage, 139–68. Chapel Hill: University of North Carolina Press, 2000.

Bates, Robin. "'The Ideal Home of the South': The Robert E. Lee Camp Confederate Soldiers' Home and the Institutionalization of Confederate Veterans in Virginia." *American Nineteenth Century History* 17.1 (2016): 23–41.

Beauvoir, Simone de. *The Second Sex*. Translated by H. M. Parshley. New York: Knopf, 1952.

Beecher, Lyman. *The Remedy for Dueling. A Sermon, delivered before the Presbytery of Long-Island, at the Opening of their Session, at Aquebogue, April 16, 1806*. New York: J. Seymour, 1809.

Beland, Daniel, and Alex Waddan. *The Politics of Policy Change: Welfare, Medicare, and Social Security Reform in the United States*. Washington, DC: Georgetown University Press, 2015.

Bernath, Michael T. *Confederate Minds: The Struggle for Intellectual Independence in the Civil War South*. Chapel Hill: University of North Carolina Press, 2010.

Berry, Stephen W. *All That Makes a Man: Love and Ambition in the Civil War South*. Oxford: Oxford University Press, 2003.

Binnington, Ian. *Nationalism, Symbolism, and the Imagined South in the Civil War*. Charlottesville: University of Virginia Press, 2013.

Blackett, Richard. *Divided Hearts: Britain and the American Civil War*. Baton Rouge: Louisiana State University Press, 2001.

Blair, Karen J. *The Clubwoman as Feminist: True Womanhood Redefined, 1868–1914*. New York: Holmes and Meier, 1980.

Blair, William A. *Cities of the Dead: Contesting the Memory of the Civil War in the South, 1865–1914*. Chapel Hill: University of North Carolina Press, 2005.

Blair, William A. *Virginia's Private Civil War: Feeding Body and Soul in the Confederacy, 1861–1865*. New York: Oxford University Press, 1998.

Bleser, Carol, ed. *In Joy and Sorrow: Women, Family, and Marriage in the Victorian South*. New York: Oxford University Press, 2001.

Blight, David. *Race and Reunion: The Civil War in American Memory*. Cambridge, MA: Harvard University Press, 2005.

Bonner, Robert E. "Slavery, Confederate Diplomacy, and the Racialist Mission of Henry Hotze." *Civil War History* 51.3 (2005): 288–316.

Bonner, Robert E. *Mastering America: Southern Slaveholders and the Crisis of American Nationhood*. Cambridge: Cambridge University Press, 2009.

Bordin, Ruth. *Woman and Temperance: The Quest for Power and Liberty, 1873–1900*. Philadelphia: Temple University Press, 1980.

Boyd, Belle. *Belle Boyd in Camp and Prison. In Two Volumes.* London: Saunders, Otley and Co., 1865.
Branch, Mary Polk. *Memoirs of a Southern Woman "Within the Lines" and a Geographical Record.* Chicago: Joseph G. Branch, 1912.
Brandt, Lydia Mattie. *First in the Homes of His Countrymen: George Washington's Mount Vernon in the American Imagination.* Charlottesville: University of Virginia Press, 2016.
Brill, Kristen. "'I Had the Men from the Start': General Benjamin Butler's Occupation of New Orleans." *Women's History Review* 26.3 (2017): 319–28.
Broomall, James J. *Private Confederacies: The Emotional Worlds of Southern Men as Citizens and Soldiers.* Chapel Hill: University of North Carolina Press, 2019.
Brown, Joshua. *Beyond the Lines: Pictorial Reporting, Everyday Life, and the Crisis of Gilded Age America.* Berkeley: University of California Press, 2002.
Brundage, W. Fitzhugh. *The Southern Past: A Clash of Race and Memory.* Cambridge, MA: Harvard University Press, 2005.
Bryan, Mary Norcott. *A Grandmother's Recollection of Dixie.* New Bern, NC: Owen G. Dunn, 1912.
Bunkers, Suzanne. "Reading and Interpreting Unpublished Diaries by Nineteenth-Century Women." *a/b: Auto/Biography Studies* 2.2 (1986): 15–17.
Burnett, Lonnie A. *Henry Hotze, Confederate Propagandist: Selected Writings on Revolution, Recognition, and Race.* Tuscaloosa: University of Alabama Press, 2008.
Butler, Lucy Wood. *The Diary of a Civil War Bride: Lucy Wood Butler of Virginia.* Edited by Kristen Brill. Baton Rouge: Louisiana State University Press, 2017.
Buck, Lucy. *Shadows on My Heart: The Civil War Diary of Lucy Rebecca.* Edited by Elizabeth R. Baer. Athens: University of Georgia Press, 1997.
Bynum, Victoria. *The Long Shadow of the Civil War: Southern Dissent and Its Legacies.* Chapel Hill: University of North Carolina Press, 2010.
Bynum, Victoria. *Unruly Women: The Politics of Social and Sexual Control in the Old South.* Chapel Hill: University of North Carolina Press, 1992.
Calcutt, Rebecca Barbour. *Richmond's Wartime Hospitals.* Gretna, LA: Pelican, 2005.
Campbell, Duncan Andrew. *English Public Opinion and the American Civil War.* Rochester, NY: Boydell, with the Royal Historical Society, 2003.
Campbell, Jaqueline Glass. *When Sherman Marched North from the Sea: Resistance on the Confederate Home Front.* Chapel Hill: University of North Carolina Press, 2005.
Campbell, William P. *The Civil War: The Centennial Exhibition of Eyewitness Drawings.* Washington, DC: National Gallery of Art, 1961.
Carmichael, Peter S. *The Last Generation: Young Virginians in Peace, War, and Reunion.* Chapel Hill: University of North Carolina Press, 2005.
Cashin, Joan E. *A Family Venture: Men and Women on the Southern Frontier.* New York: Oxford University Press, 1991.

Cashin, Joan E. *First Lady of the Confederacy: Varina Howell Davis's Civil War.* Cambridge, MA: Harvard University Press, 2008.

Casper, Scott E. *Sarah Johnson's Mount Vernon: The Forgotten History of an American Shrine.* New York: Hill and Wang, 2008.

Censer, Jane Turner. *The Reconstruction of White Southern Womanhood, 1865–1895.* Baton Rouge: Louisiana State University Press, 2003.

Chesebrough, David. *Clergy Dissent in the Old South, 1830–1865.* Carbondale: Southern Illinois Press, 1996.

Chesnut, Mary. *A Diary from Dixie.* Edited by Isabella D. Martin and Myrta Lockett Avary. New York: D. Appleton and Co., 1905.

Chesnut, Mary. *Mary Chesnut's Civil War.* Edited by C. Vann Woodward. New Haven, CT: Yale University Press, 1981.

Chesnut, Mary. *The Private Mary Chesnut: The Unpublished Civil War Diaries.* Edited by C. Vann Woodward and Elisabeth Muhlenfeld. Oxford: Oxford University Press, 1984.

Chesson, Michael B. "Harlots or Heroines? A New Look at the Richmond Bread Riot." *The Virginia Magazine of History and Biography* 92 (April 1984): 131–75.

Chirhart, Ann Short, and Betty Wood, eds. *Georgia Women: Their Lives and Times,* Vol. 1. Athens: University of Georgia Press, 2009.

Clay-Clopton, Virginia. *A Belle of the Fifties: Memoirs of Mrs. Clay of Alabama Covering Social and Political Life in Washington and the South, 1853–66,* 3rd ed. Tuscaloosa: University of Alabama Press, 1999.

Clinton, Catherine. *The Plantation Mistress: Woman's World in the Old South.* New York: Pantheon Books, 1982.

Clinton, Catherine. *Public Women and the Confederacy.* Milwaukee, WI: Marquette University Press, 1999.

Clinton, Catherine. *Stepdaughters of History: Southern Women and the American Civil War.* Baton Rouge: Louisiana State University Press, 2016.

Clinton, Catherine, ed. *Southern Families at War: Loyalty and Conflict in the Civil War South.* Oxford: Oxford University Press, 2000.

Clinton, Catherine, W. Fitzhugh Brundage, Karen L. Cox, Gary W. Gallagher, and Nell Irvin Painter. *Confederate Statues and Memorialization.* Athens: University of Georgia Press, 2019.

Clinton, Catherine, and Nina Silber, eds. *Divided Houses: Gender and the Civil War.* New York: Oxford University Press, 1992.

Coryell, Janet L., Thomas H. Appleton Jr., Anastasia Sims, and Sandra Gioia Treadway, eds. *Negotiating Boundaries of Southern Womanhood: Dealing with the Powers That Be.* Columbia: University of Missouri Press, 2000.

Coski, John. *Capital Navy: The Men, Ships and Operations of the James River Squadron.* El Dorado, Hills, CA: Savas Beatie, 1996.

Cott, Nancy. *The Bonds of Womanhood: "Woman's Sphere" in New England, 1780–1835.* New Haven, CT: Yale University Press, 1977.

Coulter, E. Merton. *The Confederate States of America, 1861–1865*. Baton Rouge: Louisiana State University Press, 1950.
Coulter, E. Merton. *James McPherson, Battle Cry of Freedom: The Civil War Era*. New York: Oxford University Press, 1988.
Cox, Karen. *Dixie's Daughters: The United Daughters of the Confederacy and the Preservation of Confederate Culture*. Gainesville: University of Florida Press, 2003.
Crawford, Martin. *The Anglo-American Crisis in the Mid-Nineteenth Century: The Times and America, 1850–1862*. Athens: University of Georgia Press, 1987.
Crofts, Daniel W. *Reluctant Confederates: Upper South Unionists in the Secession Crisis*. Chapel Hill: University of North Carolina Press, 1989.
Cullop, Charles P. *Confederate Propaganda in Europe, 1861–1865*. Miami, FL: University of Miami Press, 1969.
Cumming, Kate. *The Journal of Kate Cumming: A Confederate Nurse, 1862–1865*. Edited by Richard Harwell, 2nd ed. Savannah, GA: Beehive Press, 1975.
Cunningham, H. H. *Doctors in Gray: The Confederate Medical Service*. Baton Rouge: Louisiana State University Press, 1958.
Current, Richard Nelson. *Lincoln's Loyalists: Union Soldiers from the Confederacy*. Boston: Northeastern University Press, 1992.
Davidoff, Leonore, and Catherine Hall. *Family Fortunes: Men and Women of the English Middle Class, 1780–1850*. Chicago: University of Chicago Press, 1991.
Davis, Varina Howell. *Jefferson Davis, Ex-President of the Confederate States of America: A Memoir*, vol. 2. New York: Belford, 1890.
Downs, Laura Lee. "If 'Woman' Is a Just an Empty Category, Then Why Am I Afraid to Walk Alone at Night? Identity Politics Meets the Postmodern Subject." Comparative Studies in Society and History 35.2 (1993): 414–37.
Doyle, Don. *The Cause of All Nations: An International History of the American Civil War*. New York: Basic Books, 2014.
Edmonds, Amanda Virginia. *Journals of Amanda Virginia Edmonds: Lass of the Mosby Confederacy, 1859–1867*. Edited by Nancy Chappelear Baird. Stephens City, VA: Commercial Press, 1984.
Edwards, Laura. *Scarlett Doesn't Live Here Anymore: Southern Women in the Civil War Era*. Urbana: University of Illinois Press, 2000.
Elder, Angela Esco. "Married to the Confederacy: The Emotional Politics of Confederate Widowhood." PhD diss., University of Georgia, 2016.
Ellison, Mary. *Support for Secession: Lancashire and the American Civil War*. Chicago: University of Chicago Press, 1972.
Engel, Jonathan. *Poor People's Medicine: Medicaid and American Charity since 1965*. Durham, NC: Duke University Press, 2006.
Escott, Paul D. *After Secession: Jefferson Davis and the Failure of Confederate Nationalism*. Baton Rouge: Louisiana State University Press, 1978.
Escott, Paul D. *Many Excellent People: Power and Privilege in North Carolina, 1850–1900*. Chapel Hill: University of North Carolina Press, 1988.

Escott, Paul D. *Military Necessity: Civil-Military Relations in the Confederacy*. Westport, CT: Praeger, 2006.

Escott, Paul D. "The Moral Economy of the Crowd in Confederate North Carolina." *Maryland Historian* 13 (Spring/Summer 1982): 1–18.

Evans, Augusta Jane. *Macaria; or, Altars of Sacrifice*. Richmond: West and Johnston, 1864.

Farnham, Christie. *The Education of the Southern Belle: Higher Education and Student Socialization in the Antebellum South*. New York: New York University Press, 1994.

Faust, Drew Gilpin. "Altars of Sacrifice: Confederate Women and Narratives of War." *Journal of American History* 76.4 (1990): 1200–28.

Faust, Drew Gilpin. *The Creation of Confederate Nationalism: Ideology and Identity in the Civil War South*. Baton Rouge: Louisiana State University Press, 1988.

Faust, Drew Gilpin. *Mothers of Invention: Women of the Slaveholding South in the American Civil War*. Chapel Hill: University of North Carolina Press, 1996.

Faust, Drew Gilpin. *This Republic of Suffering: Death and the American Civil War*. New York: Alfred A. Knopf, 2008.

Felton, Rebecca Latimer. *Country Life in Georgia in the Days of My Youth*. Atlanta, GA: Index Printing, 1919.

Foner, Eric. *The Fiery Trial: Abraham Lincoln and American Slavery*. New York: W.W. Norton, 2010.

Foster, Gaines M. *Ghosts of the Confederacy: Defeat, the Lost Cause, and the Emergence of the New South, 1865–1913*. Oxford: Oxford University Press, 1989.

Fox-Genovese, Elizabeth. *Within the Plantation Household: Black and White Women of the Old South*. Chapel Hill: University of North Carolina Press, 1988.

Frank, Lisa Tendrich. "Bedrooms as Battlefields: The Role of Gender Politics in Sherman's March." In *Occupied Women: Gender, Military Occupation, and the American Civil War*, ed. LeeAnn Whites and Alecia P. Long, 33–48. Baton Rouge: Louisiana State University Press, 2009.

Frank, Lisa Tendrich. *The Civilian War: Confederate Women and Union Soldiers during Sherman's March*. Baton Rouge: Louisiana State University Press, 2015.

Franklin, John Hope. *The Emancipation Proclamation*. New York: Wiley-Blackwell, 1994.

Freeman, Douglas Southall. *A Calendar of Confederate Papers*. Richmond, VA: The Confederate Museum, 1910.

Friedman, Jean E. *The Enclosed Garden: Women and Community in the Evangelical South, 1830–1900*. Chapel Hill: University of North Carolina Press, 1985.

Fulton, Maurice Garland, ed. *Southern Life in Southern Literature*. Boston: Antheneum, 1917.

Gallagher, Gary W. *The Confederate War: How Popular Will, Nationalism, and Military Strategy Could Not Stave Off Defeat*. Cambridge, MA: Harvard University Press, 1997.

Gardner, Sarah. *Blood and Irony: Southern White Women's Narratives of the Civil War, 1861–1937*. Chapel Hill: University of North Carolina Press, 2004.

Garrioch, David. "The Everyday Lives of Parisian Women and the October Days of 1789." *Social History* 24.3 (1999): 231–49.

Garrioch, David, Harriet Branson Applewhite, and Mary Durham Johnson, eds. and trans. *Women in Revolutionary Paris, 1789–1795*. Urbana: University of Illinois Press, 1979.

Garvey, Ellen Gruber. "Anonymity, Authorship and Recirculation: A Civil War Episode." *Book History* 9.1 (2006): 159–78.

Gaston, Paul M. *The New South Creed: A Study in Southern Mythmaking*. New York: Alfred A. Knopf, 1970.

Geary, Daniel. *Beyond Civil Rights: The Moynihan Report and Its Legacy*. Philadelphia: University of Pennsylvania Press, 2016.

Gellner, Ernest. *Nations and Nationalism*. Oxford: Basil Blackwell, 1983.

Genoways, Hugh H., and Mary Ann Andrei, eds. *Museum Origins: Readings in Early Museum History and Philosophy*. New York: Routledge, 2008.

Ginzberg, Lori. *Women and the Work of Benevolence: Morality, Politics, and Class in the Nineteenth-Century United States*. New Haven, CT: Yale University Press, 1990.

Glymph, Thavolia. *Out of the House of Bondage: The Transformation of the Plantation Household*. Cambridge: Cambridge University Press, 2008.

Glymph, Thavolia. *The Women's Fight: The Civil War's Battles for Home, Freedom, and Nation*. Chapel Hill: University of North Carolina Press, 2019.

Gordon, Linda. *The Moral Property of Women: A History of Birth Control Politics in America*. Chicago: University of Illinois Press, 2002.

Gorgas, Josiah. *The Civil War Diary of Josiah Gorgas*. Edited by Frank E. Vandiver. Tuscaloosa: University of Alabama Press, 1947.

Grant, Susan Mary. "The Lost Boys: Citizen-Soldiers, Disabled Veterans, and Confederate Nationalism in the Age of People's War." *Journal of the Civil War Era* 2.2 (2012): 233–59.

Green, Carol C. *Chimborazo: The Confederacy's Largest Hospital*. Knoxville: University of Tennessee Press, 2004.

Green, Elna C. *This Business of Relief: Confronting Poverty in a Southern City, 1740–1940*. Athens: University of Georgia Press, 2003.

Greenbaum, Susan. *Blaming the Poor: The Long Shadow of the Moynihan Report on Cruel Images about Poverty*. New Brunswick, NJ: Rutgers University Press, 2015.

Greenberg, Kenneth S. *Honor and Slavery: Lies, Duels, Noses, Masks, Dressing as a Woman, Gifts, Strangers, Death, Humanitarianism, Slave Rebellions, the Proslavery Argument, Baseball, Hunting, and Gambling in the Old South*. Princeton, NJ: Princeton University Press, 1996.

Greenhow, Rose O'Neal. *My Imprisonment and the First Year of Abolitionist Rule at Washington*. London: Richard Bentley, 1863.

Gross, Jennifer Lynn. "'And for the Widow and the Orphan': Confederate Widows, Poverty and Public Assistance." In *Inside the Confederate Nation: Essays in Honor of Emory M. Thomas*, ed. Lesley J. Gordon and John C. Inscoe, 209–29. Baton Rouge: Louisiana State University Press, 2005.

Hall, Stuart. "Encoding/Decoding." In *Culture, Media, Language: Working Papers in Cultural Studies, 1972–1979*, ed. Stuart Hall, Dorothy Hobson, Andrew Lowe, and Paul Willis, 117–27. London: Routledge, [1980] 2005.

Hamburger, Susan. "'We Take Care of Our Womenfolk': The Home for Needy Confederate Women in Richmond, 1898–1990." In *Before the New Deal: Social Welfare in the South, 1830–1930*, ed. Elna C. Green, 61–77. Athens: University of Georgia Press, 1999.

Harper, Judith E. *Women during the Civil War: An Encyclopedia*. New York: Routledge, 2004.

Harris, M. Keith. *Across the Bloody Chasm: The Culture of Commemoration among Civil War Veterans*. Baton Rouge: Louisiana State University Press, 2014.

Harrison, Kimberly. *The Rhetoric of Rebel Women: Civil War Diaries and Confederate Persuasion*. Carbondale: Southern Illinois Press, 2013.

Hearn, Chester G. *When the Devil Came Down to Dixie: Ben Butler in New Orleans*. Baton Rouge: Louisiana State University Press, 1990.

Hilde, Libra R. *Worth a Dozen Men: Women and Nursing in the Civil War South*. Charlottesville: University of Virginia Press, 2012.

Hodes, Martha. *White Women, Black Men: Illicit Sex in the Nineteenth-Century South*. New Haven, CT: Yale University Press, 1997.

Hoff, Joan. "Gender as a Postmodern Category of Paralysis." *Women's History Review* 3.2 (1994): 149–68.

Home for Needy Confederate Women. *Report of the Commission to the Governor and General Assembly of Virginia, House Document No. 11*. Richmond: Virginia Division of Purchasing and Printing, 1947.

Hoole, W. Stanley. *Vizetelly Covers the Confederacy*. Tuscaloosa, AL: Confederate Publishing, 1957.

Jabour, Anya. *Scarlett's Sisters: Young Women in the Old South*. Chapel Hill: University of North Carolina Press, 2007.

Janney, Caroline E. *Burying the Dead but Not the Past: Ladies' Memorial Association and the Lost Cause*. Chapel Hill: University of North Carolina Press, 2008.

Janney, Caroline E. "Written in Stone: Gender, Race and the Heywood Shepherd Memorial." *Civil War History* 52.2 (2006): 117–41.

Johnson, Gerald. *Mount Vernon: The Story of a Shrine*. New York: Random House, 1953.

Jones, Howard. *Blue and Gray Diplomacy: A History of Union and Confederate Foreign Relations, 1861–1865*. Chapel Hill: University of North Carolina Press, 2010.

Jones, Howard. *Union in Peril: The Crisis over British Intervention in the Civil War*. Chapel Hill: University of North Carolina Press, 1992.

Jones, J. B. *A Rebel War Clerk's Diary at the Confederate States Capital*. Philadelphia: Lippincott, 1866.
Jones-Rogers, Stephanie E. *They Were Her Property: White Women as Slave Owners in the Old South*. New Haven, CT: Yale University Press, 2019.
Kenzer, Robert. "The Uncertainty of Life: A Profile of Virginia's Civil War Widows." In *The War Was You and Me: Civilians in the American Civil War*, ed. Joan E. Cashin, 61–77. Princeton, NJ: Princeton University Press, 2002.
Kerber, Linda. *No Constitutional Right to Be Ladies: Women and the Obligations of Citizenship*. New York: Hill and Wang, 1998.
Kerber, Linda. "Separate Spheres, Female Worlds, Women's Place: The Rhetoric of Women's History." *Journal of American History* 75.1 (1988): 9–39.
Kerber, Linda. *Toward an Intellectual History of Women*. Chapel Hill: University of North Carolina Press, 1997.
Kerber, Linda. *Women of the Republic: Intellect and Ideology in Revolutionary America*. Chapel Hill: University of North Carolina Press, 1980.
Kierner, Cynthia A., and Sandra Gioia Treadway, eds. *Virginia Women: Their Lives and Times*, vol. 1. Athens: University of Georgia Press, 2015.
Kimball, William J. "The Bread Riot in Richmond, 1863." *Civil War History* 7.2 (1961): 149–54.
Landes, Joan B. *Women and the Public Sphere in the Age of the French Revolution*. Ithaca, NY: Cornell University Press, 1988.
Larsen, William. *Montague of Virginia: The Making of a Southern Progressive*. Baton Rouge: Louisiana State University Press, 1965.
Lebsock, Suzanne. *The Free Women of Petersburg: Status and Culture in a Southern Town, 1784–1860*. New York: W.W. Norton, 1984.
Lee, Jean B., ed. *Experiencing Mount Vernon: Eyewitness Accounts, 1784–1865*. Charlottesville: University of Virginia Press, 2006.
Leonard, Elizabeth D. *All the Daring of a Soldier: Women of Civil War Armies*. New York: W.W. Norton, 1999.
Link, William A. "'This Bastard New Virginia': Slavery, West Virginia Exceptionalism and the Sectional Crisis." *West Virginia History: A Journal of Regional Studies* 3.1 (2009): 37–56.
Link, William A. *Roots of Secession: Slavery and Politics in Antebellum Virginia*. Chapel Hill: University of North Carolina Press, 2003.
Lockley, Timothy James. *Welfare and Charity in the Antebellum South*. Gainesville: University Press of Florida, 2007.
McClurken, Jeffrey W. *Taking Care of the Living: Reconstructing Confederate Veteran Families in Virginia*. Charlottesville: University of Virginia Press, 2009.
McCurry, Stephanie. *Confederate Reckoning: Power and Politics in the Civil War South*. Cambridge, MA: Harvard University Press, 2010.
McCurry, Stephanie. *Women's War: Fighting and Surviving the American Civil War*. Cambridge, MA: Harvard University Press, 2019.

McDonald, Cornelia Peake. *A Diary With Reminiscences of the War and Refugee Life in the Shenandoah Valley, 1860–1865*. Nashville, TN: Cullom and Ghertner, 1934.

McGuire, Judith White. *Diary of a Southern Refugee, During the War*. New York: E. J. Hale and Son, 1868.

McLeod, Stephen A. *The Mount Vernon Ladies' Association: 150 Years of Restoring George Washington's Home*. Mount Vernon, VA: Mount Vernon Ladies' Association, 2010.

Maggiano, Ron. "Captain Sally Tompkins: Angel of the Confederacy." *Organization of American Historians Magazine of History* 16.2 (2002): 32–38.

Manarin, Louis H., ed. *Richmond at War: The Minutes of the City Council, 1861–65*. Chapel Hill: University of North Carolina Press, 1966.

Mason, James M. *The Public Life and Diplomatic Correspondence of James M. Mason, with Some Personal History*. Edited by Virginia Mason. Roanoke, VA: The Stone Printing and Manufacturing Co., 1903.

Mason, Matthew. *Apostle of Union: A Political Biography of Edward Everett*. Chapel Hill: University of North Carolina Press, 2016.

Maury, Betty Herndon. *The Civil War Diary of Betty Herndon Maury: Daughter of Lieut. Commander M. F. Maury 1861–1863*. Edited by Alice Maury Parmelee. Washington: Privately Printed, 1938.

May, Robert, ed. *The Union, the Confederacy and the Atlantic Rim*. West Lafayette, IN: Purdue University Press, 1995.

Mitchell, Judith Anne. "Ann Pamela Cunningham: 'A Southern Matron's' Legacy." Master's thesis, Middle Tennessee State University, 1993.

Molloy, Marie S. *Single, White, Slaveholding Women in the Nineteenth-Century American South*. Columbia: University of South Carolina Press, 2018.

Morgan, Sarah. *The Civil War Diary of Sarah Morgan*. Edited by Charles East. Athens: University of Georgia Press, 1991.

Muir, Dorothy Troth. *Mount Vernon: The Civil War Years*. Mount Vernon, VA: Mount Vernon Ladies' Association, 1993.

Myers, Barton A. *Rebels against the Confederacy: North Carolina's Unionists*. Cambridge: Cambridge University Press 2014.

Neely, Mark E., Jr., Gabor S. Boritt, and Harold Holzer. *The Confederate Image: Prints of the Lost Cause*. Chapel Hill: University of North Carolina Press, 1987.

Oates, Stephen B. "Henry Hotze: Confederate Agent Abroad." *Historian* 27.2 (1965): 131–54.

O'Brien, Michael, ed. *An Evening When Alone: Four Journals of Single Women in the South, 1827–67*. Athens: University of Georgia Press, 1993.

Ott, Victoria. *Confederate Daughters: Coming to Age during the Civil War*. Carbondale: Southern Illinois Press, 2008.

Owsley, Frank Lawrence. *King Cotton Diplomacy: Foreign Relations of the Confederate States of America*. Chicago: University of Chicago Press, 1931.

Palmer, Brian, and Seth Freed Wessler. "The Cost of the Confederacy." *Smithsonian Magazine* (December 2018), https://www.smithsonianmag.com/history/costs-confederacy-special-report-180970731, last accessed October 1, 2021.

Parrott, Angie. "'Love Makes Memory Eternal': The United Daughters of the Confederacy in Richmond, Virginia, 1897–1920." In *The Edge of the South: Life in Nineteenth-Century Virginia,* ed. Edward Ayers and John C. Willis, 219–38. Charlottesville: University of Virginia Press, 2000.

Pember, Phoebe Yates. *A Southern Woman's Story: Life in Confederate Richmond.* Edited by Bell Irvin Wiley, 2nd ed. Atlanta, GA: Mockingbird Books, 1974.

Pomeroy, Sarah. *Spartan Women.* Oxford: Oxford University Press, 2002.

Pryor, Sarah Agnes Rice. *My Day: Reminiscences of a Long Life.* New York: Macmillan, 1909.

Quigley, Paul. *Shifting Grounds: Nationalism and the American South, 1848–1865.* Oxford: Oxford University Press, 2011.

Rable, George. *Civil Wars: Women and the Crisis of Southern Nationalism.* Urbana: University of Illinois Press, 1989.

Rable, George. *The Confederate Republic: A Revolution against Politics.* Chapel Hill: University of North Carolina Press, 1994.

Roberts, Giselle. *The Confederate Belle.* Columbia: University of Missouri Press, 2003.

Roos, Julia. *Weimar through the Lens of Gender: Prostitution Reform, Woman's Emancipation, and German Democracy, 1919–33.* Ann Arbor: University of Michigan Press, 2010.

Rosenburg, R. B. *Living Monuments: Confederate Soldiers' Homes in the New South.* Chapel Hill: University of North Carolina Press, 1993.

Rubin, Anne Sarah. *Shattered Nation: The Rise and Fall of the Confederacy, 1861–68.* Chapel Hill: University of North Carolina Press, 2005.

Rubin, Anne Sarah. *Through the Heart of Dixie: Sherman's March and American Memory.* Chapel Hill: University of North Carolina Press, 2017.

Ryan, Mary P. *Women in Public: Between Banners and Ballots.* Baltimore, MD: Johns Hopkins University Press, 1990.

Scarborough, Ruth. *Belle Boyd: Siren of the South.* Macon, GA: Mercer University Press, 1997.

Schultz, Jane E. *Women at the Front: Hospital Workers in Civil War America.* Chapel Hill: University of North Carolina Press, 2004.

Scott, Anne Firor. *Natural Allies: Women's Associations in American History.* Urbana: University of Illinois Press, 1991.

Scott, Anne Firor. *Southern Lady: From Pedestal to Politics, 1830–1900.* Chicago: University of Chicago Press, 1970.

Scott, Joan W. "Gender: A Useful Category of Historical Analysis." *American Historical Review* 91.5 (1986): 1053–75.

Sebrell, Tom. *Persuading John Bull: Union and Confederate Propaganda in Britain, 1860–65*. New York: Lexington Books, 2014.

Sexton, Rebecca, ed. *August Jane Evans: A Southern Woman of Letters*. Columbia: University of South Carolina Press, 2002.

Shackelford, George Green. *George Wythe Randolph and the Confederate Elite*. Athens: University of Georgia Press, 1988.

Sheehan-Dean, Aaron. *Why Confederates Fought: Family and Nation in Civil War Virginia*. Chapel Hill: University of North Carolina Press, 2007.

Silber, Nina. *Gender and the Sectional Conflict*. Chapel Hill: University of North Carolina Press, 2008.

Silber, Nina. "Intemperate Men, Spiteful Women, and Jefferson Davis." In *Divided Houses: Gender and the Civil War*, ed. Catherine Clinton and Nina Silber, 295–305. New York: Oxford University Press, 1992.

Silber, Nina. *The Romance of the Union: Northerners and the South, 1865–1900*. Chapel Hill: University of North Carolina Press, 1993.

Smith, Anthony D. *Theories of Nationalism*. London: Duckworth, 1971.

Spence, James. *The American Union: Its Effect on National Character and Policy*. London: Richard Bentley, 1861.

Spence, James. *On the Recognition of the Southern Confederation*. London: Richard Bentley, 1862.

Steinitz, Rebecca. *Time, Space, and Gender in the Nineteenth-Century British Diary*. Basingstoke: Palgrave Macmillan, 2011.

Sternhell, Yael A. "The Afterlives of a Confederate Archive: Civil War Documents and the Making of Sectional Reconciliation." *Journal of American History* 102.4 (2016): 1025–50.

Stevens, Rosemary, Charles E. Rosenberg, and Lawton R. Burns. *History and Health Policy in the United States: Putting the Past Back In*. New Brunswick, NJ: Rutgers University Press, 2006.

Stewart, Victoria. *Women's Autobiography: War and Trauma*. New York: Palgrave Macmillan, 2003.

Storey, Margaret M. *Loyalty and Loss: Alabama's Unionists in the Civil War and Reconstruction*. Baton Rouge: Louisiana State University Press, 2004.

Stowe, Steven M. *Keep the Days: Reading the Civil War Diaries of Southern Women*. Chapel Hill: University of North Carolina Press, 2018.

Thane, Elswyth. *Mount Vernon Is Ours: The Story of Its Preservation*. New York: Duell, Sloane and Pearce, 1966.

Thomas, Emory M. *The Confederate Nation: 1861–65*. New York: Harper and Row, 1979.

Thomas, Emory M. *The Confederate State of Richmond: A Biography of the Capital*. Baton Rouge: Louisiana State University Press, 1971.

Thompson, E. P. "The Moral Economy of the Crowd in the Eighteenth Century." *Past and Present* 50 (1971): 76–136.

Thompson, W. Fletcher, Jr. *The Image of War: The Pictorial Reporting of the American Civil War*. New York: Thomas Yoseloff, 1959.
Tice, Douglas O. "'Bread or Blood!: The Richmond Bread Riot." *Civil War Times Illustrated* 12 (February 1974): 12–19.
Tyler-McGraw, Marie. *At the Falls: Richmond, Virginia, and Its People*. Chapel Hill: University of North Carolina Press, 1994.
Underwood, Reverend J. L. *Women of the Confederacy*. New York: Neale Publishing Company, 1906.
Vandergriff, Cara. "'Petticoat Gunboats': The Wartime Expansion of Confederate Women's Discursive Opportunities Through Ladies' Gunboat Societies." Master's thesis, University of Tennessee, 2013.
Van Zelm, Antoinette G. "Virginia Women as Public Citizens: Emancipation Day Celebrations and Lost Cause Commemorations, 1863–1890." In *Negotiating Boundaries of Southern Womanhood: Dealing with the Powers That Be*, ed. Janet L. Coryell et al., 71–88. Columbia: University of Missouri Press, 2000.
Varon, Elizabeth R. *Southern Lady: Yankee Spy: The True Story of Elizabeth Van Lew, a Union Agent in the Heart of the Confederacy*. Oxford: Oxford University Press, 2005.
Varon, Elizabeth R. *We Mean to Be Counted: White Women and Politics in Antebellum Virginia*. Chapel Hill: University of North Carolina Press, 1998.
Vickery, Amanda. "Golden Age to Separate Spheres? A Review of the Categories and Chronology of English Women's History." *Historical Journal* 36.2 (1993): 383–414.
Vorenberg, Michael. *Final Freedom: The Civil War, Abolition of Slavery and the Thirteenth Amendment*. Cambridge: Cambridge University Press, 2004.
Wallace, Elizabeth Curtis. *Glencoe Diary: The War-Time Journal of Elizabeth Curtis Wallace*. Edited by Eleanor P. Cross and Charles B. Cross Jr. Chesapeake, VA: Norfolk Historical Society, 1968.
Wallenstein, Peter, and Bertram Wyatt-Brown, eds. *Virginia's Civil War*. Charlottesville: University of Virginia Press, 2005.
Watkins, Sam R. *Co. Aytch: A Confederate Memoir of the Civil War*, 2nd ed. Wilmington, NC: Broadfoot Publishing Co., 1987.
Weiner, Marli F. *Mistresses and Slaves: Plantation Women in South Carolina, 1830–80*. Urbana: University of Illinois Press, 1998.
Wei-Siang Hsieh, Wayne. "'I Owe Virginia Little, My Country Much': Robert E. Lee, the United States Regular Army, and Unconditional Unionism." In *Crucible of the Civil War: Virginia from Secession from Commemoration*, ed. Edward L. Ayers, Gary W. Gallagher, and Andrew J. Torget. Charlottesville: University of Virginia Press, 2006, 35–57.
Welter, Barbara. "The Cult of True Womanhood 1820–1860." *American Quarterly* 18.2 (1966): 151–74.
Wheeler, Marjorie Spruill. *New Women of the New South: The Leaders of the Woman Suffrage Movement in the United States*. New York: Oxford University Press, 1993.

White, Deborah Gray. *Ar'n't I A Woman?: Female Slaves in the Plantation South*. New York: W.W. Norton, [1985] 1999.

Whites, LeeAnn. *The Civil War as a Crisis in Gender, Augusta, Georgia, 1860–1890*. Athens: University of Georgia Press, 1995.

Whites, LeeAnn. *Gender Matters: Civil War, Reconstruction and the Making of the New South*. New York: Palgrave, 2005.

Whites, LeeAnn, and Alecia P. Long, eds. *Occupied Women: Gender, Military Occupation, and the American Civil War*. Baton Rouge: Louisiana State University Press, 2009.

Wight, Margaret. *A Refugee of Hanover Tavern: The Civil War Diary of Margaret Wight*. Edited by Shirley A. Haas and Dale Paige Talley. Charleston, SC: History Press, 2013.

Winterer, Caroline. *The Mirror of Antiquity: American Women and the Classical Tradition, 1750–1900*. Ithaca, NY: Cornell University Press, 2007.

Zagarri, Rosemarie. "The Rights of Man and Woman in Post-Revolutionary America." *William and Mary Quarterly* 55.2 (1998): 203–30.

Zimring, David R. "'Secession in Favor of the Constitution': How West Virginia Justified Separate Statehood during the Civil War." *West Virginia History: A Journal of Regional Studies* 3.2 (2009): 23–51.

Zweig, Bella. "The Only Women Who Gave Birth to Men: A Gynocentric, Cross-Cultural View of Women in Ancient Sparta." In *Woman's Power, Man's Game: Essays on Classical Antiquity in Honor of Joy K. King*, ed. Mary DeForest, Wauconda, IL: Bolchazy-Carducci, 1993, 32–53.

INDEX

Adams, Charles Francis, 95
Alabama, 14, 26, 58
Alexandria, Virginia, 24, 28, 30, 32, 43, 65, 81
American Union, The (Spence, 1861), 84
Anderson, Benedict, 30
Antietam, Battle of (1862), 96
Appomattox, xxviii, 40, 93, 111, 113
Arkansas, 14, 26
Arlington House, Virginia, 31, 137n42
Army of Northern Virginia, xxiv
Atlanta, 14, 143
Avary, Myrta Lockett, 91

Barber, E. Susan, 43, 58
Baton Rouge, 68
Beauregard, P. G. T., 18, 26–27, 48, 95
Beecher, Henry Ward, 84
Bell, John, 13
Belle Boyd in Camp and Prison (Boyd, 1865), 91
Benjamin, Judah P., 94
Berkeley, Cornelia A., 45
Bermuda, 78, 87–88
Black Lives Matter, 123
Boteler, Alexander, 87, 97
Boyd, Belle, 7, 75, 85, 91–95, 98
Breckinridge, John C., 13
Britain, 73–75, 77–78, 82–98, 149n2, 151n31
Broad Street Methodist Church, Richmond, xxvii, 50
Bryan, Mary Norcott, 68

Buck, Lucy, 78
Burckmyer, Charlotte, 80
Burhans, Janet, 111, 113–15
Butler, Benjamin, 7, 69, 95–96, 144n14
Butler, Lucy Wood, 77

Calhoun, Anna Maria, 23
Calhoun, John C., 23
California, 107
Callender, Bessie, 71–72
Campbell, Jacqueline Glass, 18
Caperton, George, 68
Caperton, Mary, 68
Chace, Elizabeth, 25
charity, 37, 71–72, 83, 100–101, 105, 109–13, 125n4, 146n24
Charleston, South Carolina, 22, 36, 123
Charleston Emmanuel African Methodist Episcopal Church, 123
Charlottesville, 77, 123
Chesnut, James, Jr., 27, 86
Chesnut, Mary Boykin, 1, 27, 61, 68, 86, 125n2, 141n62, 145n24
Chesnut, Mary Cox, 27
Chesson, Michael, 65
Chimborazo Hospital (Richmond), 1, 37
Christianity, 61, 135n3, 141n56
citizenship, 9–11, 26, 36, 39, 43, 46, 52, 56, 72, 90, 98, 120
Civil Rights movement, 103
Civil War, 1–3, 7, 9–13, 17–20, 22, 32–33, 39–40, 50, 64, 71, 74, 76, 81, 83–87, 96–97, 103, 110, 115, 119, 125n4, 133n51,

179

Civil War (*continued*)
  142n62, 144n13, 149n1. *See also*
  Confederate army; Union army
Clack, Louise, 69
class: conflict, 15, 57, 70, 147n58; elites,
  15–16, 18, 23, 25, 34, 38–39, 56, 61,
  69, 71–72, 74, 76–77, 80–81, 94,
  110–11, 125n4, 128n21, 129n24, 132n48,
  134n65, 138n6, 139n26, 140n29,
  144n14, 147n48, 155n7; lower class,
  18, 56, 61–62, 67, 69; the poor, 59–60,
  63–65, 76, 104
Clopton, Adelaide, 37
Clopton, John Bacon, 42
Clopton, Maria Gaitskell, 34–35, 37, 39,
  42, 44–45, 53
Comegys, Margaret, 29
Committee of Naval Affairs, 79
Confederate Aid Society, London, 82–83
Confederate army, 1, 24, 29, 68, 101–2
Confederate Congress, 27, 44, 67, 78–79
Confederate Conscription Act (1862), 60
Confederate leadership, 6, 46
Confederate memory, 33, 100–101, 103,
  107–8, 110, 113, 115–17, 120, 124
Confederate Museum (Richmond), 106
Confederate nationalism, 3–10, 12, 14–16,
  18–21, 27, 29–30, 35–36, 38, 43, 46–47,
  49–52, 55–56, 73, 82, 93, 117–20, 124,
  128n21, 130n32, 137n2, 143n4
Confederate Ordnance Laboratory
  (Richmond), 43
Confederate War Department, 54
Confederate Women's Home,
  Fayetteville, 115
Confiscation Acts (1861, 1862), 96
Congress, U.S., 22
Conrad, Charles M., 79
conscription, 15, 56, 60–61, 66, 71,
  73, 146n31
conservative women, 8, 10–11, 14, 16, 21,
  24, 26, 31, 33–34, 36, 43, 46, 48–49,
  52, 56–57, 71–72, 75–77, 81–82, 85, 90,
  98, 100–101, 103–4, 108, 111–12, 115–17,
  120, 131n46, 132n48, 140n30
Constantine, Grand Admiral, 78
Constitutional Union Party, 13, 21, 30
Coolidge, Calvin, 111
Coolidge, Grace, 111
coverture, 9–10, 130n41
CSS *Virginia II*, 43, 51–53. *See also* ladies'
  gunboat associations
Cuba, 79
Cunningham, Ann Pamela, xiv, 15, 21–32
Cunningham, Louisa Bird, 21
Cunningham, Robert, 23
Curd, Samuella Hart, 13

Dalí, Salvador, 2, *4*, 123
Danville, Virginia, 40
Darden, Colgate W., Jr., 111–12
Darden, Mrs. Colgate W., 111–12
Davis, Jefferson, 17, 27, 40, *41*, 42, 57, 62,
  77, 81, 85–86, 101, 123
Davis, Varina Howell, 13, 62
Davis administration, 3, 6, 79
DeCredico, Mary A., 55
Delaware, 27, 29, 92
democracy, 11, 120
diaries, xv, 5, 13, 18, 27, 42, 64, 77,
  79, 126n2, 128n20, 140n34,
  142n62, 146n24
diplomacy, 78, 81
Downs, L. McCarthy, 112
Duncan, Blanton, 39

economy, 8, 12, 57, 144n16
Edmunds, Amanda Virginia, 77
elites. *See under* class
Emancipation Proclamation
  (1863), 96–97
Evans, Augusta Jane, 47–49, 78
Everett, Edward, 15, 21, 23, 30–32

families, xiii, 10, 15, 26, 31, 38, 40, 60,
  71–72, 82, 111

Faust, Drew Gilpin, 49, 66
Fayetteville, North Carolina, 14, 115
Federal District Court, 115
federalism, 9, 22, 74
Fillmore, Millard, 30
First Battle of Bull Run (1861), xiv, 12, 133n56
Florida, 14, 26
Floyd, George, Jr., 122
Fogg, Mary Middleton Rutledge, 26
Ford, West, 14
Fort Delaware, 92
Fort Sumter, 24, 74
Fort Sumter, Battle of (1861), 13, 23
France, 74, 77–78, 80, 86, 94
fundraising, 35–41, 43, 99, 106, 109–10, 122, 130n34

Garrison, William Lloyd, 24–25
gender roles. *See* masculinity; motherhood; womanhood
General Order 13 (1861), 20, 28–33
George E. Pickett Camp of Confederate Veterans, 104, 107
Georgia, 33, 36, 38, 40, 45, 50, 87
Gettysburg, 77
Glymph, Thavolia, 9, 11–12, 19, 66, 69, 102, 129n24, 132n49, 148n55
Gorgas, Amelia Gaye, 42
Gorgas, Josiah, 42, 62–63
Gouldin, Caroline, 105
Greenhow, Robert, Jr., 86
Greenhow, Rose, 2, 7, 15, 75, 85–98
gunboats associations. *See* ladies' gunboat associations

Hamburger, Susan, 103, 112
Hammond, John Swainston, 93
Hardinge, Samuel Wylde, 91
Henningsen, Charles Frederick, 42
Henningsen, Wilhelmina, 37, 39, 42
Herbert, Upton, 23–24
Higgs, Chelsea Wise, 123

Hill, Eliza Oswald, 42
Hoban, James, 115
Home for Needy Confederate Women (Richmond), 2, 14, 99–117, 158n36
honor, 28, 37–41, 49, 79, 83, 101–2, 105–6, 109, 139n24, 140n29, 142n58
Hotze, Henry, 77, 85
House of Commons (British), 95
Hugo, Victor, 76
humanitarianism, 15, 83, 90, 93, 96–97

Ironclads, Battle of the (1862), 35, 43
Irwinville, Georgia, 40

Jabour, Anya, 76
Jackson, Mary Anna, 57, 71
Jackson, Thomas "Stonewall," 2, 18, 70, 122–23
James River, 42, 52, 53
Jamestown, 120
Jefferson, Thomas, 60, 121
Johnson, Robert Ward, 27
Johnson, Sarah Frances Smith, 26–27
Jones, J. B., 54
Jones, Philip de Catesby, 45
Jones-Rogers, Stephanie E., 11, 66, 129n24, 140n26
journalism, 24, 29, 42–43, 52, 58, 85–87, 95, 111, 113, 144n13. *See also* newspapers

Kentucky, 107
Kerber, Linda K., 9–11

Ladies' Aid Association of Richmond, 61
Ladies' Auxiliary of the George E. Pickett Camp, 104
Ladies' Confederate Naval Association, 24
Ladies' Defense Association, 34–53, 75, 78, 130n34
ladies' gunboat associations, 14, 35–36, 45, 51

Lafayette, Marquis de, 17
Lebsock, Suzanne, xv
Lee, Mary Custis, 108–10
Lee, Robert E., 2, 8, 18, 31, 40, 77, 108–9, 116, 123–24
Lee Camp Soldiers' Home, 115
Letcher, John, 59
letter writing, xiv–xv, 5, 18, 23, 25, 28–29, 32, 39, 44, 48, 62, 66–68, 74, 77, 79–80, 86–89, 93, 94, 98, 112–14, 130n34, 158n36
Le Vert, Octavia Walton, 26
Lew, Elizabeth Van, 13
Lexington, Virginia, 28
Lincoln, Abraham, 13, 18, 67–68, 92–93, 96
Lindsay, William Schaw, 96
Lipscomb, Ellise, 113
literacy, 9, 126n6
Liverpool, 77, 83, 94
Logan, Anna, 44–45
London, 82, 85–86, 88
Lost Cause ideology, 2, 21, 33, 49–50, 99–108, 110, 116–17, 124, 138n10, 157n17, 158n31
Lynchburg, Virginia, 44–45
Lynn, Clara Minor, 71, 76

Macaria; or, Altars of Sacrifice (Evans, 1864), 48–49, 78
Maine, 33
Mallory, Stephen R., 42–43, 45
Manchester, 93
Maryland, 86, 107
masculinity, 22, 36–41, 50, 58, 79, 105, 138n10
Mason, James Murray, xiv, 77–78, 94
Massachusetts, 15, 21
Maury, Betty Herndon, 42, 78–80
Maury, Martha, 42
Maury, Matthew Fontaine, 28, 42–43, 50, 78, 123
Maury, William A., 78

Mayo, Joseph, 59–60
McClellan, George, 15
McClure, Alexander, 110
McCurry, Stephanie, 8, 54–55
McGuire, John, 64–65
McGuire, Judith White McGuire, 64–65
McMakin, Mary, 23–24
McPherson, James, 38
McWillie, Catherine Morris Anderson, 26
McWillie, William, 26
memorialization, 15, 33, 104–5, 107, 116, 124, 158n31
Mexican-American War, 40
military service, 10, 39, 51, 57, 66–67, 71–72
Minish, James A., 27
Miserables, Les (Hugo, 1862), 76
Mississippi, 14, 26
Missouri, 107
Mitchell, Jim, 25
Mobile, Alabama, 14
Montague, Andrew Jackson, 108, 110–11
Montague, Elizabeth Lyne Hoskins, 110–12, 116
Monument Avenue (Richmond), 2, 116, 123–24
Moore, Samuel Preston, 1
motherhood, 5, 11, 46–53, 56, 73, 95, 102, 119, 141n56
Mount Vernon, xiv, 11, 14, 17–35
Mount Vernon Ladies' Association of the Union, xiv, 13–15, 17–35, 135n7
Moynihan Report, 114
Murat, Achille, 26
Murat, Catherine Willis Grey, 26
My Imprisonment and the First Year of Abolition Rule in Washington (Greenhow, 1963), 88

nationalism. *See* Confederate nationalism
National Register of Historic Places, 114
Naval Observatory, U.S., 42, 78

navy: Confederate, 42–43, 45, 51, 78, 102; Union, 78, 92
neutrality, 15, 17, 19–21, 23–24, 27–28, 30–34, 74, 78, 148n1
New Bern, North Carolina, 68
New England, 8, 131
New Orleans, 7, 14, 69, 95, 144n14
newspapers, 1–2, 4, 58, 82, 87, 91, 112, 143n15. *See also* journalism
Nicholls, Namie (Clopton), 37
Noble, Emily, xv
Norcom, Ralph, 120
Norfolk Female Institute, 1
North Carolina, 12, 14, 26, 38, 68, 90, 115
Nullification Crisis (1832), 23
Nunnally, Janet Montague, 111
nursing, 2, 100, 143

Ohio, 13
Oklahoma, 107
On Confederate Recognition (Spence, 1861), 84
Ould, Isabella, 65

Palmerston, Lord, 95
Palmeter, Lucy, 58
Paris Exhibition (1855), 26
Parker, Edmund, 25
Peake, Cornelia McDonald, 78
Pennsylvania, 13, 27
Pennybaker, Margaret, 69
Petersburg, Virginia, 14
Petigru, James Louis, 22
Philadelphia, 23, 28
Phillips, Eugenia, 69, 95
Pickens, Francis, 33
Pickens, Lucy Holcombe, 33

Pinkerton, Allan, 86
plantation household, xv, 9–10, 19, 66, 119, 125n1, 128n18, 132n48
policy, 16, 44, 54–56, 60, 66, 70, 73, 79, 96, 100, 102–3, 116

political culture, xiii, 5–7, 11–12, 14, 16, 21, 35, 52, 55, 61, 64, 73, 75, 81, 98, 100, 119–20, 131n48
Pomeroy, Sarah, 49
poor, the. *See under* class
Porter, Felicia Grundy, 26
Potomac River, 17, 19, 21, 31
power relations, 10–12, 14, 25, 35–38, 40, 42, 48–49, 52, 66, 75, 90, 97–98, 101–2, 110–11, 119–20, 124
Preston, Mary, 68
Prince Edward Ladies' Aid Association, 45
print culture, 4, 30, 87, 98, 105–6. *See also* newspapers
Pryor, Roger Atkinson, 64
Pryor, Sarah Agnes Rice, 64

Quesenbery Commission, 112

race, 5, 8, 38, 46, 49, 55–56, 75, 82–83, 87, 95, 98, 102, 114, 122
Randolph, George Wythe, 60–61, 66–67
Randolph, Janet Henderson Weaver, 106
Randolph, Mary, 61
Reagan, Ronald, 116
reform, 25–26, 48, 50, 70–72, 84, 98, 101, 120, 125n4
Republican Motherhood. *See* motherhood
Revolutionary War, American, 17, 130n45
Richmond, Virginia: Capitol Square, 54, 57, 120–22; Chimborazo Hospital, 1, 37; Circuit Court, 115; city, xv, 1–4, 12–15, 17, 23, 34, 36–37, 39–47, 52–73, 81–82, 86–87, 99, 101, 104, 106–10, 122–24; City Hall, 65; Confederate Museum, 106; Confederate Ordnance Laboratory, 43; Free Market, 60; Methodist Church, Broad Street, 11; Monument Avenue, 2, 116, 123–24; Old Capitol Prison, 86, 91;

Richmond, Virginia (*continued*)
Robertson Hospital, 1–2, 4, 101, 127n3, 146n24; Sheppard Street, 99, 106; St. James Episcopal Church, 2–3; Virginia Museum of Fine Arts, 115, 124; Virginia Museum of History and Culture, 4. *See also* Home for Needy Confederate Women
Richmond bread riot (1863), 14–15, 53, 54–73, 126n6, 144n14, 146n26
Richmond City Council, 55, 59–60, 62–63, 65, 67–70
Riddell, Lila Lee, 115
Robert E. Lee Camp, 2, 108–9, 113
Robertson, John, 1

Salisbury, North Carolina, 14
Savannah, 36
Schaar, Susan Clarke, 121
Schwartz, Ivan, 121
Scott, Winfield, xiv, 20, 30–31
self-sacrifice (culture of), 1, 5, 48–49, 51, 94, 110, 128n18
Seven Pines, Battle of (1862), 45
Seward, William, 78–79, 83, 86
Sherman, William Tecumseh, 38, 50, 143n14
Sickles, Daniel, 29
Silber, Nina, 40
slaveholding, xiii, xv, 1–2, 7, 9, 12–13, 18, 23, 25, 38, 40, 66, 119, 123, 147n43
slavery, xv, 2, 7–13, 19, 24–27, 66, 90, 96–97, 119, 134n3, 147n43
Slidell, John, xiv, 77–79
Soldiers' Aid Society, 26
South Carolina, 27–28, 30, 33, 36, 38
Southern Prisoners' Relief Fund, 83
Spartan motherhood. *See* motherhood
Speed, Catherine, 44–45
Spence, James, 77, 83–84
Stanton, Edwin, 19, 89, 92
Stanton, Elizabeth Cady, 25–26

St. Louis, 93
Strange, Col, 45
Sweat, Margaret, 33
symbolism, 3–8, 12, 14–16, 19–20, 35–36, 45, 51, 53, 55–56, 70–71, 75, 84–85, 95, 97–98, 100–104, 107–8, 114–17, 124, 139n18

Tatum, Henry Augustus, 37
Tennessee, 12, 14, 26
Tompkins, Sally Louisa, 1–2, *3, 4,* 6, 101, 122–24
Tracy, Sarah, xiv, 23–24, 27–29, 32
transatlanticism, 73, 78, 82–84, 87, 151n18
Trent Affair, 78
Trent's Reach, Battle of (1865), 52–53
Trinkle, Elbert Lee, 109
Tutwiler, Hal, 58
Tutwiler, Netta, 58
Twenty Slave Law (1862), 60, 63, 66–68, 147n48

Union army, xiv, 5, 17, 20, 29–30, 40, 69
unionism, 8, 13, 22
Union navy, 78, 92
Union Secret Service, 86
United Confederate Veterans, 108–9
United Daughters of the Confederacy (UDC), 33, 99–102, 105–8, 114, 116, 142n58, 155n7, 157n17, 158n31, 159n53
Unite the Right Rally (2017), 122

Vernon, Mrs., 47, 139n30
Victoria, Queen, 74
violence, xiv–v, 9–12, 25, 38, 55, 57–60, 62–64, 67–68, 72, 96, 123, 139n26, 148n58
Virginia: demographics, 12, 64, 115; Fauquier County, 25, 77; General Assembly, 99, 103–5, 109, 111, 113–16, 120; Norfolk County, 77; Prince George County, 71; Shenandoah

Valley, 69; Supreme Court, 115, 123. *See also* Charlottesville; Mount Vernon; Richmond
Virginia Museum of Fine Arts (Richmond), 115, 124
Virginia Women's Monument, 15, 120–21, *122*
Vizitelli, Frank, 86

Walker, Georgiana Freeman Gholson, 87–88
Walker, LeRoy Pope, 1
Walker, Letitia Harper Morehead, 26
Wallace, Elizabeth Curtis, 77
Waring, John Lancaster, 58
Waring, Warner, 58
War of Independence. *See* Revolutionary War, American
Washington, D.C., 17, 19, 24, 63, 86, 88, 92, 113, 155n7
Washington, George, 17–31, 33
Washington, John Augustine, III, 22, 28
Washington, Martha, 31, 122–23
Waveland plantation, 25
welfare, 8, 17, 54–56, 60–62, 67, 70–72, 84, 100–101, 114–15

West Virginia, 13, 91
White, Robert F., 113
White House, the, 115
Wight, Margaret, 64
Wilder, Georgia Page King Smith, 33
Wiley, Kehinde, 123–24
womanhood, 3–5, 7, 9, 19, 23, 25, 37, 48–49, 55–56, 58, 73, 93, 106, 108, 116–17, 144n14
women: collective organizing, xiii–xiv, 10–11, 24, 33, 38–39, 41, 47, 49–51, 60–61, 121; international diplomacy, 75, 79, 81, 87–88, 90, 95, 98, 149n3; political actors, 55, 73, 98, 142n2; resistance, 13, 66; rights campaigners, 10, 25–26, 117, 120; wartime experiences, xiii, 5, 85. *See also* conservative women; womanhood
Women of the Confederacy Memorial Committee, 2
Works Progress Administration, xv
worthiness, 15, 55–56, 59–60, 62–64, 70, 93, 106, 160n62
Wynne, Bill, 2, 4

Recent books in the series
A NATION DIVIDED: STUDIES IN THE CIVIL WAR ERA

Young America: The Transformation of Nationalism before the Civil War
Mark Power Smith

Black Suffrage: Lincoln's Last Goal
Paul D. Escott

The Cacophony of Politics: Northern Democrats and the American Civil War
J. Matthew Gallman

My Work among the Freedmen: The Civil War and Reconstruction Letters of Harriet M. Buss
Edited by Jonathan W. White and Lydia J. Davis

Colossal Ambitions: Confederate Planning for a Post–Civil War World
Adrian Brettle

Newest Born of Nations: European Nationalist Movements and the Making of the Confederacy
Ann L. Tucker

The Worst Passions of Human Nature: White Supremacy in the Civil War North
Paul D. Escott

Preserving the White Man's Republic: Jacksonian Democracy, Race, and the Transformation of American Conservatism
Joshua A. Lynn

American Abolitionism: Its Direct Political Impact from Colonial Times into Reconstruction
Stanley Harrold

A Strife of Tongues: The Compromise of 1850 and the Ideological Foundations of the American Civil War
Stephen E. Maizlish

The First Republican Army: The Army of Virginia and the Radicalization of the Civil War
John H. Matsui

War upon Our Border: Two Ohio Valley Communities Navigate the Civil War
Stephen I. Rockenbach

Gold and Freedom: The Political Economy of Reconstruction
Nicolas Barreyre, translated by Arthur Goldhammer

Daydreams and Nightmares: A Virginia Family Faces Secession and War
Brent Tarter

Intimate Reconstructions: Children in Postemancipation Virginia
Catherine A. Jones

Lincoln's Dilemma: Blair, Sumner, and the Republican Struggle over Racism and Equality in the Civil War Era
Paul D. Escott

Slavery and War in the Americas: Race, Citizenship, and State Building in the United States and Brazil, 1861–1870
Vitor Izecksohn

Marching Masters: Slavery, Race, and the Confederate Army during the Civil War
Colin Edward Woodward

Confederate Visions: Nationalism, Symbolism, and the Imagined South in the Civil War
Ian Binnington

Frederick Douglass: A Life in Documents
L. Diane Barnes, editor

Reconstructing the Campus: Higher Education and the American Civil War
Michael David Cohen

Worth a Dozen Men: Women and Nursing in the Civil War South
Libra R. Hilde

Civil War Talks: Further Reminiscences of George S. Bernard and His Fellow Veterans
Hampton Newsome, John Horn, and John G. Selby, editors

The Enemy Within: Fears of Corruption in the Civil War North
Michael Thomas Smith

The Big House after Slavery: Virginia Plantation Families and Their Postbellum Experiment
Amy Feely Morsman

Take Care of the Living: Reconstructing Confederate Veteran Families in Virginia
Jeffrey W. McClurken

Civil War Petersburg: Confederate City in the Crucible of War
A. Wilson Greene

A Separate Civil War: Communities in Conflict in the Mountain South
Jonathan Dean Sarris

www.ingramcontent.com/pod-product-compliance
Lightning Source LLC
Chambersburg PA
CBHW030344240426
43661CB00052B/1733